I0819122

COOKING THE BORDERLANDS

COOKING THE BORDERLANDS

Spice and Smoke Between Mexico and the States

CLAUDETTE ZEPEDA

Photographs by David Alvarado

Clarkson Potter/Publishers
New York

BORDERLANDS MARGARITA

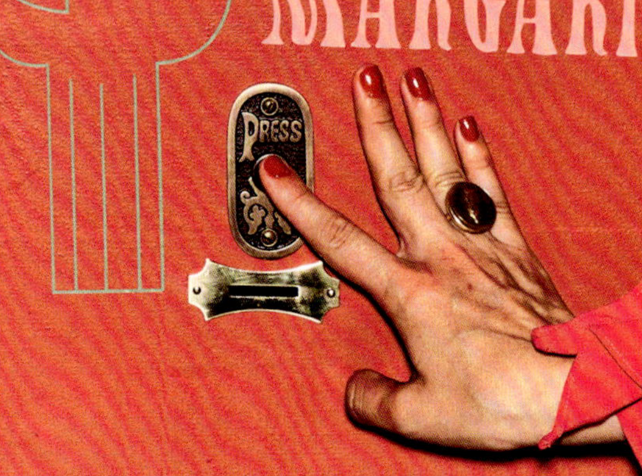

CONTENTS

Claudette
Omnia

elcome to one of the most ambitious projects that I have embarked on in my personal and professional life: Telling the stories of and celebrating the people who live in the borderlands.

There is a unique culture in the lands that surround the line drawn in the 1848 Treaty of Guadalupe Hidalgo, which divided Mexico and the US. The borderlands between the countries have always been home to beautiful tales of migration, immigration, resilient and often misunderstood people, and of course a shared love of food.

I have been a border kid for four decades, and I've cooked professionally for over half that time. So much of who I am is a result of where I was raised, the smells and sounds of my childhood, moving seamlessly—daily—between San Diego, California, and Tijuana, Mexico. But I didn't always know that's what made me who I am.

For the first decade of my career, I thought, like many indoctrinated immigrants do, that if I was going to find any kind of success, I needed to push who I am and where my family was from as far back in my mind as possible. Then, in 2014, I took a life-altering trip—my first time abroad. I had the opportunity to travel to Marrakech, Morocco. I saw the matriarchs at the markets, I saw the different religions and cultures colliding yet coexisting. I witnessed the bustling market, dowels covered with freshly butchered meat for the morning shopping rush. I smelled meat grilling over wood and kids playing soccer in the middle of the market halls. And suddenly, seven thousand miles away from home, I saw myself back in Tijuana. I tasted the air, closed my eyes, and became emotional. Why did I have to travel all the way to Africa to find home?

My aunt Lorenza told me shortly after: "Your motherland will always call you home—but you don't get to choose how the message arrives." I came back home with a fire in my belly to learn to understand myself as a first generation Mexican American: raised as a Mexican daughter in California, with a life that took me back and forth across the border daily. Part of understanding my identity is understanding the mindset of the border kid: Having a foot in two countries, being a chameleon who has the ability to be fluid, to blend in anywhere in the world (yes, even with my green hair and tattoos!).

I have also dedicated the last decade-plus to learning about the cultural and culinary anthropology of Mexico and its immigrants—the who, what, and whys of our food world. I wanted to write this book to take you with me on a journey across the borderlands, starting from where I am from on the Pacific Coast, and heading east through the Sonoran desert and cowboy country. I want you to see, smell, hear, and taste these lands with me, and hopefully feel, as I do, that there is a connection to be shared.

The biggest disclaimer I will give in this book—and any book I write—is that it is almost impossible to include every recipe from even a single square-mile area, let alone the thousands of square miles that make up our border regions. And when it comes to the recipes I've written, if your grandmother did it differently, just know that she's right and I'm wrong. (In fact, I concede power to all grandmothers. Tías—aunts—I'll exchange words with, but abuelitas? Not a chance in H-E double hockey sticks. They win every time.)

MY FAMILY

My family is unique, but at the same time, I am sure we're a lot like many others. The Zepedas, my father's side, moved from the coastal state of Nayarit to inland Jalisco and have stayed put to this day. Of the generation before me, my father was the only one who chose to become a permanent resident in the US, in the 1960s, making Los Angeles his home for twenty years. Then, during a fated trip to Tijuana in the winter of 1983, he met my madre. Forty weeks later, the earth cracked open, and I came out.

The Rodríguez side, my mother's side, was a nomadic migrant family in Mexico, always moving where the work was. My *abue* (my granny Paula, shown here) had sixteen kids during her lifetime, and nearly all of them were born in different parts of Mexico. In each state that the family lived in, she learned the regional ingredients and dishes. And I was the benefactor of this nomadic life, not only in the dishes passed down to me, but also in the skill and sense of adaptability that is part of my family's fabric. My family may not have had great financial or material means, but I am grateful to have inherited a more intangible trait—an insatiable curiosity for humanity and an ability to create and nurture using their hands, wood, and fire.

I have had the honor of traveling across all of the culinary regions of Mexico, and have swept dirt floors in exchange for my supper or a story.

My Abue, Paula Valadez de Rodriguez. Matriarch. Healer. Confidant.

While my family has had experience and made memories in all corners of the country, the fact that I grew up on the border—not just *between* Tijuana and California, but constantly crossing back and forth—informs my perspective. When you've crossed borders daily your entire life—when you're the product of movement itself—the actual border becomes less important. A sterile line that divides people, language, culture, and food becomes less and less visible. Instead, what you see is a border*land*—a place (and a mindset) that freely blends and combines in nuances and shades, not in black and white.

Life along the border requires resilience and grit. At times, I've felt "othered" by the border culture I call my own. We speak with different dialects, from the Pacific coast to the Gulf coast that divides Mexico and Texas. Certain flavors in regional dishes are dialed up in volume, distinguishing them from "dupes" elsewhere in the country. And along the border, you won't get asked if you like spicy or not—if it's supposed to be spicy, you'll know by the first bite. (That reminds me, another disclaimer: Never trust a Mexican when they tell you something's not spicy. We're built different, and believing us is a mess-around-and-find-out scenario.)

THE JOURNEY

The recipes in this book are near and dear to my heart, but they also tell the stories of the humans that make up the borderlands: The beauty that exists in our world and on the table, through the harsh desert climate and (at times) political unrest, the exchange of ingredients between both sides of the border, the *mestizaje* (blended Indigenous and European) and multicultural families that have formed a new, third-culture cuisine.

I'll start by introducing the foundation of our cuisine (and the way of life in my family), the staple elements that are always on the table: our salsas, our beans, our tortillas, and more. Chapter 1 is called "Sobremesa," meaning "on the table," and the recipes in this chapter are the soul of our food. Then, Chapter 2, "Off My Matriarchs' Hips," showcases flavors from the rest of the country that can also be found in the borderlands (as they were also highlighted in my family's kitchen). These are the recipes that the women in my family nurtured me with, leaving an imprint on my soul.

In Chapter 3, we'll take a look around the California borderlands, starting at the westernmost end, the San Diego/Tijuana port of entry, where I grew up, home to abundant seafood and the birthplace of the Caesar salad. We'll dip south to Ensenada for some more seafood classics, then head east from there. We'll end up in the streets of Mexicali, landing at the beautiful red gateway that signals that you are entering "*La Chinesca*," the Chinatown of Mexicali, where generations of Chinese immigrants have found home and raised their families. It is also where you will find, in my opinion, the most delicious Cantonese and Szechuan food outside of China, because it's where these foods took on Mexican character and flavor.

From California we head over to the desert borderlands for Chapter 4, with Indigenous communities and *vaqueros* (cowboys) influencing much of the culinary landscape. Along the Arizona–Sonora border we see the food of an incredibly geographically diverse state, one that features the Sierra Madre Occidental mountain range with its dry desert plains, high elevation, deep valleys, and pine forests . . . as well as the warm waters of the *Golfo de California*. The microclimates in Sonora are as extreme as the heat from the state's chile, the *chiltepín*.

Valle de Guadalupe at Doña Estelas Cocina

James

Rincon de Guayabitos, Nayarit

Grilling at home for Everyday with Rachael Ray

The Three Musketeers

Tijuana Christmas with brothers

Legacy

Me and James

My brother Alex (left), Miguel (right) & me in Jalisco

My father and me at our family restaurant, Las Calandrias, in Guadalajara, 1991

Perfecting the chef pose

Tortillas on the ranch

Jardín de Niños Parade, Tijuana

James & Hailey

Abue Paula and my Uncle Cesar & Aunt Betty

James, pulling dish duty for mom

ROSARITO B.C
SUZUKI
BAÑOS

In Chapter 5 we move to Chihuahua, the land of the Tarahumara (or Rarámuri) people, who are known for running extremely long distances on foot. In Chihuahua, we will see the exchange of ideas and customs across borderlines, some political, some cultural. I also share some of my favorite pastries from the area, including a cookie that seems to only exist in the North, the *corico*. It has the same texture as the soil in the dessert—haha—but once you dunk in your coffee, it's wonderful!

Chapter 6 covers the area from Coahuila to Tamaulipas, the borderlands between Texas and Mexico, where I think there are the most cowboy-influenced, meat-centric foodways. (Generally, you will see a lot more meat dishes in the desert regions of the border.) I could lie to you and tell you that we eat salads and cook broccoli on the charcoal grill, but just between you and me: I didn't know salads had greens in them until I was in high school when I got my first restaurant job. (All my "salads" growing up had a base of either mayonnaise or condensed milk and marshmallow cream with diced fruit.) This is also the birthplace of Tex-Mex cuisine, and of course we won't leave without telling the story of how nachos were born.

These places and stories matter to me. The border is often a huge topic in politics and the media, but in many cases, the border is used as a pawn in a political game, invoked by powerful people to paint an unjust picture and reinforce a narrative that serves their interests. The reality is that in many border towns, a wall does not create or protect life—it takes away from it. In fact, border communities have long depended on the exchange of people and business between both sides of the border.

If you are anything like me, and if what you read in these pages inspires you to learn more, go to these places yourself, and eat directly from their kitchens. Then I'll have achieved what I set out to do.

A NOTE ON THE RECIPES

These recipes are meant to showcase the cuisines that are the prize of their regions. Does that mean that you can't use the carne asada recipe and make it vegetarian? Absolutely not! Modify it! Use kohlrabi, celery root, mushrooms . . . anything grilled over charcoal tastes like it's got a secret to tell directly from the fire. As you begin to navigate through the pages and cook the recipes, I hope you feel empowered to change things up and make them your own.

I like to think of recipes as outlines, and they should be approached as such. (Baking recipes . . . maybe not so much.) I hear so many stories about a person who decided to not make a recipe because they were missing one ingredient, and it makes me sad! You have my permission—go ahead and make it without the missing ingredient. Or replace the missing ingredient with something similar and experiment. You'd be surprised to know how often professional chefs land on new recipes at our restaurant by doing this exact thing. If there's a special ingredient that you cannot find locally, chances are you can find it online with a couple clicks. Many dry spices will keep for months in your pantry, so buying them can be worthwhile, especially if you start to incorporate them ingredients the rest of your cooking.

The tools used in this book are not crazy—I just want to let people cook! Don't have a *molcajete*? Use a food processor. Don't have that? Use your knife! Don't have a knife? Well, okay, please buy one.

A NOTE ON THE PHOTOS

The pictures you see in this book may not look like the ones you have seen in other Mexican cookbooks. There is a reason for that. I am a first generation Mexican American, a daughter of immigrants who was raised with one foot in each country. I have never lost sight of my roots. But I was also part of a household that celebrated cinema and music. My brothers and I learned how to speak English by watching PBS. On any given day when I was a child, you could find me running barefoot, chasing my brothers like we were Batman and Robin (the Adam West version). And after we watched *20,000 Leagues Under the Sea*, my father asked my mother to make us squid for dinner. To me, food and art are inextricable from one another, and I hope that comes through in this book.

With that in mind, these photographs celebrate not just my passion for food, but also my love of self-expression. Our creative team is made up of cinephiles—David Alvarado, Jason Sutherland Hsu, Jaclyn Kershek, Ryan Norton, Salt Worth Studio, Chef Isamar Checo, and myself—and we took inspiration from Quentin Tarantino, Robert Rodriguez, and Wes Anderson, coining the book's style, "Southwes' Anderson."

Special thanks to Jessica Resendiz, for the incredible flower crown, and to Revolution Carts for sharing your story and beautiful cart to help make our tamal shot special! Thank you both for all that you do in the Latinx food and art communities.

1.5 Mts.
SANA DISTANCIA
HUSSONG'S
CUBE

DAMIANA
Coca-Cola
Coca-Cola

SOBREMESA

RECIPES THAT CAN BE FOUND
ON OUR TABLE EVERY DAY,
SOMETIMES ALL AT ONCE

The Mexican table—and the stovetop, for that matter—are never empty. The condiments from breakfast tend to work well in the afternoon meal, the afternoon leftovers in the evening, and so on. Like those in many other food-loving cultures, we finish having breakfast and immediately start thinking about our next meal. And so, the items that are always sitting on the table—think salsas, tortillas, beans—are also the core of our food. Think of it as "casa sustainability." You don't clear the table after every meal and start from scratch; you always have delicious things at the ready to make any meal more delicious.

The number one food rule in our large family—we lived at the poverty line—was that you never throw away food. "Smell it, see! Just boil it, it's not bad," my abue Paula would exclaim. We cherished our food, and we made it damn good, even if it was simple. In our home, you could assemble an entire meal out of the items that never left the stove or table: for instance, one daily snack was "perpetual" smashed beans with a salsa made in a molcajete (mortar and pestle); a slice of queso fresco, and minced cilantro, all rolled up in the last tortilla in the tortillero (tortilla warmer). I'll never not get excited about a pot of well-seasoned rice and beans. There would be chiles "en escabeche" (pickled) in a Tupperware. And of course, there would usually be one mild salsa, often heavy on the tomato and the oregano with maybe one chile de árbol that just walked past the pot to say "¿¡*Qué onda*?!" ("What's up?!")—and a second salsa so spicy that it would make you rethink your entire life. A salsa that, as my aunt said, she wished she could see her ex-husband twist in.

The recipes in this chapter aren't just the staples we need at every meal, they're also the simplest, most foundational elements that will help you learn how to cook our food. So, start here—make a delicious pot of frijoles de la olla and rice. In reality, the majority of classic Mexican dishes we eat at home are not actually complicated. But they can be very intentional. Nothing added is by accident, and every ingredient has a role to play.

And finally, to give you some insight on why *sobremesa*—literally, "on the table"—is so beloved in Mexico: It really comes down to one word . . . *chisme*. Gossip. Catching up with family, comadres or compadres, even the mailman who stopped at just the right time. Sobremesa is always there. When we'd stand up from the table, before we even offered to clear our plates, we would usually be met with the same response by our abues, moms or aunts: "*Déjalo ahí, viene tu tío y va a tener hambre.*" ("Leave it there, your uncle will be coming over soon, and he will be hungry.") Which tío? It didn't matter. Someone was always bound to show up unannounced to help us make sure no food went to waste.

The recipes in this chapter start with both corn and flour tortillas, the latter a cornerstone of the borderlands. If this is your first attempt at making corn tortillas, read the instructions thoroughly and have a bit of patience with yourself; the swift motion to get the tortilla on the comal or pan may take a little practice, but it's so worth it.

Once you master tortillas, you can move on to the other recipes that are key to customizing any dish to your liking. From spicy, pickled vegetable escabeche, to salsas of varying degrees of heat, this is where you can play with your food. Each salsa has flavors and ingredients that pair well with specific dishes. For instance, the Salsa Verde Cruda is my go-to salsa when cooking pork carnitas. But it's really all up to you and your preferences; if you are a one-salsa kinda persona and just want to use that for everything, that is fine! Welcome to the borderlands, where everyone is invited to our table. Enjoy the delicious adventure.

TORTILLAS DE MAÍZ

(CORN TORTILLAS)

Do you have to make your own corn tortillas by hand? No. Should you? I believe the answer is a resounding yes!

When you think of Mexican food, you likely think of tortillas. And while the concept of flatbread used as a vessel for a meal isn't unique to our cuisine, tortillas *are* uniquely tied to ancient Mexican folklore and myth. Every Mexican kid learns about how the Aztec god Quetzalcoatl gave *maíz* to humans after seeing an ant carrying a corn kernel. And we learn that the Mayans told stories of how man was born from corn. Regardless of which of the stories of corn you've been told, or which ones you agree with, we can all agree that the tortilla is delicious. Plus, it means you have to wash fewer dishes—your tortilla is your utensil!

Making tortillas by hand, like any other dish you make from scratch, allows you to control the quality and flavor of ingredients. You can get supermarket masa harina (dehydrated nixtamalized maíz corn flour, sold under the name Maseca) almost anywhere—and at the very least enjoy the satisfaction of homemade just-cooked tortillas—I recommend looking for non-GMO masa harina, which will give you a deeper corn flavor. Each variety of maíz has distinct flavor notes, and heirloom varieties of masa harina are increasingly available from producers like Masienda (available online).

There's an unusual ingredient in this tortilla recipe—water infused with tomatillo husks. It's the best secret straight from abuela; I learned it when I was little. There are natural compounds found in the tomatillo husks: the pectin in them slightly modifies the water absorption and binding properties, helping make the tortillas soft and flexible, and malic acid helps break down the proteins and saponins, helping the dry masa flour hydrate more evenly. The lift that the tortillas get with that pH-enhanced water will guarantee the iconic puff without a leavening agent! (You can use the same trick to make your tamales light and fluffy.)

Once you get comfortable, you can also experiment with adding flavor to your tortillas. You flavor them with the chile adobo from Tía Lore's Pozole (page 77), add herbs into to the masa, or even press edible flowers into the face of the tortilla for a beautiful taco base.

I hope this recipe empowers you at the start of your Mexican cooking journey. I do encourage you to use a tortilla press, but you don't need to go out and get any special equipment if you don't already have one. Women from every corner of Mexico, past and present, flatten tortillas using just their hands. It's intimidating and beautiful all at once. Whether you use a press or not, don't worry if you can't get the shape perfectly the first time, or the second, or the third. Tortilla-making is mastered through years of repetition. So get started here and see where it takes you!

Makes 12 (4-inch) tortillas

2 cups Tomatillo Husk Water (recipe follows)
2 level cups masa harina, plus more if needed
½ teaspoon Diamond Crystal kosher salt (or ¼ teaspoon Morton salt)

Special equipment
Tortilla press
Thin plastic bag, cut into two 6-inch squares
Tortilla warmer or clean kitchen towel

MAKE THE DOUGH:

1. In a small pot over low heat, bring the prepared Tomatillo Husk Water to body temp.

2. In a medium mixing bowl, combine the masa harina and salt. Slowly add the warm tomatillo husk water to the bowl, mixing the masa continuously with your hands, until the water is evenly incorporated into the dry ingredients and you have a cohesive dough. The dough should feel slightly tacky to the touch and will stick to your hands.

Recipe continues

TORTILLA TIPS

- The day you make the masa is the day you should use the masa. If you have leftover dough, I recommend just making it into tortillas right then and there. You can refrigerate or freeze cooked tortillas, and rewarm them later. Or make them into chips (see below)—no one hates tortilla chips.
- When you're ready to eat, open the cloth-lined tortilla warmer and flip the entire stack of tortillas so that the tortilla you cooked first is on top (and will be eaten first). Why is this important? Well, the last tortilla you cooked (at the top of the basket) hasn't had enough time to steam in the basket and become soft. But the first one you made on the bottom? It is perfectly rested, steamy and ready to enjoy.
- I wrap leftover tortillas in a paper towel and store them in a resealable plastic bag or airtight container in the fridge. Store them for no more than 3 to 4 days.
- When reheating tortillas, sprinkle them with a little water to help them steam as they heat. This will ensure they stay as soft as when they were freshly made. Heat over a comal or griddle on medium heat until warm.
- To make tortilla chips or tostadas, lay a single layer of tortillas (or tortillas cut into wedges, for chips) on a baking sheet. Bake in the oven at 350°F for 10 minutes; then flip them and continue baking for another 8 to 10 minutes, until golden brown and crispy. (You can also make tostadas on the stovetop—grill over medium heat, flipping every 3 to 4 minutes, until nice and crispy on both sides.)

3. Knead the dough. Roll the dough into a ball and press it down flat with the heel of your hand. Then, with a swift motion, drag the flattened dough back into a ball. Repeat this motion for 5 to 8 minutes—you don't have to worry about overworking the dough like you would with bread. The dough should be well-hydrated, but once it's kneaded, it shouldn't leave residue on your hand when you lift your palm.

4. At this point, you can flavor your masa by kneading in herbs or spices.

5. Wrap the masa in a clean, damp kitchen towel and allow it to rest for 5 minutes to fully hydrate.

6. Don't wash your hands after kneading—the residue of the masa will help create a nonstick surface, so you won't need oil or flour during cooking.

PRESS THE TORTILLAS:

7. Prepare the plastic sheets to line the tortilla press (thin plastic produce bags are best, not thick zip-top bags). First, cut off the closed seam of the plastic bag, then cut along both sides. You'll end up with two rectangles—trim them to the size of your tortilla press (about 6 by 6 inches).

8. Test the dough: Roll a 2-ounce ball of dough (about the size of a golf ball) and place it in between the plastic sheets in the tortilla press. Press it flat—if you see the edges are jagged and cracked, the dough is too dry. If the tortilla feels tacky and sticks to the plastic when you try to peel it off, the dough is too wet.

9. If dough is too dry, add a bit more liquid, a few tablespoons at a time, and knead until fully incorporated. If too wet, add masa harina, a pinch at a time and knead in. Continue testing the dough until it's neither too tacky nor too dry.

10. When the dough is at the correct consistency, portion it into 2-ounce (golf ball–size) balls. Store the dough under a damp towel until ready to press.

11. Place a masa ball in the middle of the plastic sheet on the tortilla press, using light pressure with your hand to flatten it a bit. Lay the second plastic sheet over the masa and press down to flatten. You want the tortilla to be about ⅛ inch thick (the height of two stacked quarters). If you flatten it any thinner, it may be tricky to handle.

12. Lift the tortilla press lid and carefully remove the top plastic sheet. Then remove the tortilla from the press and flip it gently so the exposed side lands in your nondominant palm. Carefully peel off the second plastic sheet.

13. You should be able to transfer the tortilla between hands without it tearing. The dough is forgiving, so if it does tear, simply roll it back into a ball and press it again. Again, don't wash your hands after this step!

COOK THE TORTILLAS:

14. Set the comal or griddle over medium heat.

15. Set a clean dish towel (or tortilla warmer lined with a thin cloth) next to a comal or heavy griddle.

16. Start with the tortilla in your nondominant hand. Gently place one end of the tortilla on the outstretched index and middle fingers of your dominant hand and drape the other end of the tortilla onto the comal. With a graceful, deliberate sweeping motion, lay the hanging tortilla onto the hot cooking surface, then pull your hand out from under it. (It's like the opposite of flipping the tortilla onto the comal or griddle; just slide your hand away and let the tortilla drop down flat.)

17. Cook the tortilla on the first side for about 30 seconds, long enough to cook the masa and have it set—it should release easily from the comal. Flip the tortilla and cook on the other side for another 30 seconds. Flip once again, and this time let it cook for 1 minute—the tortilla should puff up within a few seconds. If it needs encouragement, gently press the tortilla with a damp towel and watch it rise.

18. Place the cooked tortilla in the cloth (or tortilla warmer) immediately and fold the other end of the towel over it to keep it warm. If you think the tortilla is overcooked, rest assured that in the cloth will help it steam and soften up a bit.

19. Repeat the pressing and cooking steps for each tortilla, stacking them in the tortilla warmer and keeping them covered so they stay soft. Serve and eat immediately.

TOMATILLO HUSK WATER

Makes 2 cups

Husks from 10 tomatillos

In a small pot over low heat, add 2¼ cups of water and the tomatillo husks and simmer for 10 minutes.

Remove the pot from the stove. Strain the tomatillo husks into a heatproof measuring cup and discard the husks. Add water as needed to bring the measure to 2 cups.

Store the tomatillo husk water in the refrigerator for up to 1 month or freeze in silicone trays to use as needed.

TORTILLAS DE HARINA

(FLOUR TORTILLAS)

When you grow up in the North, you have a very special allegiance to the flour tortilla, the blanket of the flatbread family. By the time I had kids, I was already a pro at swaddling babies: You just roll them up like a burrito with extra-special fillings.

Making tortillas in my house was a family affair (much like tamales, page 267). Once the dough finished resting, there were rollers, cookers, eaters. (Conveniently, I was always an eater.) Trust me when I tell you that the first fresh flour tortilla that comes off the comal should be immediately slathered with salted butter, a pinch of sea salt, maybe a drizzle of honey, and nothing more—eat it right away!

The story that the flour tortilla doesn't come from Mexico has a kernel of truth to it; wheat seeds did in fact land on our soil through the spice trade and the arrival of Spanish colonizers. It's possible that in different parts of the land that is now known as Mexico, Indigenous and migrant field workers planted various seeds found at the bottom of sacks of other grains, seeds, and legumes. In the northern regions, the climate was not favorable for growing corn; wheat, however, turned out to grow beautifully.

In Sonora, there is a particular tortilla the size of a tire called "*sobaquera*," or "tortilla that gets shaped with your underarms"—yeah, words don't always translate smoothly. The women who make sobaqueras perform aerial maneuvers with the dough that look something like a rhythmic gymnastics ribbon event, creating a paper-thin tortilla the length of an arm. Then, as if covering a sleeping baby with a blanket, they gently lay the see-through sheet of dough onto a comal with a roaring wood fire underneath. The sobaquera cooks in a matter of seconds—it's hypnotic. And the global influence is notable—you'll also see nearly this exact preparation and cooking in the Middle East, South Asia, and parts of Africa. So, although wheat flour is not original to our cooking, its impact is not to be ignored. *Somos de maíz, pero somos de harina también.* (We are of maiz, but we are also of wheat flour too.)

This basic wheat flour tortilla recipe is a perfect starting point for anyone who is intimidated by making flatbreads. It truly doesn't matter if you don't get a perfect circle—tortillas can be all sorts of crazy shapes (as long as you're not using them to roll a burrito).

Makes 12 (6-inch) tortillas

- 3½ cups all-purpose flour, plus more for rolling
- 1½ teaspoons baking powder
- 2 teaspoons sea salt
- ½ cup lard or solid vegetable shortening, room temperature
- 1½ cups Tomatillo Husk Water (page 25) or water, hot (102°F to 110°F)

MAKE THE DOUGH:

1. In a large bowl, or the bowl of a stand mixer fitted with the paddle attachment, mix together the flour, baking powder, and salt. Using your hands or a pastry blender, cut the lard or shortening into the flour, making sure that it is completely incorporated. Once combined, the mixture should have the texture of wet sand.

2. If using a stand mixer: Switch from the paddle to the dough hook attachment. With the mixer on medium speed, slowly add the Tomatillo Husk Water to the mixture in thirds. Continue kneading until a smooth dough forms, 10 to 15 minutes.

3. If kneading by hand: Add the Tomatillo Husk Water to the flour mixture. Once the water is fully incorporated, transfer the dough to a smooth surface and knead until the dough becomes smooth and pliable, 20 to 30 minutes . . . or until your arm falls off. To check if the dough is ready, pinch a small piece of dough and stretch it between your hands; if it can stretch and thin out far enough so that you can see light through it before ripping, it's ready. (We call this the windowpane test.)

Recipe continues

4. Transfer the dough to a lightly greased bowl and cover with a damp towel. Let rest for 30 minutes.

5. Portion the dough into 12 equal pieces and roll into uniform balls. Let them rest on the counter for 10 minutes, covered with a damp cloth.

MAKE THE TORTILLAS:

6. Set a dry kitchen towel folded in half, or a tortilla basket/warmer, on the counter next to your comal or griddle on the stove.

7. With a floured rolling pin and a lightly flour-dusted surface, roll out a ball of dough into a thin circle, rotating the dough 90 degrees after each roll to ensure an even thickness. You have two options here: You can roll and cook the tortillas on the griddle right away, one at a time, or roll them all out at once to cook later. If you're doing the latter, stack the raw tortillas after rolling, separating them with pieces of parchment paper (or wax paper) in between each of them.

8. Set a comal or a heavy griddle over medium heat. (If you've been frustrated making corn tortillas, know that the rolled-out flour tortillas are much sturdier than corn.) Lift a tortilla from the parchment and carefully pass it between your hands (similar to handling a pizza dough or other flatbread) to gently shake off excess flour and transfer onto comal, gently laying it down closest to the edge of the comal with a sweeping motion releasing the rest onto the hot surface.

9. Cook for about 2 minutes on the first side, flip, and repeat. An indicator that they are fully cooked is seeing them puff up after flipping and having golden brown spots form over the surface of the bubbles. You may flip them once more to ensure a good puff if needed. Lower the heat a bit if the spots are getting too dark.

10. When fully cooked, place the tortilla inside the kitchen towel, folding the top over to keep them warm. The tortillas are best consumed immediately.

SOPA DE ARROZ

(RED RICE)

Sopa de arroz is a dish my abue made, not really a soup, but a loose-ish pan of long-grained rice, saucy and delicious, meant to be a side to *guisados* (braises) or meats, or eaten alone with tortillas. Many rice dishes I grew up with have a base of sofrito made with tomato, onion, and garlic (and sometimes herbs). The tomato isn't necessarily the star of this dish, but you'll know it's there. The liquid was usually chicken stock, but if money was tight, water with chicken bouillon would do just fine. When you add the chicken stock to the pan, you can also add in veggies like peas and corn; you can even throw in some chicken thighs for a quick, delicious riff on arroz con pollo (rice with chicken). This is a simple, starter red rice that you can feel free to get creative with, and I hope you will!

Serves 6

2½ cups chicken broth
¼ medium onion
1 Roma tomato, quartered
¼ cup neutral cooking oil or bacon drippings
1 cup jasmine rice
1 bay leaf
2 garlic cloves, minced
Diamond Crystal kosher salt

"SPANISH" RICE

• Can we dethrone the whole "Spanish rice" title that seems to get thrown on any tomato-based rice? Spaniards are most known for paella, which classically contains only trace amounts of tomato. So, why the name? Well, in a book that I found from 1914, only 66 years after the Treaty of Guadalupe was signed, Anglos referred to the rice dishes of Mexico as "Spanish rice" because the "Spanish-speaking natives" ate it. Echoing the words of my father, I yelled out, "*No seas mamón!*" . . . a more colorful way of saying, "You've got to be kidding me!"

• The Spaniards love a rich, fortified broth in their paellas and aim for a glorious "*socarrat*," or rice crust, on the bottom. Our rice dishes are closer to pilafs: fluffy, some containing tomato, some only garlic and onion, others with more vegetables added in to steam alongside the rice—or my favorite, rice topped with fried plantains.

1. In a blender, combine the chicken broth, onion, and tomato. Blend the ingredients on high until completely smooth. Set aside.

2. In a wide pan over medium heat, add the oil and heat until shimmering. Add the rice and the bay leaf and sauté, stirring constantly. Add the garlic, stirring constantly to ensure the garlic does not burn. Continue cooking the rice until it is no longer translucent and it begins to toast and brown in spots; it should take between 5 and 7 minutes.

3. Pour the purée from the blender into the rice and season it with a few pinches of salt. Stir to incorporate and bring the ingredients to a boil. Then immediately adjust the heat to the lowest setting. Cover the pan and let the rice cook undisturbed for 15 minutes.

4. After 15 minutes, remove the lid. Take out the bay leaf and discard. Stir the rice vigorously—this helps to release its starches. If the rice has absorbed all of the liquid at this point, you can add an additional ½ cup of water or chicken stock; you want a loose, saucy texture. Adjust salt as needed to taste.

5. Remove the rice from heat, cover it again, and let it sit for 5 to 10 minutes. Serve hot.

FRIJOLES DE LA OLLA

(AROMATIC STEWED BEANS)

Beans. This magical food is one of the largest parts of our DNA (second only to maíz, of course).

Frijoles de la olla are beans cooked in what I can only describe as the holy grail of clay pots. (Everything cooked in *la olla* tastes different, or maybe the secret ingredient is in the hands of the women who wield its power.) Push through the hypnosis of the citrus, alliums and herbs in the air to make yourself a perfect bowl. Growing up, a generous ladle of the irresistible-smelling, herb-infused beans (and the broth that they cooked in), plus chunks of *queso panela*, hand-torn cilantro and epazote, salsa, all served with a warm rolled-up tortilla, could put a smile on any one of our faces.

And after we'd eat our fill, we'd leave the beans out; we wouldn't put them away. My entire childhood, I remember there being a pan of crusted-over smashed beans on the table in the morning. It was the same pan from at least a week before—or at least it seemed like it was the same one. I always thought our kitchen (and the women in it) were magical. My abue or mom would casually walk up to the stove in the morning and add water to the pot to reinvigorate the beans, as if watering their favorite plant. This is what I now call the "perpetual beans," a never-ending story of sustenance—the "bean mother," if you will, seeded by the frijoles de la olla.

But before you go leaving your beans on the stove for a week at a time, let me stop you: Don't do it! Always refrigerate your leftover beans and reheat them when you want to eat them. The stories are fun, but food safety comes first. (I was built different, raised on MSG and lead candy.)

Makes 8 cups

1 medium yellow onion, halved crosswise
2 Roma tomatoes, quartered lengthwise
4 garlic cloves
1 pound dried beans, cleaned (pinto, cranberry, or Mayocoba)
1 fresh hoja santa leaf
1 bay leaf
2 dried avocado leaves
Peel of 1 lemon
Diamond Crystal kosher salt

Optional garnishes

½ pound panela cheese, cut into ½-inch cubes
1 large ripe Hass avocado, cut into ½-inch cubes
Chile de árbol, ground in a molcajete
Crispy tortilla strips
Warm tortillas, for serving

1. On a lightly oiled skillet or comal set over medium high heat, char the onion, tomatoes, and garlic until blackened on all sides. Remove from heat.

2. In a large pot, combine the beans, charred onion, tomato, and garlic, the hoja santa, bay leaf, avocado leaves, and lemon peel. Fill the pot with 3 inches of water to cover and stir everything together.

3. Set the pot over high heat and bring to a boil. Reduce the heat to low and bring the beans to a gentle simmer. Cover and cook for 2 hours, or until the beans are tender. Check on the water level periodically, and add more water as needed. Generally there should be about 3 inches of water over the beans.

4. Once the beans are cooked, season them well with salt to taste. Remove and discard the chunks of onion, the leaves, and the lemon peel before serving. My favorite way to enjoy fresh frijoles de la olla is to ladle a large portion into a bowl (liquid included) and garnish with cubed panela and avocado, ground chile de árbol, and fresh tortillas. Hits every nook and cranny of my tired heart.

BEAN TIPS

- If you see the pot wanting to bubble over while the lid is on, lower the heat and place the lid slightly offset from the pot, so a bit of steam can escape.
- Resist the urge to salt the beans before they are fully tender. Don't ask me why; I just don't want the ghosts of the ancestors to come back and yell at me for not warning you.
- However! When I have time, I do like to brine beans in salted water prior to cooking. It ensures that I don't get a bean blowout (no, not that kind). Why does it work? The salt penetrates the skin of the beans, giving them a softer and more pliable texture that prevents the skins from splitting. I love science!
- To brine, for 1 pound of dried beans, add 3 tablespoons of Diamond Crystal kosher salt (or 1½ tablespoons of Morton or table salt) to 4 quarts of water. Let the dried beans soak in the brine solution for 8 to 24 hours. A presoak/brine will also cut down your cooking time; you can start checking for the beans for doneness after 1 hour or so.

REALLY FRIED BEANS

The next day, we'd put leftover frijoles in a hot sauté pan with a swirl of oil or, better yet, a dollop of rendered pork fat. We'd mash them with a steel grate–looking tool. (I never knew its name; I just knew it as, "*la chingadera para machucar los frijoles*"—the damn thing to smash the beans with.)

This is what most refer to as "refried beans." The assumption of most people is that the name comes from the beans being "fried" twice. The actual name is a bad translation: "*Re*" to us means "very," so "*refrito*" actually means "really fried." (If you find the name confusing, know that *Norteños*, or northern Mexicans, have a distinctive way of speaking, a dialect and cadence that sets us apart from the rest of the country. Because many of us are farmers and/or ranchers, we are a bit country.) But whatever the name, cozy up with a warm bowl of freshly cooked beans the first day, then start with your bean "mother" the next day for your "really fried" perpetual beans.

VERDURAS ENCURTIDAS

(PICKLED VEGETABLES)

Chiles encurtidos—or sometimes a mix of pickled carrot, onion, and jalapeños—are an absolute must in my opinion. They're typically consumed after you take a bite of something that needs a kick to follow it. Take a bite of your carnitas taco, but want a bit more spice? Take a pickled chile or carrot. Why don't you just put them directly in the taco? Because that would be too easy! I don't make the rules, I just follow them . . . some of them, at least.

I like to go heavier on the vegetables compared to what you might see in other recipes, maybe because we live in California, and preserving summer vegetables in a spicy pickle is a perfect way to freeze time. You can mix and match the vegetables as you prefer, or, if you're a purist, just stick with the chiles, onions, and carrots. This pickle should leave the veggies with a snap to them; the carrots should still crunch after the brine is cool.

Makes 4 cups

½ medium white onion, julienned
2 large carrots, diagonally sliced ¼ inch thick
2 jalapeño or serrano peppers, diagonally sliced ¼ inch thick
2 Persian cucumbers, diagonally sliced ¼ inch thick
1 cup cauliflower florets
1 bunch radishes, cleaned and quartered
3 cups distilled white vinegar
2 garlic cloves
2 chiles de árbol
1½ teaspoons black peppercorns
1 star anise
1 bay leaf
1 dried avocado leaf
1½ teaspoons dried oregano
½ cup Diamond Crystal kosher salt (or ¼ cup Morton salt), plus more to taste

1. In a large heatproof bowl, combine the vegetables. Set aside.

2. Fill a measuring cup with 2 cups of ice water and set aside.

3. In a large pot over high heat, combine the vinegar, garlic, chiles de árbol, peppercorns, star anise, bay and avocado leaves, oregano, and ½ cup salt. Taste and add more salt as desired if you like a saltier pickle. Allow the mixture to come to a rolling boil.

4. Add the sliced vegetables to the pot and return to a boil. Once boiling, remove from the heat and top off with 2 cups of ice water, stirring to incorporate. Cover and let the vegetables sit for 1 hour. Transfer the vegetables to a clean glass jar with a lid, pouring in enough brine to cover the vegetables. Use as many jars as needed.

5. We keep these vegetables on the table for very meal, sunup to sundown. But you can keep them in the fridge—they will last for months there, but for peak flavor and texture I'd eat them within a month.

ARROZ CON ELOTE

(WHITE RICE WITH CORN)

For a fluffier, less-soupy rice to go with our meals, we make white rice with *elote* (corn kernels). The rice comes out tender and plump—we use a bit more liquid than typical Asian recipes, but instead of water, we use a flavorful stock, which gives the rice more heft. The rice is also infused with onion, garlic, and a bay leaf. I think the corn is a delicious addition, but just leave it out if you want a "plainer" (never "basic") white rice.

Serves 4 to 6

¼ cup neutral cooking oil
1 cup jasmine rice
1 bay leaf
¼ cup onion, diced small
2 garlic cloves, minced
2 cups vegetable stock
½ cup corn kernels
Diamond Crystal kosher salt

1. In a wide pan over medium heat, add the cooking oil. When the oil is hot, add the rice and bay leaf and sauté, stirring constantly, for 1 to 2 minutes. Add the onion and garlic, stirring constantly to ensure the garlic does not burn. Sauté for 5 to 7 minutes, until the rice is no longer translucent and starts to toast.

2. Add the vegetable stock and corn to the pan and season with a few pinches of salt. Bring the stock to a boil, then immediately adjust the heat to the lowest setting. Cover the pan and let the corn and rice cook for 15 minutes, until the stock is absorbed.

3. Turn off the heat and let the ingredients sit for 5 to 10 minutes before removing the lid to serve.

CEBOLLA ROJA ENCURTIDA

(QUICK-PICKLED RED ONIONS)

Sometimes, you just need something tart, with punch, in a hurry.

Makes 1½ cups

1 large red onion, julienned
Juice of 2 limes
Diamond Crystal kosher salt

1. Place the onion in a small bowl. Squeeze the lime juice over the onions and sprinkle with a pinch of salt. Toss to coat and let them sit for 5 minutes. Toss again and let them sit once more to continue pickling for another 5 minutes. The onions will turn a beautiful magenta pink color and become soft and flimsy.

2. Store in an airtight container in the fridge, or leave on your table like my family does.

SALSAS

I love asking people what they consider to be the greatest achievement in Mexican cooking. People rattle off all kinds of ambitious answers: Tamales! Pozole! Mole! Pibil! Barbacoa! And though these answers aren't necessarily wrong, I think people are thinking about the wrong end of the spectrum. To me, the answer is salsa. The key to transforming a tortilla from a glorified spoon to a meal of its own: A good table salsa. The magic in tacos? Salsa. The special something of quesadillas? Salsa.

The star of each salsa in Mexico, from north to south, is the chile, dating back six thousand years in the Americas. Chiles then traveled the world as a result of Spanish and Portuguese traders, helping to elevate the plainest of meals to a masterpiece. These are a few of my favorite salsas, all of them foundational to your Mexican cooking repertoire.

SALSA ROJA POZOLERA / SALSA PICO DE PÁJARO

(CHILE DE ÁRBOL SALSA)

This vinegar-based salsa is also called *pico de pájaro* (bird's beak) in my family, named for the instant sting or "peck" the chile gives you. It's ubiquitous in Jalisco and always accompanies pozole (Mexican soup with pork and hominy) . . . and the greatest, sauciest sandwiches on earth, *tortas ahogadas*. It's a briny, vinegary salsa that showcases the fruity notes of one of my favorite chiles—*chile ojo de pájaro*, also known as bird's eye chile (sadly, it's not the same as the Thai bird's eye chile you may have seen in stores). Chile ojo de pájaro can be harder to find in the States, so this recipe use chiles de árbol, which have a similar flavor.

When making this salsa, do what feels right to you as far as heat level is concerned—trade a few chiles de árbol for a guajillo if needed. You can also try using some fresh bird's eye chiles if you can find them. It should be spicy but delicious—remember, flavor is more important than melt-your-face-off heat. Double the batch and bottle for a spicy gift.

Makes 1 cup

---

10 chiles de árbol, stemmed and seeded
2 dried guajillo chiles, stemmed and seeded
1 garlic clove
⅓ cup distilled white vinegar
½ teaspoon dried oregano
½ teaspoon ground cumin
1 whole clove, or a pinch of ground cloves
Diamond Crystal kosher salt

1. Fill a medium pot with 3 cups of water and place over high heat. Once the water comes to a simmer, turn the heat off and add the chiles and garlic clove. Cover the pot and let sit for 20 minutes.

2. After 20 minutes, strain the chiles and garlic, reserving them with 1½ cups of the chile water.

3. In a blender, combine the chiles and garlic, 1½ cups chile water, vinegar, oregano, cumin, and clove. Blend on high for 4 minutes, until completely smooth.

4. Strain the sauce through a fine-mesh sieve into a medium bowl. Discard the leftover pulp.

5. Season the salsa with salt to taste. Transfer to a glass jar or bottle with a tight-fitting lid. Allow to cool and store in the fridge. The salsa will last for 3 months, though no salsa ever lasts more than a week in my family.

SALSA VERDE CRUDA

(RAW TOMATILLO SALSA)

These wise words, from the first chef I ever worked for, are seared into my head: "There's a right tool for every job." Likewise, there's a right salsa for every dish. When I'm working with earthy, deep, smoky, and/or creamy flavors, I reach for accompaniments that will breathe in lightness, or what I call "green flavor." This fresh green salsa pairs great with Adobada Bao Buns (page 149), or *queso fundido* (melted cheese with poblano peppers). A smoked Texas-style brisket, slow-braised lamb shanks, grilled maitake mushrooms, or even a plain cheese quesadilla also fit the bill.

My version of tomatillo salsa calls in help from ancestral herbs, which offer not only flavor but also medicinal benefits—you know, in case I eat too much. Holy leaf, or hoja santa, is a favorite for its anise/fennel flavor, and *yerba buena* (spearmint) is a sleeping giant in a salsa. Both herbs contain soothing compounds, helping make dishes feel less heavy and dense.

This salsa isn't cooked, so the tartness of ripe tomatillos marries flawlessly with the green, herbaceous elements. A little bit of heat ties it all together into a crave-able salsa.

Makes 2 cups

---

4 medium tomatillos
½ medium yellow onion, quartered
2 garlic cloves
½ bunch cilantro, stems included
4 green onions, green parts only
1 serrano pepper
½ fresh hoja santa leaf (optional)
1 small sprig fresh mint (yerba buena or spearmint, if available)
Diamond Crystal kosher salt

1. Clean the tomatillos by removing the husks and rinsing the tomatillos under water until they are no longer sticky. (Reserve the husks for making Corn Tortillas, page 23.)

2. In a blender, combine the tomatillos, onion, garlic, cilantro, green onions, serrano pepper, hoja santa, and mint. Add ½ cup of water and a hefty pinch of salt. Blend all the ingredients together on high speed until the salsa reaches a smooth consistency, similar to that of a smoothie.

3. Taste and adjust salt if needed. If you like a thinner salsa, add water a splash at a time, blend, taste, and repeat as needed until you reach your desired consistency.

4. Store the salsa in an airtight container. It will keep for 4 days in the fridge, or a few months in the freezer.

SALSA VERDE MORITA

(COOKED TOMATILLO SALSA WITH CHILE MORITA)

The alter ego to the *salsa cruda* (raw salsa, see page 38), *salsa cocida* (cooked salsa) gives the ingredients a chance to mature and settle on your palate. This cooked tomatillo salsa mellows out the tart, sour tomatillos, and has added smokiness and a touch of sweetness thanks to *morita chiles*, which are actually smoked ripe jalapeño peppers. (You can use fresh peppers if you'd like, but I prefer the chile morita.) My mother would tell you to add a spoonful of chicken bouillon to this recipe, and I won't say she's wrong!

While I love this salsa as is, the goal of this recipe is to give you the tools to create an arsenal of salsas on your own. Add any herbs and spices you love—tarragon or fennel, za'atar, or ground or fresh ginger would all be beautiful here. Long before I had to write recipes professionally, I learned from the moment I could see over a counter that a salsa was made of whatever was on its last legs in the vegetable drawer. Have fun with it, spoon it on generously, and enjoy the flavor ride.

Makes 4 cups

---

8 medium tomatillos, husked and rinsed
1 medium yellow onion, quartered
2 garlic cloves
3 morita chiles, stemmed
½ bunch cilantro, stems included
Diamond Crystal kosher salt

1. Fill a medium pot three-quarters of the way with water and add a large pinch of salt. Place over medium heat and bring to a simmer.

2. Once simmering, add the tomatillos, onion, garlic, and morita chiles to the pot and simmer for 3 minutes. Turn off the heat and cover the pot with a lid. Allow the tomatillos to soften until the skin begins to split but not completely fall apart, about 10 minutes. Strain the pot and discard the water.

3. Transfer the softened vegetables to a blender with the cilantro. Blend on high until smooth, and season with salt to taste. If the consistency is too thick, add a splash of water to thin. Store the salsa in an airtight container in the refrigerator for up to 4 days.

SALSA DE MOLCAJETE

(MORTAR AND PESTLE TOMATO SALSA)

My molcajete, shown here, is a family heirloom, hand-chiseled from volcanic rock and gifted to my parents at their wedding. A molcajete is more than a kitchen staple in most Mexican households; it tends to take up a decent amount of space on the counter, so it's sort of like an extra member of the family.

Making a salsa in a molcajete may seem like a primitive or unnecessarily time-intensive process, since throwing things into a food processor is way faster. But many people still prefer to use a molcajete. When asked, people will give you different answers as to why—it might be that the stone grinding allows for more thorough flavor extraction, or maybe it's the ability to control texture with more precision. But for me, the most important reason is what my grandmother and mom have always told me: Remember where you come from. Using the same tools that our ancestors used taps into a generational memory bank, connecting us and passing down family wisdom in the kitchen.

You can make many salsas in a molcajete, but this is the one we make most. I like to think of it as the "salad" of the salsa family, as it's not meant to be overly spicy. The vegetables are usually toasted on a comal or charred on the grill to achieve smoky notes, and the result is an almost-fruity salsa that's incredibly versatile. Some of my family members have been known to enjoy a scoop of molcajete salsa, a wedge of cheese, and tortillas as a complete meal.

Makes 4 cups

---

1 large yellow onion, quartered
8 Roma tomatoes
6 medium tomatillos, husked and rinsed (see page 38)
1 Anaheim pepper
1 serrano pepper
4 garlic cloves
1 bunch cilantro, including stems
2 teaspoons Diamond Crystal kosher salt (or 1 teaspoon Morton salt)

Special equipment
Molcajete or blender/food processor (I won't judge!)

1. Heat a comal, griddle, or cast-iron pan over medium-high heat. (You can also use a grill.)

2. When the griddle or pan starts to slightly smoke, place the onion, tomatoes, tomatillos, and peppers on the hot surface to blister, spaced apart so they're not sitting on top of each other.

3. Once you start to see some blistering on the bottom of the vegetables, rotate them using tongs to allow another side to blister. Continue to cook, rotating each vegetable until all sides are blistered.

4. Remove the peppers and onions when they are slightly charred on the outside, and the tomatillos and tomatoes when they are cooked throughout and soft. Adjust the heat to low-medium, add the garlic cloves to the griddle, and cook until completely cooked through and soft.

5. Now it's molcajete time! Remember, texture is important in this salsa. Add the ingredients to the molcajete and mash them together, adding salt to taste. Add water a splash at a time as necessary until you reach your desired texture. I like my salsa as a rough purée with distinct chunks.

6. If you are using a blender or food processor, coarsely chop the blistered vegetables. Blend half the vegetables, pulsing to break everything down while keeping the texture chunky. Add the second half of the vegetables and pulse a few more times to your desired consistency. Add salt and/or water to taste.

7. Allow the salsa to cool to room temperature; then store in an airtight container. It will keep for 4 days in the fridge.

omnia Pa

WHITE WIDOW SALSA

This showstopping salsa will help you earn (and edit) your list of friends. It may be hard to believe, but habanero peppers are naturally quite floral in flavor before the heat shows up. When you combine them with dairy (in this case, cream cheese, crema, and milk), garlic, and cilantro, you'll end up with a complex salsa that heats and cools all at once, leaving you wanting more. (It works great with seafood or any tomato-based dish.) Scientifically speaking, the dairy helps lock up your tastebuds right after the charred habanero rips them open. Does it really work like that? I don't know, try it and tell me.

Makes about 2 cups

¼ pound habanero peppers, stemmed and seeded (see Note)
5 garlic cloves
1½ teaspoons avocado or another neutral oil
¼ cup (about 2 ounces) cream cheese, at room temperature
2 tablespoons mayonnaise
¼ cup Mexican crema
6 tablespoons whole milk
½ bunch cilantro, stems included
Diamond Crystal kosher salt

1. Preheat the oven to 400°F. Line a baking sheet with parchment paper.

2. Toss the habaneros and garlic in the oil, and spread them evenly on the prepared baking sheet. Roast on the highest rack in the oven for 10 minutes. Then crack a window in the kitchen to get some airflow, switch the oven to the broil function, and broil on high until the habaneros and garlic start to blacken. Set aside to cool.

3. In a blender, combine the cream cheese, mayonnaise, crema, milk and 6 tablespoons of water. Blend until thoroughly incorporated.

4. Add the roasted peppers, garlic, and cilantro. Blend on high until smooth, and season with salt to taste.

5. Store the salsa in an airtight container in the refrigerator for up to a week.

Note: Removing the habanero seeds is optional—it's so you can to control the heat level of the salsa. If you remove the seeds, the salsa will still be very hot, but not scorching. Always wear gloves when handling habaneros, including when you're cleaning up. Use tongs to transfer the peppers from the baking sheet to the blender. Your eyes (and other parts of your body) will thank you!

SALSA MACHA

(NUTTY MEXICAN CHILE CRUNCH)

Countless recipes have folklore behind their origins and names. This salsa—an oil-based sauce made with fried chiles, garlic, and often seeds and nuts—causes a ton of debate. Prior to colonization, the Indigenous people of what is now known as Mexico ground chiles with palm oil and native seeds, and this salsa changed over time as new ingredients arrived. Sesame seeds were a notable evolution to the salsa, brought over on slave ships docking in Orizaba, Veracruz. We have the Afro-Mestizos to thank for the use of peanuts in this recipe. There are over two hundred recorded versions of salsa macha, and it's definitely one of my favorites.

The name "salsa macha" is also up for debate. Some translate it directly as "brave salsa." Others say the name refers to the process by which the salsa is ground—"machacada"—on a metate, a curved, rectangular mortar and pestle–like tool. I don't know which version you believe, but I will say this: "Whatever your grandma told you, she's right."

Makes 2 cups

---

2 tablespoons sesame seeds
2 cups grapeseed oil
2 dried chiles de árbol, stemmed
2 dried pasilla or ancho chiles, stemmed and seeded
½ medium white onion, diced medium
6 garlic cloves, thinly sliced
½ cup raw Spanish or redskin peanuts
Diamond Crystal kosher salt

1. Toast the sesame seeds in a dry pan over medium heat, moving the seeds constantly until they begin to turn a golden color. Immediately transfer the seeds onto a plate. Set aside.

2. In a deep cast-iron skillet or Dutch oven, add the oil. Set over medium heat until the oil reaches 350°F on a kitchen thermometer. If you do not have a thermometer, use tongs to place a chile de árbol into the oil. When the oil is hot enough, the chile should immediately puff up and turn a deep red color.

3. Once the oil is hot enough, fry the chiles in separate batches (first the chiles de árbol, then the pasilla or ancho chiles), about 30 seconds for each batch. Use a slotted spoon to position the chiles spaces apart to ensure even frying. With tongs or the slotted spoon, carefully remove the fried chiles from the oil, taking care to drain out any oil completely. Transfer the chiles to a large metal or glass bowl.

4. In the same oil you used to fry the chiles, add the onion and fry until the bits turn golden brown and float to the surface. This indicates that the water has evaporated from the onion. Using a slotted spoon, carefully remove the onions from the skillet, straining out the oil, and add them to the bowl of chiles.

5. Next, add the garlic slices to the oil. Like the onion, fry until golden brown and floating at the surface. Strain out with a slotted spoon, and add to the bowl.

6. Last, add the peanuts and fry until golden brown. Strain and add to the bowl of chiles. Turn the heat off and cool the oil to about 100°F, reserving it for the blend.

7. Fill the blender cup a quarter of the way with the fried mixture. Once the frying oil has cooled, ladle it into the blender, using enough to ensure the ingredients are submerged, with an additional inch of oil sitting on top. Blend on low speed or pulse until everything is broken down and combined, but stop before it's completely puréed into a paste. Transfer into a bowl. You're looking for a chile crisp–like texture.

8. Pour the salsa into a clean bowl. Top off with any remaining frying oil, stir in the sesame seeds, and season with salt to taste. Store in a glass jar or other airtight container. It will keep in the fridge for up to a month.

SALSA BORRACHA

(DRUNKEN SALSA)

I can remember the exact moment I first took a bite of a taco with fresh-out-of-the-pit lamb barbacoa, with salsa borracha poured over the top. It's a core memory of sensorial bliss. The lamb, cooked underground for hours, was a delight, but the magic was in the salsa borracha: A marriage of pre-Hispanic cookery and eighteenth-century hacienda meals, this unique salsa commonly includes fruit, dried chiles, onions, garlic, and an alcohol component, which makes it "borracha." Its combination of sweet, savory, smoky, and salty flavors makes it a welcome addition to my culinary repertoire.

In the regions where cactus and maguey (agave plants) cover the majority of uninhabited terrain, and lamb barbacoa is an heirloom family recipe passed down through generations, salsa borracha will usually contain *xoconostle* (cactus fruit). The fruit's high acidity and texture match that of tomatoes. The fermented sap of maguey plants, called *pulque*, is often used as the alcohol in the drunken salsa (yes, it's a relative of tequila).

Farther north, these ingredients can be changed out for a combination of tomato and light beer or *bacanora*, a less-smoky mezcal. Swap ingredients in and out of this recipe to fit whatever you have access to!

While the garnishes on this salsa are optional, they're delicious together, and turn the salsa into a snack on its own. Grab a warm tortilla and spoon some salsa, queso, and avocado, and you have a delicious vegetarian taco.

Makes 2 cups

½ cup light beer, or your favorite tequila (see Note)
2 pitted prunes
½ cup freshly squeezed orange juice
4 dried pasilla chiles, stemmed and seeded
2 Roma tomatoes
¼ white onion
1 garlic clove
Diamond Crystal kosher salt

Garnishes
1 avocado, thinly sliced
Coarse sea salt
¼ cup pulled strings of queso Oaxaca
Cilantro leaves

1. In a medium saucepan over low heat, combine the beer or tequila, prunes, ¼ cup water, and the orange juice. Allow to warm.

2. Meanwhile, in a dry comal or sauté pan, toast the pasilla chiles, tomato, onion, and garlic. Each vegetable will char at a different speed, so pay attention! As one side of the vegetable blackens, turn to char on the other side.

3. Add the charred vegetables to the liquid in the saucepan. Adjust the heat to medium and bring the mixture to a simmer.

4. Once simmering, reduce the heat to low and cover with a lid. Continue simmering for 10 minutes; then remove from the heat and allow the mixture to cool slightly, about 15 minutes.

5. Transfer all of the vegetables and liquid to a blender. Pulse on low until you have a coarse salsa and then season with salt to taste.

6. Pour the salsa into a serving bowl. When ready to serve, slice and fan out the sliced avocado, season it with coarse sea salt, and lay it on surface of the salsa. Space the pulled cheese strips apart around the avocado, and finally, garnish with a few cilantro leaves. If serving later, you can store the salsa in an airtight container in the refrigerator for up to 4 days.

Note: Obviously, using tequila instead of beer will make this salsa a lot more borracha!

CHILTEPÍN SALSA

There are not enough words to express my love for this complex, misunderstood, unknown-to-many, small-but-mighty little bb of a chile. Known as the "mother of all wild chiles," chiltepín was the first self-germinating chile pepper in the Americas, growing wild under the most unforgiving conditions in the hills and valleys of the Sonoran Desert. Chiltepíns pack a serious punch. Eaten fresh, they will send your body into a slight shock, waking up every nerve ending from your hair follicles to your toes. When dried, they can warm you to your core and humble the boldest eaters in the world with its spice. This salsa is best enjoyed with meat, or anything with depth, smoke and char. It transforms its fellow ingredients into a Hans Zimmer–quality score in your mouth—that is, in terms of drama. Disclaimer: Do not spoon this salsa generously—a little bit goes a long way. Avoid excess, and you'll be able to enjoy your stomach lining for years to come.

Makes 2 cups

---

2 large heirloom tomatoes (about 1 pound)
¼ medium white onion
1 garlic clove
7 dried chiltepín peppers
1 pinch dried Mexican oregano
Diamond Crystal kosher salt
Freshly ground black pepper
1 teaspoon apple cider vinegar

1. In a medium pot over high heat, bring 1½ cups of water to a boil. Carefully add the tomatoes, onion, and garlic and boil for 3 minutes. The onions will be translucent and the tomato will be slightly plump and the skins will be slightly lifted.

2. Remove the vegetables from the pot with a slotted spoon and transfer them into a blender (you can discard the water). Add the chiltepín peppers, oregano, a pinch each of salt and black pepper, and the vinegar. Blend on high until smooth.

3. Taste for heat level, and add more chiltepín if you're looking for an even spicier salsa. Adjust salt and pepper to taste as needed.

4. Let the salsa cool before serving, and store in an airtight container. It will keep in the fridge for up to 4 days.

CALDILLO
(ALL-PURPOSE TOMATO AND OREGANO SAUCE)

I know what you're thinking already, having read the title of this recipe: This isn't a salsa! Well, to that I say, tomate, tomato. Caldillo is a fast-cooked tomato-based seasoning sauce that can be placed on the table as a condiment, but is also a key finishing touch in Shredded Chicken Tostadas (page 84), Chicken Sopes (page 59), Quesadillas (page 80), and tons of other dishes. The main stars of the sauce are Roma tomatoes and dried oregano. Tomatoes contain glutamic acid, providing us with the wonderful flavor bomb we know as "umami," and they're even more potent here, where we use the entire tomato (rather than seeding it).

Caldillo can be ladled over any bite of food—it makes everything pop with flavor and helps you feel satisfied and satiated. And note that oregano is as important an herb as cilantro. When shopping, always buy Mexican oregano—it goes better with our cuisine's chiles, meats, and beans. I add one chile here, but by all means, add more if you want! Want to make a tomatillo caldillo instead of using Romas? Go nuts—I won't stop you!

Makes 2 cups

---

2 Roma tomatoes
½ medium yellow onion, quartered
4 garlic cloves
1 chile de árbol, stemmed
Diamond Crystal kosher salt
2 teaspoons dried Mexican oregano
Freshly ground black pepper

1. In a medium saucepan, add 1 cup water and bring to a simmer over high heat. Add the tomatoes, onion, garlic, and chile de árbol to the pot and reduce the heat to medium-low. Continue cooking the ingredients for 10 minutes, or until the onion is translucent.

2. Strain the vegetables through a fine-mesh strainer and discard the water. Transfer the vegetables to a blender. Blend on high until you have a smooth purée and season with salt to taste.

3. Return the blended salsa to the saucepan and set it over medium heat. Cook the sauce for about 15 minutes, or until most of the liquid has evaporated, stirring continuously to avoid burning it. The sauce will end up with a regular tomato sauce–like consistency, but it will be lighter in color. When it's ready, it should coat the back of a spoon. If it is too thick, adjust by adding a splash of water; if it's too thin, continue cooking to reduce until the consistency is just right.

4. Add the dried oregano, crushing the leaves between your thumb and index fingers as it goes into the sauce to release more aroma. Season with salt and pepper to taste. Stored in an airtight container in the fridge, it will keep for up to 2 weeks.

OFF MY MATRIARCHS' HIPS

RECIPES FROM OUR HOME AND FAMILY

Since 1848, the Mexico–US border has been home to people from all over Mexico, Central and South America, and really, the whole world, who travel north in order to find opportunities unavailable in their respective pueblos or countries. When writing about the borderlands and the people who have inhabited the area since the line was drawn in the dirt, I also have to include the matriarchs of my own family. While both my maternal and paternal families are from Jalisco and Nayarit, at my house in Tijuana, we grew up eating food from the entire republic. My mother's mom, my abue, was born into extreme poverty, and once she married my grandfather, they began moving wherever work was available. As their family grew, so did their list of addresses. Each of my sixteen aunts and uncles were born in a different city over the course of nearly twenty years. By the 1970s, they landed back in Tijuana, where they stayed put. In this chapter, you'll find all the highlights of our family's pan-Mexican table, and the stories that come with each staple in our house.

2 recipes Corn Tortillas dough (page 23)
Grapeseed or other neutral oil, for frying

For Serving
2 cups Cowboy Beans (page 216), or other cooked beans
4 cups Braised Shredded Chicken (recipe follows)
Shaved iceberg lettuce
Quick-Pickled Red Onions (page 33)
Thinly sliced radishes
1 recipe Tomato and Oregano Sauce (page 52)
Mexican crema
Crumbled Cotija cheese
3 limes, cut into cheeks

Special equipment
Tortilla press
Thin plastic produce bag, cut into two 6-inch squares
Clean dish towel or tortilla warmer

LAS CALANDRIAS CABALLITOS

(CHICKEN SOPES)

When I think about the time I spent in my aunt Lorenza's restaurant, Las Calandrias, in Guadalajara, Mexico, I'm flooded with the many core memories I made in that space, until it closed in 2003. At five years of age, I was waking up and heading to the wholesale market to run restaurant errands, then opening the gates at the restaurant to welcome the staff and start my daily chores. One of my payments was an order of "caballitos" (little horses). "Caballitos" were sopes, given the name in reference to the restaurant—a *caballo* (horse) comes with a *calandria* (carriage). Basically little masa cakes, sopes can carry a lot of delicious ingredients—my aunt's go-to was shredded chicken and meaty beans, with a topping of pickled onions, savory tomato sauce, and rich crema.

Sopes are made and served across the entire country. Some have a thicker masa base, some have an incredibly thin base, some are hard-fried, some are simply comal-heated, remaining very soft. There are ones you can pick up with your hands and others that you MUST eat with a fork and knife or risk ruining your outfit. You can adjust all of that to your liking, by making your sopes thicker or thinner, and varying your cooking time or method. My recipe uses the same dough that's used in my tortillas de maíz. I like to parcook my sopes on the comal or in a pan, finish shaping them, and then fry them for flavor and texture.

Once you read through this recipe, you will understand the buildable, mix-and-match nature of the ingredients. My standard is frijoles with shredded chicken (in a pinch, a store-bought rotisserie chicken is fine, but my braised shredded chicken recipe is great to keep in your back pocket), but you can use braised beef, vegetable *guisado*, chicken with chipotle tinga, birria—the options are endless.

Serves 6

SHAPE THE SOPES:

1. Line your tortilla press with the sheets of plastic. Roll the masa into twelve 4-ounce (lemon-sized) portions.

2. Preheat a comal, griddle, or skillet over medium high heat. Line a baking sheet with a clean dish towel and set aside near the comal.

3. Working one at a time, place a ball of dough in the center of the plastic-lined tortilla press. Lightly press the lid down to make a 3-inch-wide, ¼-inch-thick disk. (You can also do this with your hands if you don't have a tortilla press.)

4. Carefully peel the masa disk off the plastic and place directly on the heated comal. Cook for 2 minutes, flip, and repeat until light brown on both sides—you don't want the sopes cooked through

Recipe continues

at this point. Move the parcooked sopes to the dish towel–lined baking sheet and let them cool slightly. Once cool enough to handle, pinch their edges all the way around to form a ½-inch-high masa wall. Repeat the process with all the sopes; then cover the pinched sopes with a second clean, damp towel. (As you get the hang of it, you can cook and shape several sopes at a time, of course. But start slow!)

FRY THE SOPES:

5. Fill a large skillet with about an inch of oil and set it over medium-high heat. Test if the oil is hot enough by dipping the corner of one of the sopes into the oil. When the temperature is just right, the sope should immediately be covered in tiny bubbles, but it shouldn't be roaring hot, definitely not smoking. (The sopes will immediately get way too dark or burn.) If it gets too hot, drop it to medium heat and let it cool down a bit. Test a corner of a sope before dropping them in.

6. Carefully lay the sopes in the oil two to three at a time, being careful to not crowd your pan. Fry on both sides, about a minute on each side, carefully flipping the sopes with tongs, until golden brown. Remove the sopes and drain them on a paper towel–lined plate, with the pinched wall facing down on the towel.

TO SERVE:

7. Top your sopes with a mound of warm Cowboy Beans, Braised Shredded Chicken, and toppings to your liking.

BRAISED SHREDDED CHICKEN

Makes 4 cups

- 1 (2–3 pounds) whole chicken, giblets removed
- 2 carrots, peeled, diced large
- 2 ribs celery, strings removed, diced large
- ½ white onion, diced large
- 1 bay leaf
- 1 dried avocado leaf
- 1 teaspoon dried oregano
- 1 teaspoon freshly ground black pepper
- Diamond Crystal kosher salt

In a large stockpot over medium heat, add 1 gallon of water, the whole chicken, carrots, celery, onion, bay and avocado leaves, oregano, and black pepper. Bring to a simmer and cook the chicken, skimming off any foam or scum that forms on the surface of the water every 30 minutes. Cook for 3 hours, or until the chicken falls off the bone.

Remove the chicken from the pot and transfer it to a medium bowl to cool. Strain and reserve the chicken broth left over in the pot. Discard the bay leaf; you can purée the remaining solid vegetables and freeze to use as a soup base.

Once cooled, separate the chicken meat from the bones. Shred the meat, using two forks or a stand mixer fitted with the paddle attachment. Transfer to an airtight container and add 1 cup of the chicken broth back to the shredded chicken after shredding (you can save the rest for another use). Store the chicken in the fridge for up to 3 days, or freeze for up to 1 month. Same goes with the broth.

ENCHILADAS SUIZAS

(CREAMY TOMATILLO ENCHILADAS)

Regionally, enchiladas vary widely. They use all kinds of different salsas, some are folded, some are rolled, some are made with masa that is flavored, then filled, then deep-fried. There are lots of great ones, but my personal favorite version is enchiladas *Suizas* (meaning Swiss).

Suizas are (for the most part) made with shredded chicken and a green tomatillo salsa base, with heavy cream and cheese added to achieve a milder heat. The richness of the dairy balances the acidity and brightness of the tomatillos beautifully, for enchiladas that keep you wanting more.

Their origins, like countless other dishes, are debated to the brink of familial dissolution. There's the story of the former Austrian archduke-turned-emperor, Maximilian I of Mexico, who allegedly demanded milder enchiladas (so his cook added cream to the recipe). Then there's the rumor that the owner of Sanborns department stores said these enchiladas look like the snowcapped Swiss Alps. The true story is anyone's guess. I chose to believe there's some truth in all myths. What I know for sure is that the Suizas at Las Calandrias were stellar. My mother learned the secrets from the cooks in Guadalajara and mastered them in Tijuana. Whenever we saw her making them, we knew it was going to be a good night. You can make these in a giant pan—enough to feed a whole sports team—or do like I do, and freeze the sauce into small batches to make just enough for the people in your house (or even a serving for one).

Serves 4 to 6

Suiza Sauce

- 2 cups vegetable stock or water
- 1 pound tomatillos, husked and rinsed (see page 38)
- ½ medium yellow onion, coarsely chopped
- ½ cup coarsely chopped cilantro, stems included
- 2 serrano peppers, stemmed
- 1 cup heavy cream
- ¼ cup shredded Emmentaler cheese (or Gruyère or Munster)
- ¼ cup pepitas
- Diamond Crystal kosher salt
- Ground white pepper

For Assembly

- 12 Corn Tortillas (page 23), or store-bought
- 4 cups Braised Shredded Chicken (page 60)
- 2 cups shredded Emmentaler cheese (or Gruyère or Munster)

For Serving

- ½ head iceberg lettuce, shaved
- Cilantro leaves
- Green onions, green parts only, thinly sliced
- 1 cup Mexican crema
- 4 radishes, thinly sliced

MAKE THE SAUCE:

1. In a medium pot over medium-high heat, bring the vegetable stock, tomatillos, and onion to a simmer. Reduce heat to medium-low and continue to simmer for 10 minutes, or until the onions become translucent.

2. Remove the pot from the heat, let it cool slightly, and transfer the mixture to a blender with the cilantro, serranos, cream, ¼ cup of shredded cheese, pepitas, and salt and pepper to taste. Blend until smooth and set aside.

ASSEMBLE AND BAKE THE ENCHILADAS:

3. Heat the tortillas on a griddle to soften, and place in a folded towel or cloth-lined tortilla warmer to keep warm and soft for rolling enchiladas.

4. Preheat the oven to 375°F and position a rack on the top shelf of the oven. Spread a thin layer of the Suiza sauce to cover a 9 × 13-inch baking dish.

Recipe continues

5. Place roughly 3 tablespoons of shredded chicken down the center of a tortilla. Add about 2 tablespoons of sauce and 2 tablespoons of grated cheese on top of the chicken. Roll tight to wrap the tortilla around the filling and place it carefully, seam-side down, into the baking dish. Repeat with the remaining tortillas to fill the baking dish.

6. Top the rolled enchiladas with the remaining sauce, then the remaining shredded cheese. Cover the dish with aluminum foil, place on the highest rack in the oven and bake for 10 minutes, until heated through and bubbling.

7. Carefully remove the foil and switch the oven to the high broil setting. Broil on high for about 5 minutes, or until the cheese is browned, keeping an eye on it and rotating if needed to ensure even browning.

8. To serve the enchiladas, top them with lettuce, a few cilantro leaves, a spoonful of green onions and a drizzle of crema, with a few radish slices on the side.

NANCY'S ALBÓNDIGAS AL CHIPOTLE

(MOM'S MEATBALLS)

It's a question we've all been asked: "It's your last day on earth—what dish do you want to eat?" My answer is always the same: My mom's albóndigas, the perfect storm of beef (or pork) with herbs, rice, and lots of seasoning, filled with a chunk of hard-boiled egg and baked in a tomato and chipotle sauce.

This is a recipe you can prep in large batches, freezing the raw meatballs to cook later. I often serve this with a side of rice and vegetables—I usually roast whatever vegetables I have on hand that are on their last legs, during the last 30 minutes the meatballs are cooking. I love this with large chunks of carrots, potatoes, chayote, or zucchini for contrasting texture. Of course, always enjoy with a stack of fresh Corn Tortillas (page 23).

Serves 6

Albóndigas

- ½ cup bread crumbs
- ½ cup whole milk
- ½ cup jasmine rice, soaked in water for 1 hour
- 2 pounds ground beef or pork
- 2 large eggs
- 2 garlic cloves, minced
- ½ cup A.1. Sauce
- 2 tablespoons Worcestershire sauce
- 5 fresh mint leaves, minced
- 3 tablespoons Diamond Crystal kosher salt or Knorr Suiza chicken bouillon (or 1½ tablespoons Morton salt)
- 6 hard-boiled eggs, cubed, or 1 cup cubed mozzarella cheese, for stuffing (optional)

Sauce

- 3 tablespoons olive oil
- ½ yellow onion, chopped
- 4 garlic cloves, minced
- 2 (14.5-ounce) cans crushed tomatoes
- 5 canned chipotle peppers in adobo sauce
- Leaves from 2 sprigs mint
- 2 tablespoons fresh Mexican oregano leaves
- 2 cups beef or vegetable stock
- Diamond Crystal kosher salt or Knorr Suiza chicken bouillon (see Note)

Note: According to my ama (my mom), Knorr Suiza, a.k.a. Knorr Caldo de Pollo, aka Knorr chicken bouillon powder, is a nonnegotiable must for seasoning. As a self-proclaimed lover of MSG, I support her message, but do what feels right to you. It's between you and your deity/priest/monk/astrologer—this is a zero-judgment zone. If you do use Knorr, though, remember that it replaces the salt in the sauce and meatballs.

MAKE THE ALBÓNDIGAS:

1. In a small bowl, combine the bread crumbs and milk and allow the bread crumbs to soak for 10 minutes. Transfer the soaked bread crumbs to a large mixing bowl, discarding any excess milk.

2. Strain the soaked rice (discard the soaking water) and add it to the bowl with the soaked bread crumbs. Add the ground meat, eggs, garlic, steak sauce, Worcestershire sauce, mint, and salt (or Knorr Suiza), and mix well until combined.

3. Check the seasoning of the meatball mixture by cooking a spoonful of it in a small skillet. Taste and adjust seasoning as needed.

4. Portion the mixture into meatballs, each about the size of a lime, using a medium ice cream scoop or by rolling them with your hands. To make stuffed meatballs, hold the albondiga in one palm, and press into it with your thumb to create a dimple in the center. Place the hard-boiled egg or cheese in the center and tuck the sides inward to cover the filling. Roll once more between both hands to make it into a nice round ball again. Place the meatballs on a large baking sheet and set aside.

MAKE THE SAUCE:

5. In a large saucepan over medium heat, add the oil. Once the oil is hot, add the onions and sauté for 5 minutes, until translucent. Then add the garlic and sauté for another 3 minutes, until fragrant.

6. Add the canned tomatoes, chipotles in adobo, mint, and oregano and bring to a simmer. Simmer for 15 minutes—the excess moisture will begin to evaporate, and the herbs will become fragrant.

7. Add the stock, stir to incorporate, and season with salt (or Knorr Suiza) to taste. Remove the sauce from the heat, then use an immersion blender to purée the sauce until smooth. (Alternatively, carefully transfer the sauce to a blender, blend until smooth, and return it to the pot.)

8. Set the pan of sauce over low heat. Carefully place the albóndigas in the sauce, one by one, ensuring that they are submerged completely in the sauce. Do not use a spoon to move them after you set them in the pot, or you'll risk breaking them apart.

9. Cover the pot with a lid and simmer on low heat for 40 minutes. After 40 minutes, check for doneness by carefully removing an albondiga from the sauce and cut it open. The rice should be translucent all the way to the center and completely cooked through, with no crunch or bite. If more time is needed, add 5 minutes and check for doneness again. Serve hot.

PICADILLO A LA CUBANA

(SWEET-AND-SOUR BEEF SAUTÉ)

2 tablespoons olive oil
½ teaspoon ground cumin
½ teaspoon ground coriander
½ medium yellow onion, diced small
1 medium poblano pepper, charred, peeled, seeded, and diced small
1 tablespoon minced fresh ginger
3 garlic cloves, minced
1 pound lean ground beef
½ cup pitted sliced green olives
6 dried apricots, diced small
2 tablespoons golden raisins
1 tablespoon dried oregano
1 Roma tomato, seeded and diced small
½ (14.5-ounce) can tomato sauce (about 1 cup)
2 waxy yellow potatoes (such as Yukon Gold), diced small
2 large carrots, peeled and diced small
2 tablespoons Worcestershire or Maggi sauce
1½ cups beef broth
1½ tablespoons apple cider vinegar
Diamond Crystal kosher salt

For Serving/Garnishes

White Rice with Corn, (page 33)
Fried plantains (optional)
Chopped fresh parsley
Pickled Vegetables (page 32)

Like her albóndigas, my mom's picadillo is a hybrid of several different versions of the dish that you can find across Mexico—reflecting that while my maternal family eventually settled in Tijuana, they remembered the many places they lived before arriving in "el norte." In fact, my favorite thing about a good picadillo is its chameleon-like quality: It can be anything from the star of a dish, with rice on the side, to the filling in an empanada or tamale. Picadillo's notable Caribbean/Afro-Latino–influenced flavors give it a sweet-and-sour complexity.

This recipe gives me a moment to close my eyes and experience flavors that don't seem like they would go together, but they actually do. The earthy flavors of cumin and coriander match the charred poblanos. You won't find poblano in many picadillo recipes, but like I mentioned, my matriarchs brought their favorite flavors with them as they moved around Mexico, and we're all the luckier for it. The same goes for the ginger, most commonly associated with Asian food, which my mom discovered she loved after eating Chinese-Mexican classics in Tijuana. I think the ginger works here as a sort of flavor-boosting cymbal crash. The sweet notes of apricots and raisins will break the salinity of the overall dish and provide delicious texture in each bite. Toss in some slivered almonds or pine nuts for even more texture—that was the special occasion add-in at our house.

Serves 4 or 5

1. In a Dutch oven or medium heavy pot over medium-low heat, add the olive oil. Stir in the ground toasted cumin and coriander and sauté for 1 minute, until fragrant.

2. Add the onion, poblano, ginger, and garlic. Adjust the heat to medium and sauté, stirring often, until the onion is soft, about 5 minutes.

3. Add the ground beef, olives, apricots, raisins, and oregano. Cook, breaking up the meat with a spoon, until it is no longer pink—but not yet browned—about 8 minutes.

4. Add the diced tomato, tomato sauce, potatoes, carrots, Worcestershire or Maggi sauce, beef broth, and apple cider vinegar and stir to incorporate. Add salt to taste. Bring the mixture to a simmer, then adjust the heat to low, so you have a slow simmer.

5. Cover with a lid and continue simmering for 30 minutes. After 30 minutes, remove the lid and give the picadillo a stir. The sauce should have thickened and the vegetables should be tender—if they're not, keep cooking. Adjust seasoning to taste.

6. Serve hot on top of rice, ideally garnished with fried sweet plantains and parsley leaves, with pickled vegetables on the side.

SIETE MARES

(SEVEN SEAS SOUP)

Every coastal family has their recipe for *Siete Mares*, the soup of the Seven Seas. The perk of being raised in the cradle of the Pacific Ocean is that I've always had access to the highest quality seafood year-round. This soup is a celebration of that privilege.

The rich tomato adobo–esque seafood broth is brightly acidic while still deep and rich in flavor, with abundant vegetables that you can swap in and out depending on what's in season. You can include one kind of seafood, or ten—go with my suggestions here or use whatever quality seafood you have available.

You'll notice that the recipe makes a lot of soup, so gather your friends and some big bowls. Of course, you can halve the recipe if you want, but to me, this is best when shared with all your favorite people, on the hottest of days, served with plenty of lime and corn tortillas.

Serves 6, very generously

Fish Stock

Bones and head from a 3- to 4-pound red snapper (fillets reserved for the soup)
1 medium white onion, halved
8 garlic cloves
1 cup large dried shrimp (see Note)
3 whole allspice berries
Diamond Crystal kosher salt
1 tablespoon whole black peppercorns

Soup

1 bunch cilantro stems (leaves reserved for garnish)
2 sprigs fresh epazote
1 bay leaf
1 fresh hoja santa leaf
2 Roma tomatoes,
3 jalapeño peppers
½ cup olive oil
1 medium white onion, diced small
2 garlic cloves, minced
2 dry ancho chiles, stemmed, seeded, and cut into ¼-inch strips
1 teaspoon dried Mexican oregano
2 pounds waxy potatoes (such as Yukon Gold), cubed
3 chayotes, peeled and cubed
5 large carrots, peeled and sliced into ¼-inch rounds
2 pounds red snapper fillets from whole red snappers, skins removed, cut into large chunks (use the carcass for broth)
1 pound extra-large shrimp (preferably Mexican brown shrimp), peeled and deveined
1 pound lump crab meat
Diamond Crystal kosher salt
Freshly ground black pepper

Garnishes

Limes, cut into cheeks
Cilantro leaves
Crushed dried chiles de árbol or dried chiltepín peppers

MAKE THE FISH STOCK:

1. In a large stockpot, combine 5 quarts of water, the fish carcass, onion, garlic, dried shrimp, allspice, salt and pepper. Bring to a boil over high heat.

2. Once the mixture is boiling, reduce the heat to medium-low and cook for 1 hour, skimming off the foam from the surface of the water as it collects.

3. Remove the pot from heat, strain the stock into a large bowl, and set aside. Discard the solids and rinse and dry the stockpot—you'll use it again for the soup.

MAKE THE SOUP:

4. Tie the cilantro stems, epazote sprigs, bay leaf, and hoja santa leaf together with twine to create a bouquet garni (herb bundle). Set aside.

5. Char the tomatoes. Line a comal or heavy skillet with aluminum foil and heat over medium-high. When very hot, add the tomatoes and let the skin blister and char. Turn the tomatoes so you get a good char all over. Remove from heat and let cool for a few minutes. Set aside.

6. Char the jalapeños on a dry comal or skillet on medium high heat until blackened all around. Once charred, remove the stem and seeds and julienne the peppers. Set aside.

7. In the same stockpot over medium-high heat, heat the olive oil and sauté the onion and garlic with olive oil until translucent, about 5 minutes.

8. Slice the charred tomatoes into ¼-inch rounds and add them to the pot. Add the julienned jalapeños, ancho chile, and oregano.

Reduce the heat to medium-low and cook, stirring often, until the vegetables begin to form a thick, jammy paste, about 20 minutes.

9. Pour in the strained fish stock, then add the potato, chayote, carrots, and bouquet garni. Season with salt and pepper. Adjust the heat to medium and allow the mixture to reach a simmer. Cook, uncovered, for 40 minutes, or until the vegetables are all tender and the broth has a rich flavor.

10. When almost ready to serve, discard the bouquet garni and add the red snapper pieces, fresh shrimp, and crab to the soup. Cook for 8 minutes, just until the seafood is fully cooked but still tender. Adjust seasoning to taste.

11. When serving this soup, the right vessel is important—a pozole bowl or tall soup bowl (with 4-inch walls) work beautifully. Ladle the vegetables into the bottom of the bowl; then top with a ladleful of the broth. Arrange the seafood on top. Garnish with a few cilantro leaves among the seafood and serve with a small dish on the side with limes and crushed chile de árbol.

Note: Dried shrimp are available in most Mexican/Asian markets or online.

ARISC
Camarón
Camarón
Camarón
ENSENADA
MEXICO

Camarón
$210
PELIGRO
PELIGRO
VOLTAJE

ZEPEDA FAMILY BIRRIA

When you come from a family of rich culture and low finances, you tend to grow up alongside animals that eventually become dinner—and we were no different. We'd often visit my uncle in an area of Tijuana called El Florido, where we'd run around the hillsides, generally causing chaos and occasionally helping him feed the family goat. One day, it would be time to celebrate a baptism, wedding, birthday. That's when we'd enjoy one of the tastiest, classic Jalisco-born dishes—*birria de chivo* (goat birria).

Birria, a word coming from the Spaniards circa the sixteenth century—meaning "person or thing of the lowest value or quality." The word refers to the cheaper cuts of meat often used in the dish, but rest assured it is not an accurate reflection of the resulting flavors. Birria is typically made in an underground oven, with the meat roasting just above a stockpot that has the adobo sauce inside it (so the sauce catches all of the meat drippings). The meat is shredded and served in a bowl, with a ladle of sauce enrobing it all. Garnishes are up to the consumer.

While goat is the classic meat, beef, pork, and even fish have been subbed in, and I've also used meaty mushrooms to make a version for my vegetarian friends. This recipe calls for two separate cuts of beef, with a possible addition of goat if you can find it. Using a combination of the two proteins helps introduce goat to those who aren't used to eating a gamier meat. You could also use goat for the whole thing—I would do goat shoulder or shanks.

Serves 6 to 8

Adobo

- 6 dried guajillo chiles, stemmed and seeded
- 4 dried ancho chiles, stemmed and seeded
- 4 dried cascabel chiles, stemmed and seeded
- 1 medium white onion, diced large
- 9 garlic cloves, smashed
- 2 inches fresh ginger, peeled and halved lengthwise
- 2 tablespoons distilled white vinegar
- 1 tablespoon Diamond Crystal kosher salt (or 2 teaspoons Morton salt)
- 1½ teaspoons freshly ground black pepper
- 1½ teaspoons dried oregano
- ¼ teaspoon ground cumin
- ½ teaspoon ground cinnamon
- ¼ teaspoon ground cloves
- 6 fresh thyme sprigs
- 3 bay leaves

Birria

- 2 pounds boneless goat shoulder or beef chuck, cut into 2-inch cubes
- 2 pounds boneless short ribs, cut into 2-inch cubes
- 2 tablespoons Diamond Crystal kosher salt (or 1 tablespoon Morton salt)

For Tacos

- 1 recipe Corn Tortillas (page 23)
- 2 bunches cilantro leaves, minced
- 2 medium white onions, minced
- 8 limes, cut into cheeks

MAKE THE ADOBO:

1. In a dry skillet or comal over medium heat, toast the guajillo, ancho, and cascabel chiles. Turn them to brown on all sides, 4 to 5 minutes.

2. Fill a medium pot with 6 cups of water. Add the toasted chiles and the onion, garlic, and ginger. Bring to a strong simmer over medium-high heat. Continue to cook, uncovered, until the chiles have softened and the onion is translucent, about 8 minutes.

3. Transfer the chile mixture and 2 cups of the cooking liquid to a blender (you can discard the remaining water). Add the vinegar, salt, black pepper, oregano, cumin, cinnamon, cloves, thyme, and bay leaves.

4. Secure the lid on the blender and remove the center cap to let steam out. Place a clean towel over the opening to prevent splattering. Blend on high until smooth, then strain the sauce through a fine-mesh sieve.

Recipe continues

5. Let the adobo sauce cool to room temperature, about 1 hour. Transfer to a container with a tight-fitting lid. Keep refrigerated until ready to use.

MAKE THE BIRRIA:

6. Place the cubed meat in a large bowl and sprinkle with salt. Toss to coat.

7. Add the cooled adobo to the meat, tossing to coat the meat evenly. Cover the bowl with a lid or plastic wrap and place in the refrigerator to marinate for at least 4 hours, or overnight.

8. Preheat the oven to 300°F.

9. Transfer the marinated meat and rendered juices to a large roasting pan or large Dutch oven, and add in 8 cups of room-temperature water. Cover the dish with foil or a lid and place it in the oven. Bake for 4 hours, or until the meat falls apart easily with a fork.

10. Remove the pan from the oven. Using a slotted spoon, carefully remove the meat from braising broth, transfer it to a large bowl, and cover with foil to keep warm. Set aside.

11. Transfer the Dutch oven with the remaining broth to the stove and set over medium heat, uncovered. (If using a roasting dish, transfer the broth to a pot or saucepan). Bring the broth to a simmer and cook for 15 to 20 minutes to reduce, until you have about 8 cups of broth. Skim off any fat that accumulates on the surface and save it in a small bowl—you'll use it later for the tacos. Season the broth with salt to taste.

12. Shred the meat in the bowl with two forks (or use your hands). Pour in 1½ cups of the broth and stir to incorporate. Taste and adjust salt as needed. Reserve the rest of the broth.

TO MAKE TACOS:

13. Set a large griddle over medium-high heat. Lightly grease the griddle with the reserved fat from the birria broth. Submerge a tortilla in the reserved birria broth; then place the tortilla on the hot griddle. Top the tortilla with ¼ cup of shredded meat and fold in half to make a taco.

14. Cook each taco on one side for 2 minutes, flip, and cook the reverse side until browned and crispy, about 2 more minutes. Repeat to make as many tacos as you'd like.

15. Transfer the tacos to a serving plate, and serve with small cups of broth for sipping, and cilantro, onion, and lime on the side for garnish.

ARROZ POBLANO

(CREAMY RICE WITH CHARRED POBLANOS)

My mom's sister, my Tía Lili, is—like my mom—a phenomenal cook. This recipe is her creation. I have no sisters, and my aunt has two daughters, so as a kid, I would beg to spend the night with my cousins. When I slept over, I could sometimes smell this dish being made, and I would always flip.

With this recipe, my aunt combined any Mexican's favorite two dishes—queso fundido with *rajas* (cheese fondue with roasted poblano peppers) and garlic butter rice. The result is a creamy, savory, onion-and-garlic–infused rice topped with charred poblano pepper strips. I've been making this arroz poblano at every restaurant I've run since 2015—and I've pleaded with my aunt to come show my whole team how to make it. The cooking method might seem unorthodox to you, but trust the process and you'll be rewarded!

I suppose this recipe is emblematic of us *fronterizos* (border people)—we're restless, so we get creative with what we have, and delicious surprises come as a result. Hopefully, this dish becomes tradition in your home, too. I especially love serving this rice with Zepeda Family Birria (page 73).

Serves 4

---

2 poblano peppers
2 tablespoons salted butter
¼ medium white onion, diced
4 garlic cloves, minced
2 cups jasmine rice
1 cup whole milk
3 cups chicken stock
Diamond Crystal kosher salt

CHAR THE POBLANOS:

1. Place the poblanos over an open flame, such as over the burner of a gas stove or under a broiler. Toast on all sides—the skin should become glossy, and the peppers should blister and blacken in spots. Place the peppers in a bowl while they're still hot and cover the bowl with plastic wrap to steam and soften for 5 minutes.

2. After the peppers have softened, peel the charred skin off by rubbing the peppers with a damp paper towel. Using a knife, slice each pepper along one side from stem to tip, in order to butterfly it. Open each pepper like a book and remove the seeds and stem. Then julienne the peppers. Set aside.

MAKE THE RICE:

3. In a large saucepan over medium heat, melt the butter. Add the onion, garlic, and rice and sauté until the onion is translucent and the rice starts to brown, about 5 minutes.

4. Add the milk and the stock to the pan, season with salt, and bring the rice mixture to a boil. Turn the heat to the low, cover the pan with a lid, and continue cooking for 15 minutes.

5. After 15 minutes, turn the heat off and let the rice sit, still covered, for 5 more minutes. Add salt to taste and fluff with a fork. Served topped with the charred poblano strips.

TÍA LORE'S POZOLE

Pozole Broth
1 (3-pound) pork shoulder, deboned and cut into 2-inch cubes (bones reserved for broth)
2 (8-inch) sheets dried kombu
3 bay leaves
2 medium white onions, halved
8 garlic cloves
2 pounds fresh nixtamalized corn kernels or hominy (see Note)

Adobo
5 dried ancho chiles, stemmed and seeded
5 dried guajillo chiles, stemmed and seeded
4 garlic cloves, peeled
1 medium yellow onion, peeled and quartered
2 dried avocado leaves (optional)
½ cup bonito flakes (optional)
Leaves from 3 sprigs fresh oregano (or 2 tablespoons dried Mexican oregano)
1 tablespoon white distilled vinegar
Diamond Crystal kosher salt

For Serving/Garnishes
Shaved iceberg lettuce
Thinly sliced radishes
Dried oregano
Limes, cut into cheeks
Chile de Árbol Salsa (page 37)
Tostadas raspadas (store-bought)

Pozole, which has origins in pre-Hispanic Mesoamerica, has evolved in many directions from the original Aztec recipe. These days, it's a stew that varies widely by region; the constant is the star ingredient—big, chewy kernels of nixtamalized corn (a.k.a. *maíz cacahuazintle*, or hominy). Everyone from Oaxaca to Jalisco to Guerrero has their favorite version; red pozole from Jalisco is a beloved family tradition in the Zepeda household. The rich broth bubbling away on the stove has a hypnotic quality, luring you in like a cartoon smoke hand. And the scent doesn't lie—it tastes just as good. The umami-rich pork broth is cut with intensely flavorful red chile adobo, warming spices, and a splash of vinegar for brightness.

In my recipe, you'll notice a couple of ingredients that are somewhat unusual in the Mexican pantry: kombu (dried kelp) and bonito flakes (dried, smoked, and fermented tuna). These are base layers for the Japanese mother broth known as dashi. In the northern borderlands, our Japanese (and Chinese) immigrant brothers and sisters brought their ingredients with them—and taught us how to use them. As a born-and-raised border kid, I want to show the world how much better our cuisines can be when we welcome the migrants who make our shared land—and food—so much richer and more delicious.

Serves 4 to 6

MAKE THE BROTH BASE FOR THE POZOLE:

1. In the center of a large 12 × 12-inch cheesecloth, place the pork bones, kombu, bay leaves, onions, and garlic. Draw the corners of the cheesecloth together and tie the bundle closed with twine. Add it to a large stockpot and cover with 4 inches of cold water.

2. Add the cubed pork shoulder meat and hominy to the stockpot. Set on the stovetop over medium heat and bring to a simmer. Cook until the hominy skins burst, about 2 hours.

MAKE THE ADOBO:

3. In the meantime, bring 8 cups of water to a boil in a large saucepan over high heat. Submerge the cleaned dry chiles in the boiling water; then immediately remove the pan from the heat. Let the chiles sit in the water until soft, 10 to 15 minutes, then strain, reserving the soaking liquid.

4. Place the garlic and onions on a heatproof wire rack. Set the wire rack directly over a gas burner on high heat to char on all sides. (Alternatively, char the garlic and onions in the broiler or on the grill.)

Recipe continues

5. Transfer the charred garlic and onions to a blender along with the soaked chiles, avocado leaves (if using), bonito flakes (if using), oregano, and vinegar. Blend until smooth. If needed, add some of the reserved chile soaking liquid to achieve a smooth purée. Strain the adobo purée through a fine-mesh sieve.

FINISH MAKING THE POZOLE:

6. Stir the adobo sauce into the pot with the pork and hominy. Adjust the heat to high and bring the soup to a simmer; then reduce the heat to low to reach a gentle simmer. Partially cover the pot with an offset lid and cook for about 3 hours, stirring occasionally, until the pork is falling apart. If the liquid level drops below the level of the solids, replenish with a cup of water at a time as needed.

7. Remove and discard the cheesecloth bundle and season the soup with salt to taste. Serve the pozole hot, in large soup bowls garnished to your liking.

Note: Fresh nixtamalized corn can be found in many Latin markets that make their tortillas in house. If you can't find fresh nixtamalized corn kernels, you can substitute 12 ounces dried hominy, soaked in water overnight, then drained. Alternatively, use canned hominy with the liquid drained (three 15-ounce cans should get you about 2 pounds of kernels).

My aunt Lorenza and me at Las Calandrias, the summer of '96

ZAPOPAN-STYLE QUESADILLAS

(FRESH MASA QUESADILLAS)

You can find some of the tastiest treats in Mexico by walking around the courtyards of churches. Anywhere you go, street food helps give you a (literal) taste of the people and culture you're experiencing. Street food is also evidence that regardless of socioeconomic status, people will always figure out how to cook something delicious based on what they have available to them. *Garnachas* (corn masa–based fried street foods) are one great example—they're some of the most affordable and best eats you can find in Mexico, made simply with masa, cheese, lard, and tomatoes.

This quesadilla recipe differs from the quesadillas you're probably familiar with, and reveals how my family's Jalisco roots show up on our plates. When I would visit my family in Guadalajara as a kid, I would often ask what was on the day's agenda, secretly hoping we'd somehow end up in the town square of Zapopan, by the cathedral, where there was always a woman selling fresh masa quesadillas. Growing up, getting these quesadillas always felt like a special occasion.

These garnacha-style quesadillas are pan-fried until crisp, accentuating the flavor of the fresh corn masa, served with garnishes, and most importantly, dipped in Caldillo (page 52), a cooked tomato and oregano sauce. I think of this dish as Mexico's answer to Spain's *pan con tomate* . . . but better. Yeah, I said it! Let's keep the five-hundred-plus-year beef going strong.

The quesadilla filling is just cheese, but of course, you can evolve it to your preference to include shredded birria, squash blossoms for an impressive appetizer, or anything else you'd like. While these can be eaten as a portable snack, trust me—plating them up with caldillo, lettuce, cream and Cotija and sitting down to enjoy them is well worth it.

Serves 6 (makes 24 small quesadillas)

2 batches masa from Corn Tortillas (page 23)
4 cups shredded Oaxaca or Muenster cheese
Grapeseed or other neutral oil, for frying

For Serving/Garnishes
Tomato and Oregano Sauce (page 52), for serving
1 small head iceberg lettuce, shaved
Quick-Pickled Red Onions (page 33)
1 cup chopped cilantro leaves
1 cup crumbled Cotija cheese
1 cup Mexican crema

Special equipment
Tortilla press
Thin plastic produce bag, cut into two 6-inch squares

1. Line a baking sheet with parchment paper and set aside. Keep the prepared masa dough covered with a clean, damp kitchen towel while you work.

2. Follow the instructions from the corn tortilla recipe to press a ⅛-inch-thick tortilla, but don't remove it from the base of the tortilla press yet!

3. Add a heaping ¼ cup of shredded cheese to the center of the tortilla, still on the press, leaving a ½-inch border around for a good seal. Using the plastic sheet at the bottom of the press, fold the tortilla in half onto itself and press the edges together gently to seal the cheese inside. Remove the quesadilla from the plastic, set it on the prepared baking sheet, and cover with another clean, damp kitchen towel. Repeat the process until you have used up the cheese and masa.

4. Line a second baking sheet with paper towels and a wire cooling rack. Set aside.

5. Fill a deep, 12-inch-wide skillet with 2 inches of frying oil and set over medium heat. Heat until the oil reaches 350°F on a kitchen thermometer.

6. When the oil is ready, use a heatproof spatula to carefully lower each quesadilla into the hot oil in batches, up to 3 in a pan (depending on the size of the pan). Do not overcrowd or you won't be able to flip safely. The oil should be hot enough that it immediately bubbles when you add the quesadilla, but it should not be smoking or burning.

7. Cook the quesadillas on one side until golden, 1 to 2 minutes, then flip and cook on the other side. When both sides are golden brown, remove the quesadilla from the oil using a slotted spoon and set on the wire rack to drain. Repeat to fry the rest of the quesadillas.

8. To serve, spoon some warm caldillo to cover the base of a rimmed plate. Place a quesadilla or two on top, and garnish with shredded lettuce, pickled onions, cilantro, Cotija, and crema.

DRIED SHRIMP AGUACHILE

I know what you're thinking: "Dried shrimp?! Yuck, no way . . . so salty." Listen, you're not wrong about the salty part, but you're sorely mistaken about everything else. Growing up, my father's end-of-day ritual included a tequila or Scotch on the rocks . . . and hours spent painstakingly cleaning dried shrimp; first by removing the heads, then squeezing the hollow space along the curvature of the back and pinching off the legs and tail, preserving only the center meat. He'd contort his face, sticking out his tongue as he made sure each one was perfect.

With more than one-third of Mexico experiencing sub-tropical to tropical weather, eating salt and acid is a practical way to stay hydrated on the hottest months. And my father brought his recipe for perfectly cut red onions, cucumbers, chile, and limón-marinated dried shrimp from coastal Nayarit to Tijuana.

Legend has it that as soon as I learned to pull to stand using the edge of the coffee table, I made a beeline to my father's plate. He watched with bewilderment as his pride and joy, his beautiful baby girl, took a dried shrimp that had been marinating in lime and habanero right to the face. After the banshee-like screams, the heat eventually subsided, I wiped my face, and went back for another bite.

Even if you're skeptical, you should give this recipe a shot. Find good-quality dried shrimp that you can tell wasn't dried years ago (see Note), and withhold your judgment until the second bite. The sea salt will hit you no doubt, but so will the deep briny shrimp flavor, with a satisfying chewy texture, and bright acidity, plus the fresh crunch of the raw vegetables. It is a full sensory experience, with the heat creeping in last. After the second bite, you'll start to understand what umami truly means, and suddenly you'll feel like you can't get enough. And if you're still wary of dried shrimp, don't worry: This aguachile base can be used with any other seafood that you want, or even with fresh fruit, for your vegan friends.

Serves 4

---

1 pound large dried shrimp, cleaned (see Note)
4 green onions (green and white parts), thinly sliced on the diagonal
2 Persian cucumbers, diced small
½ bunch cilantro, minced
Juice of 8 limes (about 1 cup)
Juice of 4 lemons (about 1 cup)
2 serrano peppers, stemmed and seeded (for more spice, use habaneros)
Diamond Crystal kosher salt

For Serving/Garnishes
½ medium red onion, julienned
½ cup cilantro leaves
Coarse sea salt
Tostadas raspadas (store-bought)
½ cup mayonnaise

1. Clean the dried shrimp by removing the heads, and do your best to remove the thin shells, reserving the body meat. Discard the heads and shells. Mince the shrimp meat with a sharp knife, or use a food processor. Add the dried shrimp to a medium bowl with the sliced green onions, cucumbers, and cilantro.

2. Make the aguachile liquid: In a blender, combine the lemon and lime juices with the serrano pepper. Blend until smooth and season with kosher salt to taste. Strain the mixture through a fine-mesh sieve.

3. Pour ½ cup of the aguachile liquid over the shrimp and vegetables and toss to coat. Taste and adjust salt if needed.

4. Spread the shrimp mixture on a large serving platter. Pour the rest of the aguachile liquid over the whole platter. Garnish with red onion, fresh cilantro leaves and more salt. Serve the aguachile with tostadas and a small bowl of mayonnaise to spread on the raspadas before enjoying.

Note: Finding good-quality dried shrimp is a skill in its own right. When I'm shopping for them, I check to make sure the color is still a vibrant orange, and the shrimp are still slightly chewy—they should bend when pressed against, instead of cracking. Plenty of Mexican and Asian markets will have dried shrimp, but Mexican *mercados* have the large orange variety that I don't normally see elsewhere. If all else fails, you can buy them online.

TOSTADAS DE POLLO

(SHREDDED CHICKEN TOSTADAS)

Tostadas are a great way to repurpose leftover proteins from other dishes. Street food options flourish along the border, where blue-collar workers need a lunch that's as quick to whip up as it is delicious. I can still close my eyes and see the table of vintage Tupperwares holding the shredded lettuce, radishes, and sauce (with a plastic ladle in it) . . . and a tired mom at the helm. As a kid, I spent countless hours watching my abue and my mom cook for us. I was amazed by their ability to turn yesterday's whole roasted chicken into tomorrow's chicken tostadas, without spending hours cooking in the kitchen. It made them superheroes to me. How many times have you stared into a packed fridge and said, "There's nothing to eat!" only to have your mom say, ". . . Hold my *chancla*."

Tostadas are also a great way to turn a sit-down meal into a light snack . . . until you eat six of them, that is. This tostada recipe is a classic meal-in-a-hurry. You can swap out the shredded chicken for anything—turn chicken tinga into tinga tostadas, etc. The one rule is that you have to get intimate with your tostada, by which I mean *use your hands*! Take time to layer the toppings so that you can pick the whole thing up and take a bite—a fork will ruin the experience here. The sauces I always include in my tostadas are a classic Caldillo (page 52) for a flavor boost, and a spicy chile de árbol for heat . . . but choose your own adventure!

Serves 4

---

4 (5-inch) tostadas (store-bought)
2 cups Cowboy Beans (page 216)
1 recipe Braised Shredded Chicken (page 60)
2 cups Tomato and Oregano Sauce (page 52)
1 head iceberg lettuce, shaved
6 radishes, thinly sliced
½ bunch cilantro leaves
1 avocado, thinly sliced
½ cup Mexican crema
½ cup crumbled Cotija cheese
3 or 4 limes, cut into cheeks
½ cup salsa of choice

To build a tostada, spread 3 to 4 tablespoons of frijoles over the base of a tostada in an even layer. Top generously with a layer of Braised Shredded Chicken, then drizzle about 2 tablespoons of caldillo over the chicken. Top generously with lettuce, radishes, and cilantro. Then layer on slices of avocado, a drizzle of crema, a sprinkle of Cotija, a squeeze of lime, and salsa to your liking. Enjoy immediately.

TACOS LILY
OAXACA
Coca-Cola
Bianchi

3 AGUAS FRESCAS

Not unlike the art of turning yesterday's dinner into tomorrow's tostadas, aguas frescas are a way for moms everywhere to turn yesterday's overripe fruit into today's delicious drink. When my family fell on hard times financially, making fun aguas was a way for my mother to keep us from knowing it (or at least stop us from thinking about it). Now, as a mother myself, I can also add that it is an effective way to get stubborn, picky kids to drink water. Some agua fresca recipes are even used as energy drinks (see pages 199 and 226).

For these recipes, I was inspired by two of my favorite aguas frescas from childhood—*agua de plátano* (banana) and *agua de fresa* (strawberry). But to change things up, I mixed them with two other classic flavors: To the banana, I add horchata (cinnamon rice milk) for a creamy treat, plus some masala chai for complexity. To the strawberry, I add tangy, fragrant *jamaica* (hibiscus tea) for a perfect refresher and a touch of cinnamon for spice. The third recipe combines three popular aguas frescas into one, using cucumber, pineapple, and chia.

BANANA CHAI HORCHATA

Makes about 2 quarts

1 cup jasmine rice
1 stick Mexican canela/Ceylon cinnamon
1 teaspoon loose-leaf masala chai blend
3 medium overripe bananas
1 (14-ounce) can sweetened condensed milk
1 quart whole milk
Pinch of Diamond Crystal Kosher salt
Ice, for serving

Optional Garnishes
Frozen strawberries, slightly thawed and puréed
Ground cinnamon or cinnamon sticks
Plantain chips

In a container or bowl, mix together the rice, cinnamon, chai, and 1 quart of water. Let soak overnight.

In a blender, combine the soaked rice mixture (with the soaking water) and the bananas. Blend on high for 4 to 5 minutes, until the rice is completely dissolved.

Strain the mixture through a fine-mesh sieve into a large pitcher (discard any leftover pulp). Stir in the condensed milk, whole milk, and pinch of salt, and mix until fully dissolved.

Top off the pitcher with ice, stir again, and serve. Stir the pitcher each time before pouring.

If you want to go the extra mile, garnish your horchata like the ones found in mercados across the border: Fill a tall glass halfway with ice and pour in the horchata. Add a couple tablespoons of strawberry purée and a dash of cinnamon or a cinnamon stick. Drink with a straw.

SPICED STRAWBERRY JAMAICA

Makes about 2 quarts

2 cups packed dried hibiscus flowers
1 cup very ripe diced strawberries
1 stick Mexican canela/Ceylon cinnamon
1 whole star anise
½ cup sugar
Peel of 1 orange
Pinch of Diamond Crystal Kosher salt
Ice, for serving

Optional Garnishes (per glass)
Hibiscus flowers
Whole star anises
Orange peel twists

In a medium saucepan, combine the hibiscus flowers, strawberries, cinnamon, star anise, sugar, orange peel, salt, and 1 quart of water. Bring to a boil over medium-high heat.

Once the mixture reaches a boil, remove from heat, cover with a lid, and let steep for 15 to 20 minutes.

Strain the steeped liquid through a fine-mesh sieve directly into a pitcher and stir in an additional 1 quart of cold water. Stir to incorporate. Save a few hydrated hibiscus flowers for garnish if you wish; you can discard the rest of the solids.

Top the pitcher off with ice and stir once more before serving. If you want to impress someone, garnish with a hibiscus flower, a star anise, and an orange peel twist.

CUCUMBER PINEAPPLE CHIA

Makes about 2 quarts

1 large cucumber, peeled and diced
1 cup diced fresh pineapple
½ cup sugar
Juice of 1 lime (about 2 tablespoons)
2 tablespoons chia seeds
Pinch of Diamond Crystal kosher salt
Ice, for serving

Optional Garnishes (per glass)
Lime wedges
Tajín
Cucumber ribbons (see Note)

Add the cucumber, pineapple, and sugar to a blender with 2 cups of water. Blend on high until smooth, about 3 minutes.

Pour the mixture into a pitcher. Stir in the lime juice, chia seeds, salt, and 1 quart of cold water. Stir to incorporate, and let sit for 10 to 15 minutes so the chia seeds can expand.

Top off with ice and stir once more before serving.

If you'd like, garnish each glass by rubbing lime over the rim of the glass; then dipping the rim in Tajín. To be extra fancy, you can also line the inside circumference of the glass with a cucumber ribbon before pouring in the agua fresca.

Note: To make cucumber ribbons, use a vegetable peeler to take layers off a cucumber with a peeler, discarding until you get to the flesh.

JERICALLA

(BURNT CINNAMON CUSTARD)

This custard comes from eighteenth-century Guadalajara, created by a Spanish nun living in Mexico. The dessert is named *jericalla* after her birthplace—Jérica, Spain. The sugar is measured with restraint, and the surface of the custard is slightly bubbled up and toasted, making it different than a crema catalana or crème brûlée. It's enjoyed best cold, straight from the refrigerator, on a porch protected from the summer sun. Jericalla is traditionally flavored with cinnamon and vanilla, but you can experiment with other spices to find your favorite combination.

As a child, every year, I would get put on a plane from Tijuana to Guadalajara, where I spent time with my dad's side of the family for half the year. Most of the time, I was glued to my aunt Lorenza's hip—so it was no surprise that from the moment that I could reach a counter, I was put to work at her restaurant. One of my most favorite jobs at the restaurant was receiving the order of fresh jericallas from a woman who made them at her house. She'd pack them in layers in a five-gallon paint bucket, and I still remember lifting up the cardboard rounds that protected each layer and being graced with the aroma of toasted milk and cinnamon. It was intoxicating to my little eight-year-old senses. Many years later, being able to make jericalla at my own restaurant was the full-circle moment I didn't know I needed. This recipe is my attempt to share with you a bit of my family history and celebrate the women who shared their love for me through food.

Serves 6

---

1 quart whole milk
2 sticks Mexican canela/ Ceylon cinnamon
1 vanilla bean pod, or 1 teaspoon vanilla bean paste or extract (see Note)
2 large eggs, room temperature
6 large egg yolks, room temperature
1 cup sugar

Special equipment
6 (8-ounce) ramekins

1. Preheat the oven to 350°F. Line a shallow roasting pan with a small kitchen towel and place six 8-ounce ramekins or custard cups on the towel.

2. In a medium pot, combine the milk, cinnamon sticks, and vanilla seeds and pod (or vanilla extract). Bring to a simmer over medium heat for about 8 minutes, or until small bubbles form consistently, before a boil. Then turn the heat off and allow the ingredients to steep for 20 minutes.

3. In a medium bowl, whisk together the eggs, yolks, and sugar until they become pale yellow in color. Set aside to allow the milk mixture to finish steeping.

4. After 20 minutes, begin whisking the steeped milk mixture, keeping the whisk toward the center of the pot to form a small whirlpool. Pour the egg mixture in a slow, steady stream into the center of the whirlpool of milk—this will help prevent the eggs from curdling. Scrape the bowl to get every last bit of egg into the milk, leaving the bowl clean. Continue whisking to form a custard. Then, strain the custard through a fine-mesh sieve from the pot back into the medium bowl.

5. Lay a kitchen towel at the bottom of a deep roasting pan, and place the ramekins in the pan. Pour a scant cup of the custard base into each ramekin; they should be filled up to ¼ inch from the rim.

Recipe continues

6. Heat water in a pot until steaming-hot; then carefully pour it into a heatproof pitcher.

7. Open the oven and pull the middle rack partway out. Carefully place the pan on the rack, then slowly pour the hot water around the ramekins in the pan. The water should reach three-quarters of the way up the outside of the ramekins. Carefully push the rack with the pan back into the oven so the water doesn't slosh around) and close the oven door.

8. Bake the custards for 35 minutes. After 35 minutes, check to see if the custard has set by gently tapping the corner of the pan. If the custard is set, it should jiggle as one mass, rather than rippling like a liquid.

9. Once the custards are set, increase the oven temperature to 400°F and continue baking for 10 more minutes to toast the surface of the custards. When ready, the custards should have a brown, puffed top. If the browning isn't even, you can broil the custards on high with the oven door slightly ajar for 3 to 4 minutes.

10. Remove the jericallas from the oven and let cool completely; then place in the refrigerator to chill for several hours, or ideally overnight, before enjoying. Serve cold.

Note: If using a vanilla bean pod, split it down the middle and use the back of a knife to scrape out the seeds. Save the pod—you can let it steep in the milk to add extra flavor to the custard.

CHURROS

I challenge you to find someone who doesn't love churros. These fried treats have a loyal following akin to groupies for a rockstar legend. There are countless variations and cousins of churros around the world—and they're popular for a reason.

My mother learned how to cook churros after she met my father. (In an early effort to satisfy my dad's sweet tooth, she bought churro box mix that came with a piping bag and tip.) This recipe is definitely more involved—the dough requires patience first and foremost, and later, hand strength. Many churro recipes that I have tried make a dough that's too soft, so the churros fall apart during frying, or worse, they don't deliver on the crunch. The secret to a crispy, crunchy churro is to let the churros air-dry after piping, since moisture is the enemy of frying. I know it's hard work, but if you follow my instructions, I promise this recipe will reward you with restaurant-grade churros in your own home.

For the sugar topping, some places in Mexico simply use plain sugar; others use cinnamon sugar. Some include a bit of orange zest in the sugar and serve the churros with a thick, melted chocolate for dunking. Whatever toppings you go with, rest assured there's no wrong way to finish them—and you *will* finish them.

Makes 18 (10-inch) churros

6 tablespoons unsalted butter
Seeds from 1 vanilla bean pod, or 1 teaspoon vanilla bean paste or extract (see Note)
1 stick Mexican canela/ Ceylon cinnamon
1 whole star anise
Zest of 1 medium orange
1 teaspoon Diamond Crystal kosher salt (or ½ teaspoon Morton salt), plus a pinch as needed
2¼ cups all-purpose flour
2 cups granulated sugar
2 tablespoons ground cinnamon
2 large eggs
Grapeseed or other neutral oil, for frying

For Serving (optional)
Cajeta
Chocolate sauce
Sweetened condensed milk

1. In a 12-inch saucepan, add the butter, vanilla bean seeds (or vanilla extract), cinnamon stick, star anise, orange zest, 1 teaspoon salt, and 2¼ cups water. Bring to a simmer over medium heat, stirring occasionally until dissolved. Once the mixture reaches a simmer, remove from heat and let steep for 10 minutes.

2. Using a slotted spoon, remove the cinnamon and star anise from the pot and discard. Return the pot to medium heat and watch carefully. As soon as the mixture is scalding hot and begins to steam (do not let it reach a boil), add in the flour all at once and quickly stir to incorporate with a heatproof spatula or wooden spoon. Continue stirring until the flour is completely incorporated; then cook for 3 more minutes, still stirring, to cook the flour.

3. Remove the pan from heat. Immediately transfer the dough to the bowl of a stand mixer fitted with the paddle attachment. Beat on medium-low speed until the dough is slightly cooled and the steam dies down, about 3 minutes.

4. While the batter is mixing, in a large bowl or shallow dish, stir together the sugar, ground cinnamon, and pinch of salt for dusting. Set aside.

5. Adjust the stand mixer speed to low. With the mixer running, add the eggs to the bowl. Let the eggs incorporate into the dough, scraping the sides of the bowl with a rubber spatula if necessary. The finished dough should be shiny in appearance and feel slightly tacky.

Recipe continues

6. Line two baking sheets with parchment paper. Double-line a pastry bag (place one bag inside another) and fit with a 1M open star piping tip.

7. Pipe 10-inch-long straight ropes of batter onto the prepared baking sheets. Refill the bag with more dough as needed. (If your pot isn't big enough, pipe shorter churros.)

8. Chill the uncooked churros uncovered in the refrigerator for at least 30 minutes, or up to 2 hours, to allow excess moisture to evaporate. After chilling, the surface should be matte and should not feel sticky to the touch. (Alternatively, if you are not cooking the churros today, freeze them on the baking sheets until solid. Then transfer the frozen uncooked churros to a large plastic freezer bag and store in the freezer for future use. The uncooked frozen churros will keep for up to a month.

9. When you are ready to fry the churros, line a baking sheet or tray with paper towels and set a wire rack on top. Pour 3 inches of oil into a large Dutch oven or heavy pot; it should be wide enough for the churros to fit lying down. Set the pot over medium-high heat until the oil reaches 375°F on a deep-frying thermometer.

10. When the oil is ready, fry the chilled or frozen churros, working in batches of 3 or 4 at a time. Flip the churros occasionally, until they rise to top of oil.

11. Once the churros float, start timing: Fry for an additional 3 minutes, or until the churros turn light golden brown, with a crispy outside and a custardy center. Remove the churros from the oil and drain on the wire rack.

12. After each batch of churros, check the temperature of the oil and adjust the heat to return the oil to 375°F before you start the next batch.

13. Once you finish frying all of the churros, transfer them to the dish with the sugar and toss to coat on all sides.

14. Serve the churros immediately as is, or with small bowls of cajeta, chocolate sauce, or sweetened condensed milk for dipping.

Note: If using a vanilla bean pod, split it down the middle and use the back of a knife to scrape out the seeds for this recipe. Save the leftover pod and add it to a container of sugar for dusting the churro—it will infuse the sugar with vanilla flavor.

THE TALE OF TWO RICE PUDDINGS

Many cultures have a rice pudding–like dessert. I wanted to share the two versions that I love, one from my infancy (which my mother makes for us to this day), as well as the old-world Asturian/Spanish version I learned to make while studying the culinary anthropology of Mexico. Both are incredibly soulful and decadent in their own ways.

I have vivid core memories of my mother peeling an orange in one smooth motion, revealing a perfect orange coil. Then she'd whip the egg whites to perfect stiff peaks, showing us her trick of turning the bowl upside down over our heads without a drop falling out. The magic of her recipe is in the meringue, which makes for the fluffiest, most melt-in-your-mouth rice pudding you'll ever taste.

The magic in the Asturian version is the creamy texture that comes from the short-grain Spanish *bomba* rice, as well as the showstopping brûléed top, which you will need a blow torch for, unless you happen to have a caramelizing iron handy. You can make both of these the night before serving—they'll taste better the next day, anyway.

MOM'S ARROZ CON LECHE

Serves 4

1 cup jasmine rice
Peel of 1 orange
1 stick Mexican canela/ Ceylon cinnamon
Pinch of Diamond Crystal kosher salt
1 (12-ounce) can evaporated milk
1 (14-ounce) can sweetened condensed milk
2 teaspoons vanilla extract

Meringue
3 large egg whites
Pinch of Diamond Crystal kosher salt
Pinch of cream of tartar
½ cup sugar
Ground cinnamon, for garnish

Make the rice pudding. In a medium pot, combine the rice, orange peel, cinnamon stick, a pinch of salt, and 5 cups of cold water. Bring to a simmer over medium heat.

Cook for 15 minutes, maintaining a consistent simmer, but don't let the mixture reach a boil. Stir frequently to prevent sticking and to encourage the rice to release starch. After 15 minutes, check the rice for doneness; it should be completely tender. If not, continue simmering, adding half a cup of water at a time as needed to replenish the absorbed liquid; each grain of rice should have a translucent, gelled starch coating.

Once the rice is fully cooked, turn off the heat and discard the cinnamon stick and orange peel. Stir in the evaporated and condensed milks and the vanilla. Set aside to cool.

Make the meringue. Add the egg whites, salt and cream of tartar to the bowl of a stand mixer fitted with the whisk attachment (or use a regular bowl with an electric hand mixer). Whisk on high until foamy. Carefully pour in the sugar a little bit at a time until the mixture is glossy, with stiff peaks.

Assemble. If the arroz con leche is still hot, allow it to cool a bit longer—it should be warm to the touch, but not piping hot. Gently fold the meringue in thirds into the warm arroz con leche.

Portion the rice pudding into individual serving dishes and sprinkle with ground cinnamon. Serve it warm, or refrigerate it if you prefer to enjoy cold. (If eating cold, I still suggest leaving it out at room temperature for 15 minutes before serving.)

Recipe continues

ARROZ A LA ASTURIANA

(ARROZ CON LECHE'S GRANDPA)

Serves 4

3 tablespoons unsalted butter
1 cup bomba or Calasparra rice
1 (3-inch) stick Mexican canela/ Ceylon cinnamon
1 whole star anise
1 vanilla bean, split lengthwise and scraped
Peel of 1 lemon
Peel of 1 orange
Pinch of Diamond Crystal kosher salt
2 cups heavy cream
2 cups whole milk, plus more as needed
1 cup granulated sugar
Confectioners' sugar, for brûléeing

In a large paella or sauté pan over medium heat, melt 1 tablespoon of butter. Add the rice, cinnamon stick, and star anise and stir constantly until the rice toasts and the butter begins to brown.

Add the scraped vanilla bean seeds (along with the scraped pod), the lemon and orange peels, salt, and 1 cup of water. Cook, stirring constantly, to release the starches and "bloom" the rice, for about 5 minutes.

Once the rice is simmering and has absorbed at least half of the water, add 1 cup of heavy cream and 1 cup of milk to the rice, continuing to stir constantly.

Reduce the heat to medium-low to avoid scorching the milk. Continue cooking until the rice has absorbed about half of the milk and cream; then add the remaining 1 cup each of cream and milk. Stir continuously until the rice has absorbed all the liquid, 25 to 30 minutes.

Check the rice for doneness; it should be slightly more tender than al dente. If the rice is still not fully cooked, add additional milk, ½ cup at a time, and continue cooking, stirring frequently, until the rice is cooked through.

Once the rice is cooked, reduce the heat to low, add the granulated sugar and remaining 2 tablespoons of butter, and stir until incorporated. Turn off the heat.

Remove and discard the cinnamon stick, star anise, vanilla bean pod, and citrus peels. Portion the rice pudding equally into serving dishes and let cool to room temperature, allowing a skin to form on the surface.

Once the surface of the rice pudding is dry to the touch, dust each serving with a layer of confectioners' sugar. Place under a broiler (or use a blowtorch to brûlée the sugar directly) until deep amber in color, with a hard shell on top. Serve immediately.

TRES LECHES GELATINA CON MANGO

(THREE-MILK GELATIN WITH MANGO)

Cake with gelatin is our version of cake with ice cream—it's the perfect birthday pairing. My mother's creativity (and her sweet tooth) helped her make the tastiest *gelatinas.* It was the first thing I learned to make with her, to bring to a sleepover at a friend's house. I remember making panna cotta for the first time as a pastry cook (now over eighteen years ago) and connecting the dots with the treats of my youth . . . my mom was more of a chef than she ever gave herself credit for.

With that said, Mexican gelatinas are stylistically very different stylistically from a classic Italian panna cotta. We like a firmer, bouncier texture, as our gelatins need to withstand sitting outside on a hot summer day, and then being cut into fifty slices. This tres leches version, with the addition of canned mango chunks, is a favorite of mine and my brothers.

Makes one 13 by 9-inch baking dish, or one large Bundt mold

- 1 (15-ounce) can mango chunks in syrup (see Note)
- 4 (7g) packets instant gelatin (28 grams total)
- 1 (12-ounce) can evaporated milk
- 1 (14-ounce) can sweetened condensed milk
- 2 cups heavy cream
- 1 teaspoon vanilla extract
- Cooking spray, for greasing

1. Strain the canned mangoes, reserving the syrup. Dice the fruit into small pieces, if needed. Set aside.

2. In a small bowl, combine the gelatin and ½ cup of cold water. Whisk to incorporate and let the gelatin hydrate for 15 minutes.

3. In a separate large bowl, combine the evaporated milk, condensed milk, heavy cream, vanilla extract, and reserved mango syrup. Whisk until incorporated.

4. Transfer 1 cup of the milk mixture to a small pot and bring it to a slow simmer over medium heat. As soon as the milk reaches a simmer, turn the heat off. Add the hydrated gelatin and whisk until fully dissolved. Using a fine-mesh sieve, strain the gelatin-milk mixture back into the bowl with the rest of the milk mixture, and whisk to combine.

5. Spray a 13 × 9-inch baking dish or a Bundt pan with cooking spray. Pour the milk mixture into the pan; then add in the diced mango, making sure it is evenly distributed throughout. Cover with plastic wrap and place in the refrigerator. Let the gelatina set for 3 to 4 hours before serving.

Note: You can use fresh mango, as long as you have access to incredibly ripe, very sweet fruit. Canned mango just gives you consistent sweetness, which is important for this recipe.

Alternative gelatina flavors/mix-ins (instead of mango): Fresh strawberry, *chongos* (caramelized milk curds), cajeta, coffee, *mazapán* (ground peanut candy)

TIJUANA, ENSENADA, MEXICALI, AND CALEXICO

CALIFORNIA'S BORDERLANDS (WITH A SIDE TRIP TO TECATE)

We'll start our journey along the US/Mexico borderlands where I grew up, on the westernmost end of the border. We'll begin with the seafood-heavy coastal cuisine of Tijuana and Ensenada, and then move inland to the twin border cities of Mexicali and Calexico, with a short stop in Tecate. But before we dive into this chapter, I'd like to acknowledge that as a San Diego–Tijuana border kid, I was raised on Indigenous Kumeyaay land. Once the land was colonized, and after the borders were drawn, the land crossings between Mexico and California became some the most highly trafficked ports of entry in the Western Hemisphere.

Hundreds of different cultures have passed through these border crossings in their relatively short history. During the nineteenth century, westward expansion in the United States required labor on the railroads and in the mines, much of it outsourced by European and Anglo corporations. Asian immigrants were the fastest growing immigrant group of the time period, arriving to the region for the promise of work and bringing with them customs, food, and ingredients.

You may be surprised to find that many of the Mexicali/Calexico recipes in this chapter are heavily influenced by Chinese cuisine. Many immigrants (most of them Chinese) made the exhausting 120-mile journey on foot from coastal Ensenada inland to Mexicali, to join the Colorado River Land Company. At times, they outnumbered Mexicans in certain areas (which wasn't hard to do in Tijuana; its population in 1900 was just 243 people). La Chinesca in Mexicali became the largest Chinatown in Mexico, home to 10,000 Chinese residents (and just 700 Mexicans) in the 1920s. It's no surprise that this place is deeply influenced by Chinese culture and food. Today, the population is over 15,000.

By the 1970s, when my mother's family moved to Tijuana permanently, you could see the global influence from many different cultures on the city, which was home to Italian, Russian, Chinese, and Japanese restaurants. Tijuana has a unique ability to welcome cultures from all over the world and bring them into our fold—and this is especially true of the culinary landscape. Baja California Norte (north) and Sur (south) continue to inspire countless young chefs and fill the void in every tourist's hungry stomach. #tijuanamakesmehappy

In the coastal town of Ensenada, many Japanese immigrants helped establish the fishing industry. What would set the Baja fish taco apart if we didn't have Japanese tempura to thank?! And what would my dad have worn on the weekends if we didn't have *guayaberas* (embroidered linen button-down shirts), which likely evolve from *barong tagalogs* worn by Filipino immigrants? What would we rim our beers with if it weren't for the Chinese and Japanese influence of salt-cured plums and hibiscus flowers that influenced the invention of *chamoy*?!

I try to honor these cultural marriages whenever I create new dishes. These recipes are a mix of old favorites and new riffs—I hope you enjoy them!

DESDE 1941
FM
HUSSONG'S
SALIDA
EXTINTOR
RESTROOMS·BAÑOS
IBC

TORTA DE CHILAQUILES

(RED CHILAQUILES SANDWICH)

My culture has an unabashed love for a little carb-on-carb action. Fideo pasta in a taco? Sign me up. A beef *tamal* stuffed inside a torta bread roll with cream and salsa? Sure thing . . . and pass the water! Some of the creations may sound downright bizarre, and we have no plans to try to make sense of or explain these dishes to outsiders. But when you're in the club, you're in the club for good—so grab a plate!

A torta de chilaquiles is one of my favorite of these quirky indulgences, and anyone you serve this to will yell in excitement when they see it. Perfectly crispy tortilla pieces are drenched in a flavorful guajillo tomato sauce, then sandwiched in a freshly baked roll—your tastebuds would cry tears of happiness if they could.

The torta de chilaquiles was born in Mexico City and then migrated, like many foods and people do. I have eaten the best ones in the northern border area (in my humble opinion, at least). The punch of flavor beats others I've had throughout the rest of the republic. Listen, I could be biased! Try it and decide for yourself. But I will tell you that this torta has a visible stronghold in Tijuana—the last time I was at a gastro park (food truck park) in TJ, several trucks were all doing their own version of chilaquiles torta . . . and they all had insane lines.

Serves 4

Chilaquiles

- 2 dried chiles de árbol, stemmed and seeded
- 5 dried guajillo chiles, stemmed and seeded
- 1 dried chipotle chile, stemmed and seeded
- 1 medium white onion, quartered
- 3 garlic cloves
- 8 Roma tomatoes (1½ pounds), halved lengthwise
- 1 tablespoon dried Mexican oregano
- 1 bunch cilantro stems (leaves reserved for garnish)
- Diamond Crystal kosher salt

Tortas

- 1 (32-ounce) package thick corn tortilla chips
- 4 torta rolls, toasted
- ½ cup Mexican crema
- 1 bunch cilantro leaves, chopped
- Quick-Pickled Red Onions (page 33)
- 2 avocados, sliced (optional)
- 2 cups crumbled Cotija cheese (optional)
- 4 fried eggs (optional)

MAKE THE CHILAQUILES SAUCE:

1. First, make the sauce. Set a large cast-iron skillet over medium heat. When the skillet is hot, begin toasting the chiles de árbol, guajillo chiles, and chipotle in the dry pan, moving them continuously and flipping to evenly toast, until they are darkened and fragrant. Add the toasted chiles to a medium bowl and set aside.

2. Add the onions to the skillet, cut-side down, followed by the garlic cloves and halved tomatoes. Cook, turning to char on all sides, until softened and blackened in spots, 8 to 12 minutes. Remove the charred vegetables from the pan and transfer them to the bowl with the chiles.

3. Combine the toasted chiles and charred vegetables in a blender, followed by the cilantro stems, oregano, and 1 cup of water. Blend on high until smooth, about 20 seconds. Pour the salsa through a fine-mesh strainer into a bowl and discard any solids. Season with salt to taste and set aside. If using later, cover and refrigerate.

MAKE THE SANDWICHES:

4. Bring the chilaquiles sauce back up to a simmer, if needed.

5. Add a portion of tortilla chips (about 3 cups) to a large bowl. Pour 1½ cups of the chilaquiles sauce over them. Toss the chips with the sauce to coat them evenly.

6. Slice a torta roll in half lengthwise. Pinch out some of the bread from the inside of the larger, domed half to make a cavity. Fill the cavity with chilaquiles. Drizzle the chilaquiles with crema, cilantro leaves, and a few slices of red onion. (Adding a few slices of avocado, crumbled Cotija, and a fried egg is also encouraged.) Close the sandwich and serve immediately.

7. Repeat with the rest of the chips, bread rolls, and toppings. Serve each one as soon as you make it to preserve that incredible crunchy-saucy factor.

THE OG CAESAR SALAD

A CLASSIC . . . THE CLASSIC

Serves 4

- 3 garlic cloves, minced
- 4 anchovy fillets packed in oil, minced
- 1 tablespoon Grey Poupon mustard (see sidebar, page 108)
- 1 large egg yolk (pasteurized, if preferred; see Note)
- Juice of 1 lime (about 2 tablespoons)
- 1 tablespoon Worcestershire sauce
- 1 teaspoon freshly ground black pepper
- ¾ cup olive oil
- ¼ cup finely grated high-quality aged Parmigiano-Reggiano, plus more for garnish
- 4 small romaine lettuce hearts, leaves separated, rinsed and well dried
- 8 (¼-inch-thick) baguette slices, toasted until golden brown and crispy

1. In a large bowl, combine the garlic, anchovies, Dijon mustard, and egg yolk. Whisk to form a paste, breaking up the ingredients. Whisk in the lime juice and Worcestershire sauce; then add the black pepper and continue whisking.

2. While whisking continuously, add the olive oil little by little in a thin stream. Do not stop whisking—this is an important step to emulsify the dressing and prevent separation. Once the dressing is emulsified, whisk in ¼ cup of the grated Parmigiano Reggiano.

3. Add the romaine leaves directly to the dressing in the bowl and toss gently to evenly coat them. Divide the salad among 4 plates, and garnish each serving with the toasted baguette slices, plus more grated Parmigiano-Reggiano to taste.

Note: I have eaten raw yolk emulsions a thousand times, but if you would feel better pasteurizing them first, an immersion circulator (what people call a "sous vide machine") is your best bet. "Cook" the eggs at 135°F for 90 minutes, then cool in an ice bath. The yolk will still be raw but safe to eat.

Topo Chico

HOTEL CAESAR'S INFAMOUS SALAD

There's no doubt that you've heard of Caesar salad, and you've probably also heard that this classic dish actually hails from Mexico—it was invented in Tijuana over one hundred years ago, in 1924. But you may not know that Caesar salad is yet another example of the borderless culture of the borderlands. So, here's the story.

During the era of US prohibition, Italian immigrant and San Diego restaurateur Caesar Cardini, tired of prohibition restrictions, crossed the border to Mexico and opened a restaurant and cantina—and later hotel—in Tijuana. Hotel Caesar's de Tijuana was smack dab in the middle of what is now called La Avenida Revolución, a street that was famous for indulging tourists and sailors alike in their search for debauchery. A century later, Caesar's is still in operation, a borderlands institution. The origin story of its famous salad is one of the, if not *the most* talked-about food stories in Mexican (and perhaps worldwide) culinary folklore.

Of course, there are many versions of the story. One popular legend says that American GIs stumbled into the restaurant just as it was closing, and Cardini, without access to the kitchen, scrambled to grab ingredients for a simple salad his mother often made him. But credit should really go to eighteen-year-old Italian immigrant Livio Santini, who was the actual chef at the restaurant. Santini based the salad on a recipe his mother called "hard times salad," because it contained a single coddled egg, a ration that she received while in an Austrian refugee camp during the First World War.

In 1924, the young Chef Santini was making lunch for Caesar himself, and decided to serve Mr. Cardini his mother's salad. A table of women visiting from Los Angeles were dining next to Caesar, noticed the salad, and asked if they could have some, too. They spread news of the salad like wildfire (never underestimate a woman's ability to pick up on the latest, greatest trend). Cardini, ever the showman and a larger-than-life host, decided to move the preparation tableside, so you could have a Caesar salad made right in front of your eyes.

I myself have a connection to the Caesar salad history, by way of the Plascencia family, who own and operate one of the largest restaurant groups in Baja California. Included in their portfolio is Hotel Caesar's, which they became custodians of in 2010. Cut to 2015, when I was preparing to help open Javier Plascencia's ambitious new restaurant project in San Diego. The project offered me a chance to do a deep-dive on the origin and ways of the famous salad—and attempt to replicate the original version. Sounds easy enough, right? *Wrong.* The phrase, "Often imitated, never duplicated," comes to mind. I had to convert ingredient quantities from a single tableside salad to make twenty-two quarts of dressing—and it had to taste exactly like the original Tijuana version, full stop.

It took months, making trips to taste the salad and study the captains who had been making the salad for years, some for two decades. I fell short time after time, subjecting myself to months of seeing the disappointment on Javier's face after every taste test. It was awful—disappointing my mentors is not something I enjoy, to say the very least.

After almost six months of what I called my "Caesar Crucible," I invited the dining room captains from Caesar's to have them inspect our process in San Diego. Now, in my retelling, I'm drawing out the drama of the story for a reason. I love to be unexpectedly trolled by the universe, and when a challenge seems insurmountable, I find that the solution is often ultimately quite simple . . . don't believe me? Keep reading.

Back to the story: The Caesar's *capis* inspected our ratios, and everything seemed in line, so they moved on to our ingredients. The Tijuana Caesar has limes, not lemons—a nonnegotiable. We had that right. The egg yolk, anchovy paste, garlic, Worcestershire sauce (good luck pronouncing that if you're an ESL kid like me), Parmigiano-Reggiano, freshly ground black pepper, the very best olive oil from olive groves established by Italian immigrants in Baja. We had all of that right. The last thing was the mustard. Mustard is a fantastic binding agent in dressings and lends huge flavor to whatever you add it to—but no two mustards are created equally. I had been buying ultra-fancy French mustard . . . like a dumbass, it turned out. The *capis* took one look at the fancy can of mustard and immediately exclaimed, gesticulating with the arms of an Italian grandmother, "Está mal!!" The correct mustard, they told me, was old-school Grey Poupon.

After making the new batch, this time with *all* of the correct ingredients, I asked Javier to come in and try it. I swear a single tear fell from his eye, and for a moment, all was right in the world. This salad is what I call a knife-and-fork salad—my favorite kind. Leaving the romaine spears whole, to cut up as you eat, stays true to the original version. I hope you all love this Caesar salad as much as I do, and now you have a few more stories to add to the salad's legendary history.

CALABACITA CON ELOTE

(BRAISED ZUCCHINI AND CORN CASSEROLE)

I ate this braised vegetable casserole–type dish at least once a week up until I moved out of my family's house at seventeen. It's a perfect dish for a large family on a budget, and oh—it happens to be delicious. It consists of three vegetables that were native to Mesoamerica, and later spread across the world after colonization: *calabacitas* (summer squash), corn, and tomatoes.

I like to think of this dish as ratatouille's Mexican cousin, packed with spice and smoke from chipotles and drenched in savory Tomato and Oregano Sauce. And don't forget the hot dogs! Many of us border kids laugh reminiscing about the number of childhood dishes that included weenies. To dress it up, you can swap the hot dogs with smoked sausage, or omit them entirely for a vegetarian dish. And yes, before you ask, you can also use this as a taco filling.

Serves 4 to 6

2 tablespoons grapeseed oil
1 white onion, diced small
3 kosher hot dogs, sliced into ¼-inch-thick rounds (optional)
3 garlic cloves, minced
1 canned chipotle pepper in adobo sauce, minced (plus more to taste)
1 cup Tomato and Oregano Sauce (page 52)
2 cups yellow corn kernels
1½ pounds calabacitas or zucchini, diced small
1 teaspoon dried Mexican oregano
Diamond Crystal kosher salt
Freshly ground black pepper
3 Roma tomatoes, diced small

For Serving/Garnishes
Mexican crema
Crumbled Cotija cheese
Minced fresh cilantro
Corn Tortillas (page 23)

1. In a large sauté pan over medium heat, add the oil and heat until shimmering. Add the onion and cook to sweat out the liquid, stirring often, until the onion is translucent—about 4 minutes.

2. Add the sliced hot dog (if using), garlic, and chipotle pepper in adobo (if you like spice, add more adobo sauce or chipotle peppers to taste). Let everything cook together, stirring often, until the mixture begins to caramelize, 7 to 10 minutes.

3. Reduce the heat to low and pour the caldillo into the pan to deglaze it, using a wooden spoon to scrape up any caramelized bits stuck at the bottom of the pan. Once all of the caramelized bits are lifted, add the corn kernels and the diced zucchini to the pan and stir to incorporate. Add in the oregano and season with salt and black pepper to taste. Cook for 5 to 7 minutes, stirring frequently.

4. Add the diced tomatoes to the pan and let everything simmer until the zucchini is tender, about 10 more minutes. Adjust the seasoning to taste as needed.

5. To serve, transfer the calabacitas to a serving dish and top with a drizzle of crema, crumbled Cotija, and cilantro. Serve with warmed corn tortillas.

TACOS GOBERNADOR

(GRILLED TACOS WITH SHRIMP AND CHEESE)

Tacos taste different in the North, even if no one from other areas will admit that there is a certain je ne sais quoi to them: the perfect storm of umami, salt, fat, acid, and heat, plus charcoal, a little bit of car exhaust, and some good music . . . okay, maybe I'm biased.

Every seafood truck in Baja sells a grilled shrimp-and-cheese taco, affectionately called "Tacos Gobernador," or "the governor's tacos." Tacos Gobernador originated in the city of Mazatlán in Sinaloa, invented by a chef at Los Arcos restaurant in the late 1980s to serve to the then-governor of the state. They were a hit and quickly became popular, and the name stuck as a tribute.

Sweet, mild shrimp are cooked with butter, garlic and onion, and then paired with sharp, creamy cheese and charred poblano pepper. Like any proper Norteño food, it is finished on a charcoal grill until the cheese is melted and tortilla is crispy. With each bite's crunch, you know you're home.

My recipe pairs this marvel of a taco with my roasted habanero White Widow Salsa, which is so addictive that you may start to question your sanity as you reach for dollop after spicy dollop.

Serves 4

---

3 tablespoons salted butter
3 garlic cloves, minced
1 pound jumbo shrimp, peeled, deveined, and cut into ½-inch pieces
Diamond Crystal kosher salt
1 poblano pepper, charred, peeled, seeded, and cut into strips
8 (5-inch) corn tortillas, store-bought or fresh (page 23)
1 cup grated Manchego cheese

For Serving
White Widow Salsa (page 47)
Limes, cut into cheeks

Special equipment
Charcoal or gas grill (see Note)
Toothpicks

Note: The purpose of using a grill in this recipe is really for the charcoal flavor, so if you only have a gas grill, I'd skip the grilling entirely and cook on the stovetop instead.

1. Fill a coal chimney with charcoal to the top, light the charcoal, and wait until the coals are completely gray, about 20 minutes. Pour three-quarters of the coals into the bottom of half of the grill, and the remaining quarter into the other half, setting two heat zones, a "hot zone" and a "hold zone." Place a clean grill grate over the coals.

2. In a large sauté pan over medium heat, add the butter and garlic. Sauté for 3 to 4 minutes, until the butter is melted, and the garlic is soft and translucent. Add in the shrimp pieces and season with a pinch of salt. Sauté, stirring continuously, until the shrimp turn light pink, about 4 minutes. Remove from the heat and mix in the charred poblano strips.

3. Set a dry, nonstick skillet or comal over medium heat (or use your grill). Add the tortillas and cook them just until they are pliable. Place the warmed tortillas on a clean work surface to assemble the tacos.

4. Fill a tortilla with 2 tablespoons of shrimp with peppers and 2 tablespoons of cheese. Fold the filled tortilla in half, and secure by threading a toothpick along the edge of the tortilla. Repeat with the remaining tortillas and filling.

5. Grill the tacos (see Note). Place the tacos directly on the hot grill and cook until the tortillas crisp up, the cheese melts, and the tacos pick up some flavor from the grill, about 3 minutes on each side.

6. If you don't have a charcoal grill, toast the tacos over a comal or in a skillet until the tortillas are crisp on both sides and the cheese is melted.

7. Serve the tacos with the White Widow Salsa and lime cheeks.

CUZALAPA #3
ABARROTES
CUZALAPA
BANOS
BAÑOS

BODEGADE
AGUILA X
020134/9135

LANGOSTA ESTILO PUERTO NUEVO

(ENSENADA-STYLE LOBSTER)

This is a dish as famous in its geographical area as its cousin, the Baja fish taco. Puerto Nuevo, established in 1793, is known as the "Lobster Village" of Baja, and is home to the tastiest preparations of the crustaceans.

This recipe is an ode to Lobster Village: Pacific spiny lobsters (sometimes called California spiny lobsters) are split, fried in lard, and served with a clarified garlic butter, alongside rice, beans, salsas, and delicious handmade flour tortillas. The swift deep-frying of the lobster ensures tender and succulent tail meat and by beautiful consequence, will create a core food memory for anyone who's had it.

Serves 4

---

4 medium whole Pacific spiny lobsters (or lobster tails)
Diamond Crystal kosher salt
Freshly ground black pepper
½ cup salted butter
2 garlic cloves, smashed
1½ cups manteca or lard, plus more as needed

For Serving/Garnishes
Flour tortillas (page 27), warmed
Beans with Cheese and Chorizo (page 187)
White Rice with Corn (page 33)
1 cup Tomato Sauce with Oregano (page 52)
¼ cup Chile de Árbol Salsa (page 37)
Limes, cut into cheeks

1. Prep the lobsters. Split the lobsters lengthwise, keeping the shells on, and clean by peeling out the intestine and removing any roe, sand sacs, and tomalley. Season the exposed meat with salt and pepper.

2. Make the clarified butter. In a small pot over low heat, melt the butter and the garlic cloves slowly, gently skimming off and discarding any butter foam that forms on the surface. (This "clarifies" the butter.) Continue cooking until the garlic is translucent, or cook longer to brown the butter slightly, if desired. Pour the butter into a small bowl for dipping and set aside.

3. Cook the lobster. In a large cast-iron skillet, add the lard and set over medium-high heat. Once melted, there should be enough lard to fill the pan with about ¼ inch of fat.

4. When the lard is melted and shimmering, add the lobsters to the pan, cut-side down. (Work in batches as needed; you might be able to only fit two lobster halves in the pan at a time.)

5. Fry the lobsters for 4 minutes, or until nicely caramelized. Flip the lobsters and fry on the other side for another 3 minutes, until the shell is bright red and the meat is just barely cooked through. Transfer the lobsters to a plate and cover with aluminum foil, or place in an oven set at a low temperature, just to keep them warm until ready to serve.

6. Serve the lobster family-style with flour tortillas and your pick of side dishes. For a salsa, combine the Tomato and Oregano Sauce and the Chile de Árbol Salsa in a small bowl.

Gold'n Soft

HUSSONG'S CANTINA MARGARITA

(THE "FIRST" MARGARITA)

Families from several bars and restaurants from Mexico and beyond have fought hard to defend their claim to the "first margarita" in history. One of the contenders in the dispute happens to be my favorite, so I'm sharing it here with all of you. (Drinks are just as legendary in our culture as many of our classic dishes. Our reputation as party-loving people who are not afraid to imbibe—whether for a special occasion or on a random Tuesday—isn't for nothing.)

Hussong's Cantina in Ensenada, a landmark in Baja California Norte, has been shaking this refreshing tequila-and-lime cocktail since 1941. Legend goes that it was shaken for a woman named Margarita Henkel Cesena, allegedly the daughter of the German ambassador to Mexico at the time. The newly shaken drink was said to be an adaptation of the Brandy Daisy, with tequila replacing the brandy, and each bar naming it after a different Margarita.

Hussong's version is my favorite because it uses licor de damiana, a Mexican liqueur made from the damiana plant, instead of triple sec or other orange liqueurs. The damiana liqueur gives the margarita an herbaceous, woodsy flavor that pairs amazingly with lime. The damiana plant is native to Baja, so this really is the version of the drink that's most connected to its region of origin. It's an ancient plant believed to have various health benefits, from regulating hormones in women to increasing testosterone in men (as an aphrodisiac).

Makes 4

---

1 cup coarse sea salt
1 Key lime, quartered, to rim glasses
4 ounces blanco Tequila
4 ounces damiana liqueur (see Note)
4 ounces Key lime juice (from about 10 limes)
Ice cubes, for serving
4 slices of lime peel, for garnish

1. Pour the salt onto a small plate. Rub the lime wedges over the rims of 4 small rocks glasses; then dip the rims in the salt.

2. Pour the tequila, liqueur, and lime juice into a large cocktail shaker. Fill the shaker with ice cubes and cover it with the lid. Shake the ingredients aggressively until the liquid is ice-cold, the shaker is frosty on the outside, and you hear less ice rattling around, about 1 minute.

3. Fill the glasses with fresh ice and strain the drink into the glasses. Garnish each glass with a lime peel right on top of the ice.

Note: I was able to find damiana liqueur for sale locally on a grocery delivery app, as well as online. I highly recommend it so you can make the real thing, but in a rush, Cointreau, or another orange liqueur, will work fine.

BORDERLANDS MARGARITA

CANTINA
1892
HUSSONG'S
EXCLUSIVO
TAXIS
AZUL Y
BLANCO
24 HORAS
GRUA
PROHIBIDA LA
ENTRADA A MENORES
DE 18 AÑOS
PROHIBITTED THE
ENTRANCE TO MINORS
UNDER 18 YEARS
NO MINOR
UNDER 18
ALLOWED
PROHIBIDA LA ENTRADA
A MENORES DE 18 AÑOS
Y A PERSONAS QUE NO
PRESENTEN IDENTIFICACION
OFICIAL.

HUSSONG'S
HUSSONG'S

LA CHINESCA-STYLE SALT-AND-PEPPER CHICKEN WINGS

This recipe is for my son James. His love for this beloved appetizer when getting Chinese takeout rivals only my own. The "salt-and-pepper" style in Chinese cooking always surprises newbies—it sounds like the most boring combination, but it really refers to a crispy, twice-fried dish seasoned with salt and a shower of fried chilies and other aromatics. The crunch on S-and-P anything is *loud*, and the flavors explode immediately, making your eyes widen for a split second before you close them out of pure bliss.

Growing up, the weekends were a chance for my father to bribe us with a mini road trip to Mexicali for Chinese food (and so he could do business on whatever legal case was working on at the time). The smells dancing through the air of the opulent banquet-hall restaurants are permanently embedded in my mind; so is the ritual of mixing the sweet-and-sour sauce with lime, a dash of Chinese mustard, and ketchup to make a dipping sauce for my crispy chow mein noodles—what I thought of as the chips and salsa of Chinese-Mexican restaurants. When the salt-and-pepper chicken and/or fish would land on the table, I'd pounce. Have I mentioned that I'm the only girl in a family with a lot of brothers? If I moved too slowly, I would be left with only crumbs from the platters to eat, because my brothers ate *everything*. I didn't learn to be scrappy for nothing!

Serves 4

Grapeseed or other neutral oil, for frying
1 cup potato starch
1 cup cornstarch
1 tablespoon Diamond Crystal kosher salt (or 1½ teaspoon Morton salt)
¾ cup Chinese cooking wine (Shaoxing)
20 chicken wings

Chili Oil
1 tablespoon freshly grated ginger
4 garlic cloves, minced
1 bunch green onions, white parts only, minced
1 serrano pepper, stemmed, seeded, and thinly sliced
1 tablespoon chili flakes
½ teaspoon ground Szechuan peppercorns
½ cup hot vegetable oil, reserved from frying

Garnishes
Finishing salt
½ bunch cilantro, leaves only
1 bunch green onions, green parts only, cut into 1-inch matchsticks

DO THE FIRST FRY:

1. Line a baking sheet with paper towels and place a wire cooling rack on top. Set aside.

2. Pour 3 inches of oil into a large Dutch oven or heavy, high-walled pot (about halfway up the pot). Set over medium-high heat and bring the oil to 350°F on a cooking thermometer.

3. In a large bowl, combine the potato starch, cornstarch, salt, cooking wine, and 1¼ cups of water. Whisk until smooth. The consistency should be very loose, not like tempura batter at all.

4. Pat any excess moisture off the chicken wings, then add them to the batter and toss to coat (work in batches if needed). Shake to allow any excess batter to drip off.

5. Use tongs to place the battered wings directly into the oil, working in batches of 5 or 6 wings at a time. Fry for 8 minutes, flipping the wings at the 4-minute mark. The wings should be very lightly golden.

6. After frying each batch of wings, remove from the oil and place them on the wire rack to drain excess oil. When all the wings are cooked, remove the pan from the heat.

MAKE THE CHILI OIL:

7. In a large heatproof bowl, combine the minced ginger, garlic, green onions, serrano pepper, chili flakes, and Szechuan pepper. Carefully ladle in half a cup of the still-hot frying oil from the pot, taking care to prevent splattering. Gently whisk to combine, then set aside.

DO THE SECOND FRY (AND SERVE):

8. Return the remaining frying oil in the pot to medium-high heat until the oil once again reaches 350°F on a kitchen thermometer. Fry the chicken wings a second time, working in batches of 4 to 5, until extra crispy and fully golden brown, 6 to 8 minutes. Remove the wings from the oil and drain again on the wire rack.

9. Add the double-fried chicken wings to the bowl of chili oil and toss to coat, then season with salt to taste. Transfer the wings to a platter and garnish with cilantro and green onions. Serve immediately.

CRAB SALPICÓN–STUFFED CHILES GÜEROS

Crab Ceviche

½ pound lump crab meat
½ cup finely diced heirloom tomato
½ cup finely diced jicama
½ cup finely diced red onion
1 small serrano pepper, stemmed, seeded, and minced
1 bunch cilantro (stems included), minced
3 tablespoons olive oil
1 tablespoon sesame oil
Zest and juice of 2 lemons (about ½ cup)
Zest and juice of 3 limes (about ⅓ cup)
½ tablespoon ground white pepper
Diamond Crystal kosher salt

Sauce

½ tablespoon Fermented Black Bean–Garlic Sauce (page 136), or store-bought)
2 tablespoons Chinese black vinegar
2 tablespoons Chinese cooking wine (Shaoxing)
1 cup soy sauce
Juice of 6 limes (about ½ cup)
Juice of 3 lemons (about ¾ cup)
1 teaspoon brown sugar

Stuffed Peppers

2 tablespoons grapeseed or other neutral oil, for blistering
8 whole yellow banana peppers (chiles güeros)
½ cup minced green onions, green parts only, for garnish

At many tables across Mexico and along the border, you'll see bowls of charred, blistered peppers accompanying meals, meant for you to nibble on while you eat as another way of adding heat. Chinese-Mexican restaurants also often serve meals with chiles, but instead of being charred and peeled—the usual Mexican way—these are blistered in oil. The result is a turned-up flavor and a beautiful marriage of culinary cultures.

In this recipe, I stuff oil-blistered banana peppers (*chiles güeros*) with a simple, fresh crab and vegetable ceviche, turning them into a proper appetizer in their own right. The sauce, though . . . this sauce is magical. Think soy sauce, but amped up with tart citrus . . . umami from top to bottom. A pro tip for even more flavor: If this dish was on my table, I would also add a spoonful of Salsa Macha (page 48).

Serves 4

MAKE THE CRAB CEVICHE:

1. Add the lump crab to a medium bowl and use the back of a spoon to break the meat up into smaller pieces. Add in the tomato, jicama, red onion, serrano pepper, and cilantro and toss to combine. Pour in the olive oil, sesame oil, lemon and lime zest and juice, and white pepper, and salt to taste. Toss to combine and add salt to taste. Set aside.

MAKE THE SAUCE:

2. In a small bowl, combine the Fermented Black Bean–Garlic Sauce, Chinese cooking wine, soy sauce, lime and lemon juice, and sugar and whisk until the mixture is homogeneous. Set aside.

PREPARE AND STUFF THE PEPPERS:

3. Add 2 tablespoons of oil to a medium skillet set over high heat. Once the oil is shimmering, add the peppers and carefully blister them, turning to blister on all sides, about 4 minutes total. Remove the peppers from the skillet and place them on a paper towel to drain and cool.

4. Once the peppers are cool enough to handle, remove their stems and slice them in half lengthwise. Remove their seeds, being careful not to rip the walls of the peppers in the process. Place the peppers cut-sides up on a medium serving platter.

5. Pack the crab ceviche into the peppers, forming a small mound in each one. Spoon the sauce over the peppers and garnish with minced green onions. Serve immediately.

RESTA
PALACÍ
Rest
9650
ABIERTO

RANT
ROYAL
Tel.
686-3422
ES 2705
PL/13072/EXP/ES/2016
Gasolinas con tecnología
PEMEX ADITEC
PEMEX Magna
PEMEX Premium

CARNITAS COLORADAS

(CHAR SIU PORK, MEXICALI-STYLE)

When this beautiful culinary creation landed on our lazy Susan, I was immediately smitten. If you're familiar with char siu pork, the bright red, sweet-and-savory honey-lacquered Chinese barbecued pork that hangs in the windows of butcher shops around Chinatown: This is the Mexicali version of it.

The bright red color in this dish actually comes from food coloring, so you can opt out of it if you'd like. To me personally, that signature red ring around the meat is sort of nostalgic, reminding me that the meal is going to be delicious, as dependable as Chinese mustard is hot.

For my ode to char siu pork, I include five-spice powder and ground Szechuan peppercorns. You'll also notice the use of unrefined piloncillo cane sugar here, which I prefer over regular brown sugar here because it contains more minerals that give it a deeper flavor.

Serves 4 to 6

---

2 pounds boneless pork shoulder
¼ cup ground or grated piloncillo
4 garlic cloves, minced
2 teaspoons Diamond Crystal kosher salt (or 1¼ teaspoons Morton salt)
1 tablespoon five-spice powder
½ teaspoon ground Szechuan peppercorns
1 teaspoon sesame oil
½ cup plus 2 tablespoons Chinese cooking wine (Shaoxing)
2 tablespoons soy sauce
2 tablespoons hoisin sauce
2 tablespoons molasses
½ teaspoon red food coloring (optional)
2 tablespoons honey

1. Cut the pork shoulder into long strips, about 2 inches wide and 1 inch thick. You can trim off some of the fat if you want, but don't trim it completely. Place the sliced pork in a 13 × 9-inch baking dish and set aside.

2. Make the marinade. In a small bowl, combine the piloncillo, garlic, salt, five-spice powder, ground Szechuan peppercorns, sesame oil, 2 tablespoons of the Chinese cooking wine, soy sauce, hoisin sauce, molasses, and red food coloring (if using). Whisk until combined.

3. Pour the marinade into the baking dish with the pork, and turn the pork to ensure it is fully coated with the marinade. Cover the dish with plastic wrap and place in the refrigerator to marinate for 24 hours, flipping the strips of pork after 12 hours.

4. After 24 hours, remove the pork from the refrigerator and allow it to come to room temperature, about 30 minutes.

5. Preheat the oven to 475°F. Line a rimmed baking sheet with aluminum foil and place a wire rack on top.

6. Arrange the pork on the wire rack, leaving space between the pieces. Place the baking sheet with the pork to the middle rack of your oven. Pour the remaining ½ cup of Chinese cooking wine and ½ cup of water into the baking sheet (below the wire rack), carefully close the oven, and roast the pork for 10 minutes.

7. While the pork is roasting, make the glaze: Combine the honey and 1 tablespoon of hot water in a small bowl and whisk together. Set aside.

8. After 10 minutes, remove the pork from the oven and brush with the glaze. Reduce the oven temperature to 375°F and return the pork to the oven for 10 more minutes, or until the glaze is no

Recipe continues

煌
酒

Royal

longer shiny. If the cooking wine and water in the baking sheet have evaporated, replenish as necessary.

9. Remove the pork from the oven, flip the pieces, and brush with the glaze again. Put the pork back in the oven for another 10 minutes.

10. Repeat this process of glazing and roasting until you run out of glaze—about 2 more rounds. (Continue replenishing the cooking wine and water as needed.)

11. Cook the pork until it reaches an internal temperature of 145°F at the thickest part. Remove the pork from the oven, tent loosely with aluminum foil, and let the meat rest so the juices can redistribute for at least 10 minutes.

12. If the pork is still not browned or charred to your liking at this point, broil it on the highest oven rack for a few minutes, with the door open. For serving, I like to slice it into thin strips and enjoy with steamed rice. Leftovers of both the carnitas and the steamed rice can be used for the House Avocado Fried Rice (page 139).

BLACK BEAN–GARLIC SKIRT STEAK WITH ASPARAGUS

This dish combines two of my favorites: the high heat–grilled skirt steak that is common in northern Mexican food, and a Chinese-style stir-fry of asparagus in fermented black bean–garlic sauce. Many dishes from my childhood stand out, but this dish lands in the top five. I remember my brothers fighting with each other for the last piece of steak on the platter . . . and my uncle slyly passing me a piece of the extra serving that he snuck onto his plate for me without them noticing.

A note on the sauce: You can buy premade fermented black bean–garlic sauce, but when you can control the salt, heat, and overall flavor by making your own, why would you? Plus, my recipe includes Mexican chiles de árbol, a variation you won't find at the grocery store. The included recipe makes a cup of sauce—more than you need for this dish—so you'll have a good amount left over to use in a quick meal. Salted fermented black beans are readily available at Asian markets, and also easy to find online. Once you get familiar with this ingredient, I guarantee you'll want to experiment with using them in other dishes in your repertoire, for their mysterious, ultra-concentrated umami flavor.

Serves 4 to 6

Skirt Steak

2 pounds skirt steak (ask for outside skirt; you want it almost 1 inch thick)
1 tablespoon minced garlic
1 tablespoon freshly grated ginger
Olive oil
Pinch of salt

Asparagus Stir-Fry

2 tablespoons grapeseed oil
1 pound asparagus, woody stems trimmed, cut into thirds
½ red onion, julienned
5 tablespoons Fermented Black Bean–Garlic Sauce with Chiles de Árbol (recipe follows)

Garnishes/For Serving

½ bunch cilantro leaves
Green onions, green parts only, thinly sliced
Limes, cut into cheeks
Steamed rice

MAKE THE STEAK:

1. Place the steak in a 9 × 13-inch baking dish. Rub the skirt steak with the garlic, ginger, oil, and salt, massaging it thoroughly. Cover the baking dish with plastic wrap and refrigerate the steak for at least 3 hours, or ideally overnight.

2. Prepare the grill. If using a charcoal grill, fill a coal chimney to the top with charcoal and light it. Wait 20 minutes, until the charcoals are completely gray; then pour the coals into the grill and place a clean grill grate on top. (Alternatively, if using a gas grill, preheat to high.)

3. Place the marinated skirt steak on the highest-heat section of the grill and cook for 4 minutes, without moving, to achieve a hard sear. Flip the steak and sear on the other side for 3 to 4 more minutes.

4. Continue cooking the steak to your desired doneness. If the steak is thicker and needs longer to cook, you can slide it over to a cooler area of the grill to avoid burning the outside. Remove the steak from the grill and allow the meat to rest for 5 minutes before slicing.

MAKE THE STIR-FRY:

5. Place a wok or large, heavy skillet over high heat and add the oil. Let the oil heat up until it starts lightly smoking, then quickly add the asparagus and onion. Sauté, stirring constantly, until the asparagus is tender but still has a slight bite, about 4 minutes.

Recipe continues

6. Add the Fermented Black Bean–Garlic Sauce and 3 tablespoons of water and cook, stirring often, until the asparagus is just done, another minute or so. If the asparagus is taking longer to cook, and the liquid evaporates, add more water a tablespoon at a time. Remove from the heat.

TO SERVE:

7. Slice the steak into thin strips against the grain and arrange on a large platter. Carefully spoon the stir-fried asparagus over the steak. Garnish with cilantro leaves, green onions, and the reserved chile de árbol from the black bean sauce. Serve with lime cheeks on the side. (Yes, Chinese food in Mexico also includes lots of lime—a beautiful culinary marriage indeed!)

FERMENTED BLACK BEAN–GARLIC SAUCE WITH CHILES DE ÁRBOL

Makes about 1 cup

- ½ cup salted fermented black beans, rinsed
- 4 green onions, white parts only, roughly chopped
- 8 garlic cloves, smashed
- 3 tablespoons freshly minced ginger root
- ¼ cup grapeseed or other neutral oil
- 3 chiles de árbol, stemmed
- 3 tablespoons Chinese cooking wine (Shaoxing)
- 3 tablespoons soy sauce
- ⅓ cup ground or grated piloncillo

In a blender, combine the black beans, green onions, garlic, and ginger. Pulse until you have a rough minced paste (not a smooth purée).

In a large sauté pan or wok over medium-high heat, add the grapeseed oil. When the oil is shimmering, add the chiles de árbol and fry them, stirring often, until they turn a dark burgundy color. Use a slotted spoon to remove the chiles from the oil, and reserve them for garnish. (Once the fried chiles are cool, finely chop them to use as a garnish.)

Add the black bean paste to the oil and fry it, stirring frequently, until you see the paste begin to separate from the oil. Then add in the Shaoxing wine, soy sauce, and piloncillo and whisk to combine thoroughly.

Cook the mixture for another 5 to 7 minutes; it will be dark and glossy and could almost be mistaken for a chocolate sauce (if you had no sense of smell, that is). Transfer the sauce to a small heatproof bowl.

If storing the sauce for later use, allow it to cool to room temperature before refrigerating. It lasts for several weeks in the fridge.

Thank You
RECYCLE
ME

HOUSE AVOCADO FRIED RICE

Fried rice is like a hug in a bowl for me—and I love it all the more because you can cook it in under 20 minutes. This easy-to-make dish is a reminder that we border kids are truly fortunate to have easy access to so many rich, nuanced flavors and cuisines—including ones that many people have never heard of.

Making stir-fries on a regular basis keeps me on my toes, and I always end up learning something about a technique or ingredient. I have no formal culinary training in Chinese cooking, but I respect the cuisine's insanely impressive understanding of food theory. I refer to the style as "double Dutch cooking," since you have to know the exact right moment to add each ingredient to ensure it doesn't burn or drop the heat in the pan too quickly.

The new Chinese-Mexican residents did have to make some adaptations when it came to ingredients, as different foods were available to them on foreign soil. The largest difference in my opinion: The inclusion of lemons, limes and avocado, and I am grateful for the addition. If you are a fried rice lover already, just wait until you try it with avocado and lemon.

Serves 3 or 4

2 tablespoons sesame oil
5 large eggs, beaten
Diamond Crystal kosher salt
4 tablespoons grapeseed or neutral oil
6 green onions, finely chopped (white and green parts separated)
6 slices bacon, cut into ½-inch pieces
3 links Chinese sausage, sliced thinly on the diagonal
½ pound jumbo shrimp, peeled, deveined, and butterflied
½ cup frozen peas
½ cup carrots, diced small (frozen is okay)
2 cups leftover cold cooked jasmine rice
3 tablespoons soy sauce
Freshly ground black pepper

Garnishes

2 avocados, thinly sliced
¼ cup chopped cilantro leaves
Lemon wedges, for serving

1. Preheat a wok over medium-high heat for 2 minutes. When the wok is hot, add in the sesame oil. Quickly pour in the beaten eggs, season with a pinch of salt, and allow them to cook thoroughly before breaking them up into pea-sized pieces with a wooden spoon or spatula. Place the cooked eggs in a medium bowl and set aside.

2. Add 2 tablespoons of the grapeseed oil to the wok. When the oil is hot, add the bacon, Chinese sausage, and white parts of the green onions. Stir-fry the ingredients, stirring frequently to prevent burning, for about 3 minutes, or until the white parts of the onions are translucent and the fat from the pork is rendered out.

3. Add the shrimp, peas, and carrots to the wok and stir-fry for about 5 minutes, until the shrimp are just cooked and the vegetables are tender. Transfer the contents of the wok to the bowl with the scrambled eggs.

4. Add the remaining 2 tablespoons of grapeseed oil to the wok, still set over high heat. When the oil is very hot, add in the rice. Spread the rice across the bottom surface of the wok and drizzle the soy sauce all over it. Stir. Cook, flattening the rice against the wok and stirring occasionally, until it is very hot.

5. Add the stir-fried ingredients from the bowl back into the wok with the rice. Fold all the ingredients together, cooking long enough just to get everything hot again. Season to taste with salt, pepper, green parts of the green onion, and soy sauce as you like. Serve hot, with avocado slices and cilantro on top and lots of lemon wedges on the side for squeezing.

CANTONESE-MEXICAN CHOP SUEY

The story goes that chop suey is a Chinese-American dish that came to life at the hands of early Chinese immigrants coming to California during the Gold Rush. (The name comes from the phrase *jaahp-seui*, which means "odds and ends.") By the end of the Gold Rush in 1855, many of those Chinese immigrants were out of work, and with the Chinese Exclusion Act passed in 1882, they were suddenly no longer welcome in the United States.

The policy resulted in another huge migration—this time south into Mexico. In this case, Mexico became the beneficiary of America's racist, short-sighted law. When we ordered this dish at restaurants growing up, it was a meat lover's dream, including shrimp, beef, pork, and chicken. A single order could legitimately feed a family of six.

Today, my kids and I eat chop suey at least a few times a month. It is my go-to packed lunch for the kids to take to in school, and even if I'm traveling, it's been part of their culinary training to make it themselves.

This recipe calls for some leftover Carnitas Coloradas (page 130), along with beef, chicken, and shrimp—I like to pretend it's the same order from my youth, the #10 House Special Chop Suey—but you can use any combination of proteins. I also go pretty heavy on the chiles here; not how Cantonese cooks would necessarily do it. (Remember what I said about how you should always be wary when a border kid tells you something isn't spicy . . .)

Serves 4 to 6

Stir-Fry Sauce

½ cup oyster sauce
3 tablespoons soy sauce
3 tablespoons ketchup
1 tablespoon cornstarch

Chop Suey

4 tablespoons grapeseed or neutral oil
1 tablespoon sesame oil
1 tablespoon crushed red pepper flakes, or seeds from a dried chile (ancho or guajillo chile seeds work great)
6 chiles de árbol, stemmed
1 garlic clove, minced
1 tablespoon freshly grated ginger
½ pound beef rib eye steak, thinly sliced
¾ pound chicken breast, thinly sliced
½ pound peeled baby shrimp
½ medium white onion, julienned
3 ribs celery, peeled and sliced thinly on the diagonal
1 carrot, peeled and sliced thinly on the diagonal
1 pound bean sprouts
½ pound leftover Char Siu Pork, Mexicali-Style (page 130), or other leftover meat
Cooked rice, for serving

MAKE THE SAUCE:

1. In a small bowl, combine the oyster sauce, soy sauce, ketchup, cornstarch, and ½ cup water. Whisk thoroughly and set aside.

MAKE THE CHOP SUEY:

2. In a wok set over medium heat, add 2 tablespoons of grapeseed oil and the sesame oil. When the oil is hot, add the red pepper flakes (or chile seeds) and the chiles de árbol and fry them until toasted but not dark, about 2 minutes. Add the garlic and the ginger and continue frying, stirring continuously for another minute, until fragrant.

3. Adjust the heat to high. Add the sliced rib eye and chicken breast to the wok, stirring constantly, until just cooked, about 5 minutes. Add in the baby shrimp and continue to sauté until all the proteins are fully cooked, about a minute longer. Remove the wok from heat, transfer the proteins to a plate and set aside.

4. In the same wok, again over high heat, add the remaining 2 tablespoons of grapeseed oil. Once the oil is shimmering, add the sliced onion, celery, and carrot. Stir-fry until tender-crisp, about 4 minutes. Add the bean sprouts, reserved proteins and Char Siu Pork to the wok and fold to incorporate, until the bean sprouts are just wilted and the meat is heated through.

5. Pour the reserved sauce over the stir-fry in the wok and toss everything together. Cook until the sauce reaches a boil and thickens slightly.

6. Turn the heat off immediately so the vegetables do not overcook; you still want them to have a bit of al dente crunch. Serve with rice.

POLLO A LA NARANJA

(ORANGE CHICKEN WITH CHAMOY)

I shouldn't need to do much convincing to get you to cook this dish. I truly do not know a single person who doesn't do a happy dance in their chair when I bring a platter of this orange chicken to the table. It ticks all the boxes: sweet, sour, salty, crunchy, spicy. The (gluten-free!) batter gives you the nooks and crannies you need so the sauce can stick to the chicken, while still maintaining its crunchy texture.

It was my daughter's idea to incorporate chamoy in the orange chicken sauce; she eats chamoy on just about everything. If you're not familiar with chamoy, it's a Mexican seasoning sauce with a complex, sweet-sour-salty flavor. It's typically made with orange juice, hibiscus, and fruit such as prunes and dried apricots, which is brined and then mixed with chili powder for spice. You've probably seen the deep-red chamoy drizzled on fresh fruit, which takes the flavor up to 100. You can find chamoy at just about any Mexican grocery store, or order it online. Fun fact: It's thought that chamoy arrived in Mexico from Asia, by way of Filipino or Chinese immigrants . . . so it's a more natural fit for this recipe than you might have assumed!

Serves 4 to 6

---

8 boneless, skinless chicken thighs, cut into 1-inch cubes
2 tablespoons cornstarch
Neutral oil, for frying
¾ cup potato starch
1 teaspoon garlic powder
Pinch of Diamond Crystal kosher salt
Pinch of freshly ground black pepper
1 large egg
1 recipe Orange Chamoy Sauce (recipe follows)

For Serving/Garnishes
3 cups steamed jasmine rice
Cilantro leaves
Sesame seeds
Limes, cut into cheeks

1. In a medium bowl, combine the chicken with the cornstarch. Toss to ensure that all the chicken pieces are evenly coated. Set aside.

2. Prepare the batter. In a large bowl, mix together the potato starch, garlic powder, salt, and black pepper. Add the egg and ½ cup water and whisk until smooth. Add the chicken pieces to the batter and stir, coating the chicken thoroughly.

3. Fry the chicken. In a cast-iron skillet or wok, add 2 to 3 inches of frying oil. Set over medium-high heat until the oil reaches 350°F on a frying thermometer.

4. While the oil comes to temperature, line a baking sheet with paper towels and place a wire cooling rack on top.

5. Carefully transfer pieces of the battered chicken directly from the batter into the hot oil, working in batches as needed to prevent crowding. I like to use a metal skewer to take the pieces out of the batter and gently lower them into the oil. This helps remove any excess batter from the pieces.

6. Fry the chicken for 6 to 7 minutes per batch, flipping the pieces with a slotted spoon, until they are golden brown on both sides. Test one piece for doneness before removing the rest from the oil. When cooked, remove the fried chicken pieces from the oil with a slotted spoon and drain on the wire rack.

7. Check the heat before you fry each new batch, making sure the oil comes back up to 350°F before you add more chicken. Once all of the chicken is fried, discard the leftover frying oil and wipe out the wok.

8. Glaze the fried chicken: Return the fried chicken to the wok and set over high heat. Pour the Orange Chamoy Sauce over the chicken and gently toss until the chicken is coated in the sauce and very hot.

9. Serve the orange chicken with rice, garnished with cilantro and sesame seeds.

ORANGE CHAMOY SAUCE

Makes about 1 cup

- Zest of ½ an orange
- ½ cup freshly squeezed orange juice (about 2 oranges)
- 3 tablespoons granulated sugar
- ¼ cup chamoy sauce
- 5 tablespoons soy sauce
- 2 garlic cloves
- 1 teaspoon peeled and chopped fresh ginger
- 1 teaspoon rice vinegar
- 1 tablespoon cornstarch

In a blender, combine the orange zest and juice, sugar, chamoy, soy sauce, garlic, ginger, rice vinegar and cornstarch. Blend until the mixture is fully incorporated and smooth.

Transfer the mixture to a small pot set over medium heat. Bring the sauce to a simmer and continue cooking until it begins to thicken, about 5 minutes. Remove the sauce from the heat immediately and set aside.

CHUN CUN DE VERDURAS

(VEGGIE EGG ROLLS)

Another dish whose name is part of Chinese-Mexican food folklore. While in the US, the Chinese term *chun guen* was translated to "spring rolls," in Mexico we just went with the transliteration—"chun cun." These are also sometimes called *taquitos chinos* (Chinese rolled tacos) . . . I think the sense of familiarity helps connect the two cultures.

My brothers and I would play rock paper scissors for the last chun cun. I like to enjoy my chun cuns fresh, crunchy, and elbow-deep in dipping sauce—it's the only way. The veggie filling is straightforward and flavor-packed, and the vegetables are our excuse to eat more of them than beef taquitos, since they're "healthier" . . . right? That's my Mexican math at work.

In terms of preparation, chun cuns demand the same strategy as tamales: If you wanna make a whole bunch of them, recruit all of your family members to help with rolling, and remind them they'll reap the benefit of getting to eat them afterward. With an assembly line setup, you will have these ready in no time.

Serves 4 to 6

Grapeseed or other neutral oil, for frying
5 garlic cloves, minced
1 tablespoon freshly grated ginger
2 large shiitake mushrooms, minced
1 carrot, grated
2 cups shaved napa cabbage
2 ribs celery, peeled and diced small
3 green onions (white and green parts), minced
½ cup bean sprouts
¼ teaspoon ground white pepper
½ teaspoon ground five-spice powder
2 tablespoons soy sauce
1 tablespoon rice vinegar
1 teaspoon sesame oil
1 (16-ounce) package large egg roll wrappers
Orange Chamoy Sauce (page 143), or store-bought sweet-and-sour sauce, for dipping

1. Make the vegetable filling: Add a couple tablespoons of oil to a large skillet or wok set over medium heat. Once the oil is hot, add in the garlic, ginger, mushrooms, carrots, cabbage, celery, green onions, and bean sprouts and mix to combine. Stir in the white pepper and five-spice powder. Cook, stirring continuously, until the cabbage wilts down, about 5 minutes. Reduce the heat to low.

2. In a small bowl, combine the soy sauce, rice vinegar, and sesame oil together. Pour the mixture over the vegetables, tossing everything to coat evenly. Cover the pan with a lid and turn off the heat. Allow the filling to cool to room temperature in the pan before making the rolls.

3. Thirty minutes before assembling the egg rolls, take the wrappers out of the refrigerator and leave them out on the counter to come to room temperature.

4. When you are ready to roll (ba-dum-tss!), fill a small bowl with room-temperature water and place it next to your rolling station.

5. To build each roll, place the wrapper on a clean work surface at a 45-degree angle, so that you have a diamond shape in front of you. Place 2 tablespoons of the vegetable filling in the center of the wrapper—do not overfill! Using your finger or a pastry brush, dab some water along the edges of the diamond's upper half. Then fold the bottom corner of the diamond up over the filling to meet the top corner—you should now have a triangle. Seal the edges of the triangle shut, carefully pressing out any air pockets along the way. This is the most important step—leaving air pockets can cause the rolls to explode during frying, potentially right in your face/arms. If the filling starts leaking out at this stage, be more gentle, or use less filling for the next roll.

6. Dab some water on each side corner of the triangle, and fold each one in tightly toward the center, so they meet in the middle. Finally, dab a little bit of water on the top triangle corner; then roll the filled base of the roll up toward the corner to seal the deal.

7. When ready to fry the rolls, line a baking sheet with paper towels, and set a wire cooling rack on top.

8. In a cast-iron skillet or large, high-walled pot, add 1 to 2 inches of oil. Set over medium-high heat until the temperature of the oil reaches 375°F on a kitchen thermometer.

9. Add the rolls to the oil a few at a time, working in batches to prevent crowding. Fry the rolls until they turn golden brown, 4 to 6 minutes, using tongs to turn every couple of minutes to ensure even browning.

10. Remove the spring rolls from the oil using tongs and set on the wire rack to drain excess oil. Continue frying the rest of the rolls, checking the heat between batches to ensure that the oil returns to 375°F before you fry the next batch.

11. Serve the egg rolls hot, with the Orange Chamoy Sauce or your favorite sweet-and-sour sauce for dipping.

GRILLED CHICKEN WITH SERRANO PONZU

For many of us in the border regions, charcoal-grilled chicken is as beloved a food as tacos. The smell of the meat hitting the charcoal grill takes me back to my early-morning commutes across the border to our new school in San Diego: It's the smell from the hundreds of food vendors starting their days.

The scene I just described is probably easy to imagine, but what you might not know is that Japanese ponzu sauce is a common staple at restaurants and in homes in Tijuana. Classic ponzu is made by simmering a mixture of soy sauce, mirin, vinegar, *katsuobushi* (smoked, dried and shaved fish flakes), and kombu (kelp), then straining and adding citrus juice. It's a personal favorite of mine, and an identifier for many Norteños or Tijuanenses: Whenever I see someone whip up a makeshift ponzu to dip food into, I start a conversation with them, asking, "Where did you grow up?"

Though relations between Mexico and Japan began forming as early as the seventeenth century, It was between 1920 and 1940 that a large population of Japanese emigrants arrived to Ensenada, Baja California. From then, Japanese influence stayed relatively confined to the coast and down the Baja peninsula, where the Japanese helped establish commercial fishing and farming. While the population isn't gigantic, Japanese-Mexican cross-pollination still gave us some of the tastiest condiments and, importantly, battered fish. (Did you ever think about how the classic fried fish taco looks a bit like tempura? Well, that's exactly what it is.)

But about the recipe. It's a classic grilled chicken with a homemade ponzu so you can have the experience of making your own. Of course, we wouldn't be Mexican if we didn't throw in some charred serrano peppers into the ponzu while we're at it. You'll probably have leftover ponzu sauce—I keep the extra sauce handy in a mason jar in the fridge, and use it to dress my steamed rice. It will keep for a week in the refrigerator, though in my house, it never lasts that long.

Serves 4

Ponzu

2 whole serrano peppers
3 green onions (white and green parts)
2½ cups soy sauce
½ cup rice vinegar
1 stalk lemongrass, smashed and cut into 2-inch pieces
2 tablespoons freshly grated ginger root
3 tablespoons cornstarch
2 cups freshly squeezed orange juice

Grilled Chicken

2 pounds boneless chicken thighs
2 tablespoons grapeseed oil
Diamond Crystal kosher salt
Ground white pepper

For Serving

½ cup minced cilantro
Zest of 2 limes
2 limes, cut into cheeks
Steamed rice

CHARGRILL THE VEGGIES:

1. Fill a coal chimney with charcoal, light it, and wait 20 minutes, until the charcoals turn completely gray with ash. Dump the coals into the bottom of a charcoal grill and place a clean grill grate over them. (Alternatively, set a gas grill to medium-high heat.)

2. Place the serrano peppers and green onions on the grill. Grill them whole, using tongs to turn them so they char on all sides. Once they are charred, remove them from the grill, and set aside until to cool enough to handle.

3. Remove the stems and seeds, then mince the peppers and reserve for the ponzu sauce. Mince the green onions, and reserve for garnish.

MAKE THE PONZU SAUCE:

4. In a saucepan, whisk together the soy sauce, vinegar, and ¾ cup of water. Toss in the lemongrass and ginger. Place the saucepan on the stovetop and bring the mixture to a simmer over medium heat; then turn the heat off and cover the pot with a lid. Let the ingredients steep for 10 minutes to infuse flavor.

Recipe continues

5. Strain the ponzu base through a fine-mesh sieve into a medium bowl. Discard the solids; then pour the strained liquid back into the same pot, and place over medium heat to bring to a simmer.

6. Meanwhile, in a small bowl, whisk together the cornstarch and 2 tablespoons of cold water to make a slurry. Pour the slurry mixture into the ponzu, whisking continuously until the sauce thickens. Once thickened, turn off the heat and set the pot aside to cool.

7. After the sauce cools, stir in the orange juice and the minced charred serrano peppers and set aside.

MAKE THE CHICKEN:

8. Now, we're moving back to the grill. Pat the chicken thighs dry with paper towels and drizzle them with the grapeseed oil to coat on both sides. Season the chicken all over with salt and white pepper and transfer the thighs directly onto the hot grill. Cook for 5 minutes on one side, then turn each thigh and cook the other side for 5 more minutes, or until they reach an internal temperature of 165°F. Remove the thighs from the grill and allow them to rest for 5 to 10 minutes before serving.

9. To serve, spoon the ponzu onto a serving platter to cover, and place the grilled chicken on top. Garnish the chicken with cilantro, lime zest, and the charred green onions. Serve with steamed rice and lime on the side, and drizzle with remaining ponzu.

ADOBADA BAO BUNS

(THE NORTH'S VERSION OF AL PASTOR)

Is it al pastor, or adobada? Either or both . . . depending on where you happen to be. We all know the al pastor taco, one the most iconic foods in Mexico. It's basically a shawarma taco, made with achiote-marinated pork that's roasted on a spit and topped with pineapple. And that makes sense, given that *carne al pastor* emerged after the arrival of Lebanese immigrants to the state of Puebla in the early twentieth century. As the dish traveled north from Puebla, it evolved as it was exchanged through many hands, both Middle Eastern and Mexican. It arrived in the North with a punchier marinade, more acidity, and a bit of a spicy kick—becoming what we call *carne adobada.*

This recipe is what I like to refer to as a border kid special, the kind of dish I dream up when I'm feeling nostalgic and hungry. Having eaten many baos throughout my childhood, I developed a fondness for their pillowy-yet-chewy dough and delicious surprise fillings. The bao, whether in the form of a fluffy steamed bun or a pan-fried dumpling, offers a warm embrace, not so different from a tamal. This recipe is probably most similar to steamed cha siu bao, with the typical barbecued pork replaced with carne adobada. The tangy achiote and vinegar-marinated grilled pork, combined with charred pineapple and swaddled in a soft bun, make for one of my new favorite bites.

Serves 4 to 6

Carne Adobada Filling

- 4 dried guajillo chiles, stemmed and seeded
- 1 cup white distilled vinegar
- 2 (3.5-ounce) packages achiote paste
- 4 canned chipotle peppers in adobo sauce
- 1 tablespoon Diamond Crystal kosher salt (or 2 teaspoons Morton salt)
- 2 pounds pork tenderloin, sliced lengthwise into ½-inch-thick steaks
- 1 pineapple, peeled, cored, and quartered

Steamed Bao Buns

- 2 tablespoons (30 grams) grapeseed or neutral oil, plus more for greasing
- ½ cup (122 grams) warm water (100°F to 110°F)
- ½ cup (111 grams) warm whole milk (100°F to 110°F)
- 1 tablespoon (14 grams) active dry yeast
- ⅓ cup (70 grams) granulated sugar
- 3 cups plus 2 tablespoons (464 grams) all-purpose flour
- ¼ teaspoon (1 gram) Diamond Crystal kosher salt
- Cornstarch, for dusting
- Nonstick cooking spray
- Parchment paper, cut into 4-inch squares

Garnishes

- Quick-Pickled Red Onions (page 33)
- 1 bunch cilantro, leaves only
- Limes, cut into cheeks
- Salsa of choice

PREPARE THE MARINADE:

1. Toast the guajillos on a dry comal or in a skillet over medium heat, using tongs to turn on all sides, until darkened and fragrant. Transfer the toasted guajillos to a small pot and add in the distilled vinegar. Bring to a simmer over medium heat; then turn the heat off and cover the pot with a lid. Let steep for 5 minutes to soften the chiles.

2. In a blender, combine the steeped guajillos and vinegar, achiote paste, chipotles in adobo sauce, and salt. Blend on high until smooth; then pour the marinade into a medium bowl. Adjust the seasoning to taste and let cool to room temperature.

3. Once the marinade is cool, add the sliced pork loin to the bowl with the marinade. Cover the bowl with plastic wrap and place in the refrigerator to marinate for at least 2 hours, or up to 2 days.

MAKE THE BAO BUNS:

4. First, make the dough. In a large mixing bowl, combine the oil, warm water and milk, yeast, and sugar. Whisk the ingredients to dissolve and let rest for 5 to 8 minutes until bubbles form on the surface, indicating the yeast has activated.

Recipe continues

5. In the bowl of a stand mixer fitted with the hook attachment, combine the flour and salt. While mixing on low speed, gradually add the wet mixture to the dry mixture. Mix until combined; then raise the speed to medium, mixing until the dough comes together and there is no more visible dry flour.

6. Continue kneading the dough in the stand mixer for 6 minutes. The dough should be elastic and soft, and it should easily pull away from the walls of the bowl.

7. Lightly oil the bowl that held the wet mixture with more grapeseed oil. Then remove the dough from the stand mixer and place it in the greased bowl. Cover the bowl with a clean, damp kitchen towel (or plastic wrap) and place in a warm spot in your kitchen until it doubles in size. (At a temperature of 72 to 77°F, it will take about 30 minutes.)

8. Next, shape the dough. Once the dough has risen, dust a clean work surface with a thin layer of cornstarch. Roll the dough out flat, ¼ inch thick. Use a 3-inch biscuit cutter to cut out rounds from the dough—you should end up with 8 to 10 circles. Spray the surface of the dough rounds with cooking spray; then fold each dough round in half over itself. Place each half-moon of dough on its own square of parchment paper.

9. Cover the folded buns with a clean, damp kitchen towel and let them rise for another 30 minutes, until they are puffy to the touch.

10. Finally, steam the buns. Fill a wok or large pot with an inch or two of water, and place a 12-inch bamboo basket (or a steamer rack) in the pot. Set over medium-high heat and bring the water to a simmer.

11. Once the water is simmering, place the buns in the steamer in batches of 6. Cover and steam the buns for 9 to 12 minutes, until they are opaque and spring back immediately when touched. Repeat with additional batches, keeping an eye on the water level and adding more as necessary, until all of the dough is cooked.

12. Once done, keep the steamed buns covered with a cloth until ready to serve, ideally right away. If serving the next day, you can refresh them by putting them back in the steamer for 2 minutes just before filling.

GRILL THE PINEAPPLE AND CARNE ADOBADA:

13. Thirty minutes before grilling, remove the marinated pork from the refrigerator and allow it to come to room temperature.

14. Fill a coal chimney to the top with charcoal, light it, and wait 20 minutes, until the coals turn completely gray with ash. Pour three-quarters of the coals on one side of the grill and the remaining quarter on the other side to create two heat zones, a "hot zone" and a "hold zone." Place a clean grill grate over the coals. (Alternatively, set a gas grill to medium heat.)

15. Place the pineapple and marinated pork steaks on the grill.

16. Grill the pineapple, flipping occasionally, until it is charred on all sides and the sugars begin caramelizing, about 10 minutes. Remove the charred pineapple with the cooked pork to cool once charred. Cut the pineapple into thin slices.

17. Cook the pork on one side for 4 minutes, flip, and cook on the other side for 4 minutes, until you have a bit of char on the ends and the meat has an internal temperature of 145°F. Move the cooked pork steaks off the grill and let rest for 3 to 5 minutes. Once cool enough to handle, shave the pork on a bias, creating taquero-quality carne adobada.

18. To serve, fill each bao bun with the meat and a little bit of grilled pineapple, and garnish with Quick-Pickled Red Onions, cilantro, a squeeze of lime, and salsa.

TACOS DE FIDEO CON CHORIZO VERDE

(VERMICELLI TACOS WITH GREEN CHORIZO)

Fideos (thin noodles) are enjoyed in soups and in regular pasta dishes across the country. But there's another more popular variation in the northern half of Mexico, made with fideo seco—"dry" fideo—that's cooked in a bold-flavored sauce and then tucked into a corn tortilla as a taco.

Various regions have their signature fingerprint on the flavor. In Tijuana, I remember having tacos de fideo with melty cheese and chorizo, either crisped on a dry comal or grilled until crunchy, similar to Tacos Gobernador (page 112).

This recipe also includes a fresh salsa verde *and* a green chorizo filling. Chorizo verde, a creation of the city of Toluca, gives the filling a lighter, herbal green flavor (it's got more greens than pork in it). These tacos are extremely adaptable—you can make them vegetarian by leaving out the chorizo, or the filling can be served in a soft tortilla. I suggest enjoying these with White Widow Salsa (page 47).

Makes 8 tacos

Salsa Verde Chorizo

1 poblano pepper, charred, seeded, peeled, and cut into strips
2 garlic cloves
1 bunch cilantro, minced
1 cup frozen spinach, thawed and squeezed to remove water
½ fresh hoja santa leaf
Diamond Crystal kosher salt
½ pound ground pork

Fideo

¼ cup grapeseed oil
1 chile de árbol
1 (10-ounce) package fideo pasta
2 sprigs fresh thyme
1 bay leaf
1 dried avocado leaf
2 cups Raw Tomatillo Salsa (page 38)
2 cups grated Manchego cheese

For Serving/Optional Garnishes

8 (5-inch) Corn Tortillas (page 23), or store-bought
Mexican crema
Sliced avocado
Minced cilantro leaves
Limes, cut into cheeks
Salsa of choice

MAKE THE SALSA VERDE CHORIZO:

1. First, make the salsa. In the cup of a blender, combine the charred poblano, garlic, cilantro, spinach, and hoja santa. Blend the ingredients on high until smooth, and season generously with salt to taste (this salt will also season the pork). Set aside.

2. In a large skillet set over medium heat, add the ground pork and then pour in the blended salsa. Cook until the liquid has evaporated and the meat begins to caramelize, about 10 minutes. Transfer the green chorizo to a medium bowl and set aside.

MAKE THE FIDEO:

3. Line a baking sheet with parchment paper and set aside.

4. Wipe out the same skillet you used to cook the chorizo and add the grapeseed oil. Set the skillet over medium heat. When the oil is hot, add the chile de árbol and toast it until fragrant, about 1 minute.

5. Stir in the fideo, thyme, bay leaf, and avocado leaf, and stir the ingredients continuously until the noodles are toasted and golden brown.

6. Turn the heat to low and pour the Raw Tomatillo Salsa and 1 cup of water over the fideo. Stir to incorporate, and cover the pan. Cook for 7 minutes, then check that the pasta is cooked al dente and all the liquid has been absorbed.

7. Once the noodles are done, turn off the heat and transfer the fideo to the prepared baking sheet. Let cool completely before assembling the tacos.

Recipe continues

MAKE THE TACOS:

8. Gently stir the salsa verde chorizo and the Manchego cheese into the fideo. Be careful to not stir the fideo too much, or the delicate noodles will start to break down, and you'll end up with a paste. Adjust the seasoning to taste.

9. Set a nonstick skillet or comal over medium heat and warm the tortillas for a few seconds on each side until they become pliable. Keep them warm by placing them between clean kitchen towels or in a tortilla basket.

10. To assemble the tacos, place a tortilla on a clean work surface and top one side it with ¼ cup of the filling. Then fold the other side of the tortilla over the filling to close. Repeat to make tacos with the rest of the tortillas and filling.

11. Return the folded tacos to the dry comal over medium heat to toast them before serving. If you prefer, you can grill or fry the tacos instead. (If frying, secure them with a toothpick first.) Serve hot, garnished with crema, avocado, and cilantro, with lime and salsa on the side.

LOS ARCOS PLÁTANOS FOSTER

(BANANAS FOSTER, TIJUANA-STYLE)

To me, tableside service in Mexico calls to mind two things: Caesar Salad (page 106) and Plátanos Foster. Unlike the world's most famous salad, Bananas Foster is not originally a Mexican dish—it was actually invented in New Orleans—but I think it's only fair that we get to enjoy the perfection of bananas flambéed tableside, too.

My father loved going out to eat at Los Arcos, a family-friendly restaurant where he could catch up with his "compadres" while keeping us entertained with food. I still remember squirming in my seat with each passing bite, restless with excitement and anticipation of spotting the tableside flambé cart making its way through the dining room. Maybe that's where I became the pain-in-the-ass kid who always wanted to order dessert for the whole table. At Los Arcos, my undisputed favorite was the Plátanos Foster.

So, here's my version of the dish. The piloncillo—unrefined dark brown cane sugar—balances the sweetness with an earthy, almost-savory quality that you can't get if you use light brown sugar. I use orange liqueur (instead of banana liqueur) to give the sauce a more complex, whole-bodied fruit flavor. A touch of salt brings all the flavors together. Don't skip the vanilla ice cream!

Serves 4

4 tablespoons salted butter
4 bananas, sliced in half lengthwise
½ cup ground or grated piloncillo, or dark brown sugar
½ teaspoon ground Mexican canela/Ceylon cinnamon
¼ cup orange liqueur
½ cup dark rum
Pinch of sea salt
Vanilla ice cream, for serving

1. In a large skillet over medium heat, melt 2 tablespoons of the butter. Once the butter is bubbly, add the banana halves to the pan, cut-sides down. Let the bananas caramelize for about 4 minutes without touching them. (Really, do not move the bananas, even if they feel stuck!)

2. Adjust the temperature to medium-low and add the remaining 2 tablespoons of butter to the skillet, along with the piloncillo, ground cinnamon, and 2 tablespoons of water. Carefully swirl the pan in a circular motion to help the piloncillo melt and incorporate into a sauce, 3 to 5 minutes.

3. Raise the heat to medium and carefully pour in the orange liqueur and rum. Once the sauce is bubbling violently, it's time to flambé! Slightly tilt the skillet toward the flame of the stove to ignite the alcohol, or light a match and hover it over the skillet. The alcohol will catch on fire and burn off, reducing the sauce and helping the sugars caramelize (this is called the Maillard reaction). Once the flames dissipate, swirl the bananas again to make sure they're thoroughly coated in the sauce. Season the sauce with a pinch of sea salt.

4. Divide the flambéed bananas and sauce among 4 plates, top each serving with a scoop of vanilla ice cream, and serve immediately.

ORDITAS DE NAT

BORDER GORDITAS DE NATA

(CLOTTED CREAM GRIDDLE CAKES)

Crossing the border can often be a feast for the eyes. Food, art, drinks, sweets, souvenirs, all simultaneously being prepared and sold for miles to hungry travelers waiting in line to pass through the border checkpoints. If you're stuck in that line between San Diego and Tijuana, you'll probably find these sweet cakes cooking away on a flat-top griddle on wheels, the smell of butter and condensed milk wafting through the air.

These gorditas are made with *nata*, a thick cultured cream that accumulates when you boil raw milk. Using nata gives the dough a higher fat content (higher than if you used milk or even heavy cream), and the dough comes out fluffier and more tender as a result.

You may have heard the word gordita in reference to a thick corn masa cake that's hollowed out and filled with various meat and cheese fillings. This recipe is not that. These are sweet wheat cakes (Remember, in the North, we love wheat flour!) that are pale in the middle with golden-brown tops and bottoms. I love to eat them straight from the griddle while still puffy and warm, filled with butter, condensed milk, jam, cajeta, or your choice of condiment. They go especially great with a hot cup of Café de Olla (page 202). The gorditas aren't pretty after the fillings ooze out, but man, are they delicious—definitely core memory material.

Makes 16 (2-inch) gorditas

⅔ cup whole milk
1 tablespoon dry active yeast
½ cup plus 2 tablespoons sugar
1 cup Mexican nata (or substitute clotted cream, crème fraîche, or mascarpone), plus more for serving
1 tablespoon vanilla extract
1 large egg
3⅔ cups all-purpose flour
1 tablespoon Diamond Crystal kosher salt (or 2 teaspoons Morton salt)
2 tablespoons salted butter, softened, plus more for greasing

For Serving

Jam of your choice (optional)
1 (14-ounce) can condensed milk
Cajeta (optional)

1. In a small pot over low heat, bring the milk up to body temperature, around 98°F, taking care not to overheat it (use a cooking thermometer). Turn the heat off; then whisk the yeast and 1 tablespoon of sugar into the milk. Allow the yeast to bloom for about 5 minutes. The surface will look foamy as the yeast activates.

2. In a medium bowl, whisk together the remaining sugar, nata, vanilla, and egg. Then stir in the bloomed yeast mixture.

3. Add the flour and salt to the bowl of a stand mixer fitted with the hook attachment. With the mixer running on low speed, slowly stream the wet ingredients into the flour mixture, using a rubber spatula as needed to scrape down the sides of the bowl to incorporate.

4. Once the mixture is thoroughly combined, increase the mixer speed to medium and add the butter 1 tablespoon at a time, allowing it to thoroughly incorporate after each addition. Continue kneading the dough in the stand mixer for an additional 10 minutes; it should become shiny and slightly tacky to the touch. Even if you're worried that it's too sticky, do not add more flour at this point.

5. Lightly grease the bowl that contained the wet mixture with butter. Transfer the dough to the lightly greased bowl and cover it with a clean, damp kitchen towel or plastic wrap. Set the dough in a warm place to proof until doubled in size, about 30 minutes.

Recipe continues

6. With wet hands, punch the dough down; then fold it back into a tight ball and cover again with the towel to proof for about 15 minutes. Do the "poke test"—press your thumb into the dough. If the dough springs back quickly, it needs to proof longer. If it springs back slowly, your dough is ready. If you are not ready to roll out the dough, you can cover it and put it in the fridge to slow down the proofing.

7. When you are ready to cook the gorditas, flour your work surface well. Use your hand to flatten the dough into a round, and then lightly flour the surface of the dough. Roll out the dough to ½ inch thick.

8. Using a floured 2-inch biscuit cutter or a glass cup, cut out gordita rounds as close to each other as possible (to get the most out of the dough). Lay the rounds on a floured baking sheet and let them rest for 10 minutes.

9. Set a comal or dry skillet over the lowest heat setting. Once the comal is hot, carefully transfer 4 gorditas from the baking sheet to the pan. Cook the gorditas for 8 minutes on one side, then flip and cook for another 8 minutes. If necessary, flip the gordita once more to ensure it's browned evenly on both sides. You're looking for a pancake-like golden brown color; they will feel slightly crisp after the initial cook, but will soften once cooled. Repeat until all of the gorditas are cooked.

10. Let the cooked gorditas cool slightly. Then split them crosswise and fill them with jam, condensed milk, or cajeta—or go the savory route, with salted butter and ham.

ROMPOPE DE LAS MADRES BRIGIDAS DE TECATE

(SPIKED EGG CUSTARD BEVERAGE)

One day, I'll write the book on sweets and treats across Mexico, from conquest to present day, but for now, let's talk about a group of ladies who live together in the *Pueblo Mágico* (magical town) of Tecate. I'm referring to the nuns in the convent of Las Madres Brigidas, who make one insane *rompope* (think eggnog but better, made with almonds and spices). Like many of the clergy members who have made food throughout Mexico since the seventeenth century, the nuns became regionally famous for their exceptional rompope. Growing up, I didn't spend much time in Tecate, but we would drive past it on our way to Mexicali, and we always made an obligatory stop to buy rompope. Something about buying booze from clergy members still makes me giggle.

We Mexicans love all things rompope-flavored; it's a nostalgic flavor. You can find it in *paletas* (popsicles), dozens of candies, cakes, and even other cocktails, and in the winter months as a stand-alone treat. The surprise of the almonds helps give the drink luxurious body, and the flavor is delicious. I've had other rompopes made with pine nuts or pecans, so you can start here and branch out. Here's my version of the famous pit-stop rompope along the Tecate wine route.

Makes 6 cups

- ½ cup slivered blanched almonds, soaked overnight in cold water, water reserved
- 4 cups whole milk
- 2 (3-inch) sticks Mexican canela/Ceylon cinnamon
- 1 cup sugar
- 6 large egg yolks
- 1 tablespoon vanilla extract
- ⅛ teaspoon ground cloves
- ⅛ teaspoon ground nutmeg
- Pinch of baking soda
- Pinch of Diamond Crystal kosher salt
- 1 cup spiced rum

1. Strain the soaked almonds and reserve ½ cup of the soaking water. Add the almonds with the reserved soaking water to a blender, and blend on high to purée into a smooth paste. Set the blended mixture aside.

2. In a medium pot set over medium heat, combine the milk, cinnamon sticks, sugar, and the blended almond mixture. Bring to a low simmer, stirring occasionally. Once the mixture is simmering, turn off the heat and cover the pot. Let the mixture steep for 20 minutes.

3. Meanwhile, in a medium heatproof bowl, combine the egg yolks, vanilla, cloves, nutmeg, baking soda, and salt. Whisk gently until just combined, taking care not to whip too much air into the mixture (you don't want it to be frothy).

4. Temper the egg yolk mixture: Whisking continuously as you do so, add 2 to 3 large ladlefuls of the warm infused milk from the pot into the eggs, whisking continuously to incorporate. Then pour the tempered egg mixture back into the pot of milk in a steady stream, whisking continuously.

5. Return the pot to low heat and switch to a wooden spoon or heatproof spatula. Cook, stirring continuously, until the mixture thickens enough to coat the back of a metal spoon.

6. Turn the heat off and strain the rompope through a fine-mesh sieve into a medium heatproof bowl. Stir in the rum and serve hot, in mugs garnished with cinnamon sticks. To serve cold, let the rompope cool to room temperature before storing in the refrigerator. It will keep for up to 2 weeks.

SONORA

LAND OF DESERT AND OCEAN

The northern border state of Sonora is the second-largest state in Mexico and is also home to several native peoples. (I have had the honor of cooking alongside and getting know two of them—the Yaqui, near the Sea of Cortez, and the Tohono O'odham Nation, along the Arizona border.)

When I was growing up, Sonora to me meant vaqueros (cowboys), desert land, flour tortillas, and spicy aguachiles, Mexico's fiery take on ceviche. As I've learned more about this land—both its arid landscapes and its seemingly infinite miles of coastline—and researched its culinary history, it has become one of favorite states in the country. You can't go anywhere in the state, from the desert to the gulf, without seeing cowboy hats, tight Wranglers, and ornate belt buckles. The men and women of Sonora are a bit salty, sometimes hard on the exterior but with hearts of gold, and with a tan that is ubiquitous among those who work out on the ranches.

While the cowboy culture of straightforward, old-school ranch-style cooking does have a strong influence on what and how Sonorans eat, the meals that I have eaten on *rancheros* have included some of the most complex flavors I have ever tasted. Char and smoke are used extremely intentionally, deployed to level up any grilled item. The salsas are spicy as hell, yet well-balanced with sea salt and acid from Mexican limes (like Key limes).

My last trip to Sonora was to the city of Ures, where I visited a ranch whose owners welcomed a group of chefs, showing us how they have eaten for the last few hundred years. Lining the driveway were dozens of *metates* (rectangular, nearly flat mortar-and-pestle–like grinding stones) that were collected from all around the property when the family bought the land. The wear on the stones varied—some were over a thousand years old.

In some respects, not much has changed in the Sonoran diet, at least since the Spanish colonizers arrived. At the ranch, thinly sliced beef hung on clotheslines strewn across the backyard, from tree to tree, a display of Sonora's famous *carne seca* (dried meat). Once dried, the meat was ground on the metates and then used to make the state's classic *machaca*, or beef aguachile. A convex piece of sheet metal was set over a mound of firewood for making *sobaqueras* or tortillas de agua (giant, paper-thin flour tortillas). I was transfixed watching the women handle the dough, stretched from one arm to the other and so thin that it was completely see-through. Foolishly, I thought to myself, "Hey, I can do that!" . . . and then proceeded to fail miserably, ending up with tortilla dough in a large clump of my hair. This style of tortilla is also a reminder of how Middle Eastern immigrant families came here and influenced Sonoran culture and cuisine. In my research, I have come across images of Syrian women making similar flatbreads, hundreds of years before migrating to Mexico.

While I'm not from Sonora, I take so much inspiration from the food of this state, and I owe it eternal thanks for helping me to get my name out there—my take on a Sonoran hot dog, a.k.a. a *dogo*, was my first recipe to be featured in a print magazine. And my signature flavored aguachiles have made it to the UK, Australia, and Europe.

And while we're on the topic of aguachiles—let's not forget that they harness the full power of one of the spiciest peppers Mexico has to offer, the chiltepín. Much like its human coinhabitants, the beautiful, resilient chiltepín pepper plant has thrived in often inhospitable environments. (In the summertime, temperatures in Sonora can reach a blistering 120°F or higher and drop down to the 40s during winter.) I'm not sure how the first person who put one of these tiny, ball bearing–sized peppers in their mouth must have reacted, though I can imagine it included several expletives. When it comes to chiltepíns, don't try to test them, just like you wouldn't try to test a Sonoran. Just respect them and let them reveal their flavor to you.

CLASSIC
A Lo Hecho, Pecho
CALIDAD
QUALITY
mexican style

AGUACHILE NEGRO

(CHILE ASH AGUACHILE WITH SCALLOPS OR SHRIMP)

When most people think of Sonora, they probably picture the desert. But look at a map, and you'll see that's not all there is to it: Sonora boasts both desert ranches and plenty of warm gulf coastline. The state's biodiversity means that you eat extremely well there, including lots of delicious seafood. The classic seafood dish, aguachile—Northern Mexico's spicier answer to ceviche—was born in Sinaloa, but it's also super popular on the Sonoran coast.

To me, this Sonoran-style aguachile tastes exactly like where it was created, with acidity as bright as the sun over the ocean, and dried chiltepín peppers to bring you back to the desert mountains where they grow. The black ash from charred onion gives this dish an earthy flavor and a mysterious dark color that's complemented by a trio of umami-rich sauces—soy sauce, Worcestershire, and Maggi. Let sweet, fresh shrimp marinate in this aguachile, and it'll transport you to sitting under a *palapa* (thatched palm-leaf dwelling), enjoying the traveling mariachis that is going table to table, taking song requests.

Serves 4

- 1 small yellow onion
- 1 pound 11/15 jumbo, shell-on Mexican brown shrimp or jumbo scallops
- Diamond Crystal kosher salt
- ½ cup Maggi sauce
- ½ cup Worcestershire sauce
- ½ cup soy sauce
- Juice of 5 limes (about ⅔ cup)
- Juice of 3 lemons (about ¾ cup)
- 2 tablespoons ground chiltepín peppers
- ½ cup cilantro leaves
- 4 radishes, thinly sliced
- ½ red onion, julienned
- 2 Persian cucumbers, thinly sliced
- 1 avocado, cubed

1. Preheat the oven to 400°F and place a rack in the top position. Line a baking sheet with aluminum foil.

2. Make the onion ash. Slice off the root and top of the yellow onion, and then halve it lengthwise. Peel the onion and then separate the layers, and place them in a single layer on the prepared baking sheet. Place the sheet in the oven on the top rack. Bake the onion until the flesh is completely dehydrated and blackened, which can take up to 45 minutes. Remove the baking sheet from the oven and set aside to allow the charred onion to cool completely.

3. Peel and devein the shrimp, and use a paring knife to butterfly them from the back, leaving a bit of the tail still attached if you'd like. Sprinkle salt all over the shrimp and set aside.

4. In a medium bowl mix together the Maggi, Worcestershire sauce, soy sauce, lemon and lime juices, and the ground chiltepín. Taste and adjust the citrus or salt if necessary. Set the sauce aside to allow the flavors to meld together, about 20 minutes.

5. In a medium bowl, Toss together the cilantro, radish, red onion, and cucumber. Set aside.

6. Now, going back to the onion ash: Set a fine-mesh sieve on top of a separate medium bowl. Add the blackened onion pieces to the sieve and press down on them with your hand using a circular motion to push the blacked ash through the mesh. You can stop when you're just left with large pieces that won't break down. Discard the larger pieces.

7. To plate, shake any excess salt off of the shrimp. Arrange the shrimp on a large rimmed platter, and ladle on enough of the sauce to completely surround the shrimp. Place the mixed vegetables over the shrimp, leaving some shrimp still visible. Top with the cubed avocado; then sprinkle the onion ash over everything for the final touch. (I like to put the ash back in a fine-mesh sieve and gently dust it over the platter.) Serve immediately.

DOGOS

(STREET-STYLE HOT DOGS)

The dogo is a perfect example of border culture and its resulting third-culture cuisines. While American culture popularized the hot dog, along the border, and particularly in Sonora, we've done what we do best: made it a little bit "extra." In a state that has extreme summer weather, you can't help but be amazed that just like the rest of the country, they take street food and their dogos incredibly seriously.

Sometime in the 1980s, the bacon-wrapped dogo took the lead as the most ubiquitous version. Yes, everybody loves bacon, but for me, the toppings are where it gets *really* exciting: stewed beans, salsa fresca, chile colorado, etc.

I love texture, and the bacon wrapped around the hot dog isn't always as crispy as I'd like it to be, so for my version, I make a bacon crunch instead—think of it as a sort of smoky granola with crispy and sweet fried shallots and garlic. And my dogos are also creamy, savory, and fresh all at once, with charred green onion crema and soy sauce–infused salsa fresca.

Use whatever hot dog is your favorite, but I would suggest using a soft, enriched bun. There's nothing worse than biting into a dogo with amazing flavor only to find that the bread is dry. If you want to be even more extra, spread mayo on the inside of the bun and sear or grill it before adding everything in.

Makes 4 dogos

Bacon-Shallot Crunch

1 cup grapeseed or other neutral oil
1 large shallot, thinly sliced
2 garlic cloves, thinly sliced
1 tablespoon crushed red pepper
4 bacon slices, cooked until crispy, then crumbled

Salsa Fresca

½ cup small-diced heirloom tomato
½ cup small-diced yellow onion
¼ cup minced cilantro
½ serrano pepper, stemmed, seeded, and minced
Juice of 2 limes (about ¼ cup)
2 tablespoons soy sauce

For Grilling/Serving

1 tablespoon grapeseed or other neutral oil
Diamond Crystal kosher salt
4 green onions (white and green parts)
½ cup Mexican crema
4 hot dogs
4 brioche hot dog buns

1. If using a charcoal grill: Fill a coal chimney to the top with charcoal, light it, and allow the coals to burn for 20 minutes, until they are covered with gray ash. (If using a gas grill, preheat the grill to medium-high.) In the meantime, you can prepare the bacon crunch and salsa.

MAKE THE BACON-SHALLOT CRUNCH:

2. Line a plate with paper towels and set aside.

3. Add 1 cup of oil to a medium saucepan over medium heat. Let the oil heat up for 3 minutes; then test if the oil is ready by carefully adding in one piece of shallot. The shallot should immediately be covered in bubbles and start turning golden. When the oil is ready, add all of the sliced shallots to the hot oil and fry them, stirring occasionally, until they are browned and crispy, but not burnt, about 4 minutes. Remove the shallots from the oil using a slotted spoon and transfer them to the paper towel–lined plate.

4. Add the sliced garlic to the same oil. Fry the garlic, stirring occasionally and watching carefully, until golden and crispy but not too dark, 2 to 3 minutes. Transfer the garlic to the plate with the fried shallots.

5. Add the crushed red pepper to the oil; then immediately remove the pan from the heat. Let the red pepper steep in the oil for 15 minutes; then strain it out of the oil using a fine-mesh sieve. (Reserve the infused frying oil for a later use—it's great on anything.)

Recipe continues

lsa Que Pic
"A Madres"

6. Combine the crispy shallots, garlic, red pepper, and crumbled bacon in a small bowl and set aside.

MAKE THE SALSA FRESCA:

7. In a small bowl, combine the diced tomato, onion, cilantro, serrano pepper, lime juice, and soy sauce. Mix thoroughly and adjust salt and acid to taste.

GRILL AND SERVE:

8. When the charcoal is completely gray, pour the coals into a pile at the bottom of your grill (about 10 inches high at the center). Place a clean grill grate over them.

9. Combine the tablespoon of oil with some salt on a plate, and roll the whole green onions in the salted oil, coating them evenly. Grill the green onions, uncovered, until charred, 3 to 5 minutes per side. Remove the green onions from the grill and let them cool completely. Finely mince the green onions and mix them with the crema in a small bowl. Set aside.

10. Place the hot dogs on the grill, and cook uncovered until grill marks form, 3 to 5 minutes per side. Carefully toast the buns on the grill.

11. To serve, place the hot dogs in the grilled buns and top with the green onion crema, Salsa Fresca, and Bacon-Shallot Crunch.

CARNITA ASADA: A WAY OF LIFE

Every family gathering involves food . . . and our culture is no different in that respect. An *asada*, or a *carnita asada*, refers to a family cookout (we add -ito/-ita to make words sound cute and welcoming). It's a unique tradition in the environment of the North. Usually, Banda music (or Selena) is blasting away on a boombox or speaker. There is a man fanning the charcoal grill to get it going . . . and his dad nearby telling him how he did it wrong. Whether you are at a community park or on a beach, the women are probably setting up a makeshift kitchen, covering all surfaces with aluminum foil just in case you have to use them for food prep.

When you are invited to an asada, it usually means there will be grilled meat (possibly a few different kinds), rice, beans, tortillas, cheese, and lots of fresh chiles, green onions, limes, radishes. It's sort of like a regular kitchen, except your cutting boards are giant chunks of tree trunk, and the knives are cleavers, machetes, and field knives. (The same knife you used to whittle a piece of wood earlier? Now you're using it to dice tomatoes for the salsa.)

Basically, a carnita asada is our version of a potluck; everyone works together to bring together a delicious meal alfresco. On ranches, the hottest part of the day is around the same time as lunch, so the days start extremely early—and lunches can be extended as needed. Go inside, you say? That would involve changing clothes and cleaning up, only to go back outside later to finish the day. Not happening.

While we know carne asadas to be quite elaborate, the truth of the matter is that they can sometimes be quite simple and low-key. Take an extremely thin slice of a tough cut of meat, grilled with just salt, and thrown on a grilled tortilla with a squeeze of lime and crushed chiltepín: that's a luxurious meal to a vaquero or field laborer. And the DIY spirit is unshakeable: Have a warped, rusted piece of sheet metal or a steel drum? Great, put it over the meat on top of the grill—the tortillas can cook on top if the meat is taking up the space over the charcoal.

I guess what I'm saying is that the way that I can describe the entire border culture is that we're the MacGyvers of Mexico. We might not have a grill, but if we have a lonely grocery cart abandoned on the side of the road, well . . . that can make a fine grill, right? Don't have a comal, but see an aluminum folding chair nearby? Hold my cerveza. We make do with what we have, and we always end up with something delicious to eat.

THE ASADA SPREAD

These recipes are some of my family's favorites. I'm often volunteered as tribute to host the family hunger games du jour, frequently with little heads-up—but if I have more than four hours' notice, I'll make a more elaborate marinade like the one below. This marinade takes ponzu—introduced to Mexico through Japanese influence in Baja—right to the ranch, for a fruity, spicy, garlicky flavor. The guacasalsa is a delicious way to add richness to a tart salsa cruda, with avocados blended in. The grilled onions and chiles can never be missed, ever.

Honestly, this spread is everything I love. My family and I have enjoyed our asadas my entire life, and hopefully now, yours will, too.

Serves 4

The Spread

Grilled Steak (recipe follows)
Grilled Onions and Chilies with Maggi Ponzu (recipe follows)
Guacasalsa (recipe follows)
Lots of tortillas
White Rice with Corn (page 33)
Stewed Beans (page 30), or other beans

1. First, set up your grill for the asada.

2. If using a charcoal grill: Fill a coal chimney to the top with charcoal, light it, and allow the coals to burn for about 20 minutes, until the coals turn gray with ash. Pour the coals into a pile at the bottom of your grill. Carefully push three-quarters of the coals to one side of the grill, and the remaining quarter to the other side, to create a "hot zone" and a "hold zone."

3. If using a gas grill: Turn the grill to medium-high heat, with a separate medium-low zone.

4. Clean and oil the grill grates before grilling.

GRILLED STEAK

Serves 4

½ cup minced garlic (from about 2 heads)
2 tablespoons ground cumin
2 tablespoons chili powder
Juice and zest of 3 oranges (about ¾ cup juice)
3 bunches cilantro, chopped
1 cup grapeseed or other neutral oil
½ cup cubed fresh pineapple
Diamond Crystal kosher salt
Freshly ground black pepper
2 pounds skirt steak

First, make the marinade. In a blender, combine the garlic, cumin, chili powder, orange juice and zest, cilantro, oil, pineapple chunks, salt, and black pepper. Blend on high until smooth. Taste and adjust salt if necessary.

Trim the skirt steak if needed and place it in a baking dish or shallow bowl. Pour the marinade over the meat. Massage the steak to ensure it gets evenly covered with the marinade. Cover with plastic wrap and place it in the refrigerator to marinate for 4 hours or overnight.

At least 30 minutes before grilling, remove the steak from the refrigerator to take off the chill.

Place the steak on the grill over the hot zone and grill for about 4 minutes on each side, until there are grill marks. The thinner the steak, the shorter the grill time—depending on the thickness, you can move the meat to the hold zone to continue cooking to your desired doneness. Remove the steak from the grill and allow to rest at least 5 minutes before slicing.

Recipe continues

GRILLED ONIONS AND CHILES WITH MAGGI PONZU

3 garlic cloves, minced
½ cup soy sauce
¼ cup Maggi sauce
Juice of 4 lemons (about 1 cup)
Juice of 4 limes (about ½ cup)
½ cup olive oil
Diamond Crystal kosher salt
8 green onions (white and green parts)
6 whole jalapeño peppers

Make the Maggi ponzu: In a medium bowl, whisk together the garlic, soy sauce, Maggi, lemon and lime juice, and olive oil until combined. Add salt to taste.

Trim the roots off the green onions, preserving as much of the white ends as possible, and then toss the green onions and the jalapeños in the Maggi ponzu to coat. Reserve the extra sauce for serving.

Place the green onions and jalapeños on the hot zone of the grill, turning to char on all sides, about 5 to 8 minutes total. Place the green onions and jalapeños on a rimmed plate, and pour the extra Maggi ponzu over them before serving.

GUACASALSA

(AVOCADO SALSA FRESCA)

1 recipe Raw Tomatillo Salsa (page 38)
2 ripe avocados
½ bunch cilantro (stems included)
1 serrano pepper, stemmed and seeded
Diamond Crystal kosher salt

Add the prepared salsa to a blender with the flesh of the avocados, the cilantro, serrano, and a pinch of salt. Blend the ingredients on high until smooth, then adjust salt to taste. Transfer the guacasalsa to a small bowl to serve.

CHILE COLORADO

Some of the best and most classically known Mexican dishes come from *campesinos* (farmers) and vaqueros. These workers typically did not—and still don't—own their own land, but part of their job includes the physical oversight of the land for the hacienda owner. The harsh sun in the desert of the northern borderlands requires taking a lot of necessary (in fact, life-saving) short breaks between tasks. Payment usually includes a portion of meat and vegetables from the land that they tend to, and assembling a makeshift stove to prepare meals is often a highlight of their days.

Chile colorado is a braised beef commonly cooked on the ranches and farmlands in the Sonora and Chihuahua. The star ingredients are the flavorful sun-dried chiles. ("Colorado" in the name refers to the chiles' red hue, not the US state.) To this day, chiles hang from branches or are laid out on canvas mats to dry in the intense Sonoran heat. In chile colorado, the chiles are turned into a rich paste, blended with other aromatics, and used to marinate and then braise tough cuts of meat.

Ancho chiles, the ripened and dried form of poblanos, gives the sauce a deep, earthy flavor. Guajillo chiles provide a mild-to-medium spice level, but you can add in a chile de árbol or two for an additional kick. I add avocado leaf and hoja santa for their herbal notes, but you can omit them if you wish and still have a beautiful dish. If you have family or friends who are vegan, you can use vegetable broth and green jackfruit or large meaty mushrooms like king trumpet or portobello mushrooms in place of beef.

Serves 6

---

1 quart beef broth
4 dried ancho chiles, stemmed and seeded
5 dried guajillo chiles, stemmed and seeded
1 yellow onion, quartered
4 garlic cloves
2 tablespoons Mexican dried oregano
1½ teaspoons ground cumin
1 teaspoon smoked paprika
2 dried avocado leaves (optional)
1 hoja santa leaf (optional)
Diamond Crystal kosher salt
3 pounds beef chuck, cut into ½-inch cubes
2 tablespoons cornstarch
3 tablespoons grapeseed oil
1 bay leaf
Diamond Crystal kosher salt

1. Add the beef broth to a medium pot and bring to a boil over medium-high heat. When the broth begins to boil, turn the heat off and add in the dried chiles, onions, and garlic. Cover the pot and steep for 20 minutes.

2. After 20 minutes, transfer the steeped mixture (including the broth) to a blender. Add the oregano, cumin, paprika, avocado and hoja santa leaves (if using), and a few pinches of salt. Carefully cover the blender with the lid, leaving a small crack for steam to escape. Blend the ingredients until smooth; then strain the mixture through a fine-mesh sieve into a medium bowl. Discard any solids. Taste the mixture and adjust the salt as needed. Set aside.

3. In a bowl, toss the beef with cornstarch and salt well.

4. Set a large, heavy pot or Dutch oven over medium-high heat. Once hot, add the oil and heat until it starts to shimmer. Carefully add the meat in a single layer, working batches as needed. Cook until you start to see some good browning; then rotate the pieces to brown on another side. Once the cubes are caramelized on all sides, transfer them to a plate. Repeat until all of the beef is equally seared. Don't be surprised if the whole searing process takes 15 minutes or longer!

5. Once all of the beef is caramelized, return it to the pot, and pour in the chile sauce mixture. Stir to incorporate. Use a wooden spoon to deglaze the pot, scraping the bottom to release the caramelized bits known as the fond (that's where all the best flavor is).

6. Add the bay leaf and adjust the salt if it's desperately needed. (Remember that the sauce will cook and reduce, concentrating the flavor, so it's okay if it tastes slightly under-seasoned for now.)

7. Bring the chile colorado to a slow boil; then reduce the heat to low. Cover the pot and simmer the beef until the meat is fork-tender, about an hour. The sauce will thicken as it cooks, so if you want a thinner sauce, you can add additional broth or a little bit of water. Serve with rice, beans, and flour tortillas.

Coca-Cola

GALLINA PINTA

(OXTAIL STEW WITH BEANS AND HOMINY)

The name of this *caldo* (stew) is argued over by many Sonorenses. It literally translates to "speckled hen," but it contains no chicken of any kind. Regardless of the name, it lands on my top ten favorite dishes that I have eaten in my travels through the North.

Reading through this recipe, you might wonder why there are *two* starchy elements—Why beans *and* hominy? Before you start asking questions—don't. There is magic in not knowing and just eating in peace, especially when it comes to a dish as soulful as gallina pinta. The beans and hominy absorb the beef flavor as they cook, and they release their own starches into the broth, helping thicken it perfectly. The oxtail bones help with the texture and rich flavor of the stew, but if you cannot find them, simply include a bit more chuck roast for more meat, and use another stock bone in the stew for flavor (just remember to remove it before serving).

Serves 4

½ pound dry pinto beans
Diamond Crystal kosher salt
1½ pounds beef oxtails
1 pound chuck roast, cut into 1-inch chunks
2 tablespoons neutral oil
2 serrano peppers, stemmed
1 medium white onion, halved
2 garlic cloves
1 bunch cilantro stems (leaves reserved for garnish)
2 epazote leaves
2 Roma tomatoes, halved
2 teaspoons freshly ground ground black pepper
1 tablespoon dried Mexican oregano
¼ teaspoon ground cumin
1 (15.5-ounce) can hominy, drained and rinsed

For Serving/Optional Garnishes

1 white onion, minced
1 bunch cilantro leaves, finely chopped
Dried Mexican oregano
Limes, cut into cheeks
Dried crushed chiltepín peppers, or crushed red pepper flakes
Warmed Corn Tortillas (page 23)

1. Soak the pinto beans overnight in cold water to cover and a couple of pinches of salt. This will help ensure that the beans do not explode while cooking. Drain and discard the soaking water.

2. In a large stockpot, combine the soaked pinto beans, oxtails, and beef chuck, and pour in enough cold water to cover by about 3 inches. Add in a few generous pinches of salt. Place the pot over medium-high heat and bring to a simmer. Lower the heat to keep the pot at a simmer and cook for 1 hour.

3. Fill a small bowl with cold water and set it on the counter next to the pot. Using a slotted spoon, skim off any foam that rises to the top of the stew as it cooks, and then dip the spoon into the bowl of water to help remove the foam after each time. (Discard this water when you are done cooking the stew.)

4. In a medium pot set over medium heat, add the oil, serrano peppers, onion, garlic, cilantro stems, epazote, tomato, and a couple pinches of salt. Sauté until all of the vegetables are soft and translucent, about 15 minutes.

5. Once soft, transfer the vegetables to a blender and add in the black pepper, oregano, and cumin. Cover carefully with the lid, leaving a small gap for steam to escape. (I like to also place a kitchen towel over it to prevent splattering.) Blend until smooth, adding a ladle of the stew broth if needed to thin out. Strain the sauce through a fine-mesh sieve into the pot of stew. Adjust seasoning to taste.

6. After the stew has cooked for an hour, add the hominy. Cook for an additional 30 minutes, or until the beans and meat are tender.

7. Taste and adjust the seasonings one more time before serving. Serve with garnishes on the side and a stack of steaming hot tortillas.

BLACK GARLIC AGUACHILE WITH RIB EYE

One of my favorite food memories is from a trip to Hermosillo, Sonora, when I ate my first rib eye aguachile. "Aguachile" literally translates to "chile water," and it almost always refers to an acidic, spicy, flavorful broth served cold with raw seafood, meant to flavor it (but not cure or marinate it, like its cousin, ceviche).

So yes, you're probably more familiar with aguachile paired with seafood. But combined with the rich taste of grilled steak, it's arguably even better. It blew my mind to learn that Sonorenses first ate aguachiles with carne seca (dried beef) on the desert ranches *long before* the emergence of the now-classic seafood aguachile. It's just proof that everything migrates . . . humans and food. When people are exposed to new food concepts, they are quick to adapt them to fit their own environment and needs. So, this recipe honors the beefy roots of the aguachile.

Back at my restaurant, in 2018 or 2019, my sous chef Leo played with the idea of adding black garlic to the aguachile sauce (he paired it with tuna carnitas). The black garlic gives the aguachile depth of flavor and umami, similar to how Maggi functions in Aguachile Negro (page 167). This aguachile sauce is incredibly versatile: Use it with beef, tuna, shrimp, or even vegetables. If you cannot find chiltepín peppers, feel free to use chile de árbol or more serranos.

Serves 4

Aguachile Broth

1 bunch cilantro, some leaves reserved for garnish
3 garlic cloves
5 black garlic cloves
4 dried chiltepín peppers
Zest of 1 orange
Juice of 2 oranges (about ½ cup)
Juice of 6 limes (about ¾ cup)
1 shallot
6 tablespoons rice wine vinegar
½ serrano pepper, stemmed
¾ cup olive oil

Rib Eye

2 pounds boneless rib eye steaks, trimmed
Olive oil
Diamond Crystal kosher salt

Garnishes

1 small red onion, julienned
2 Persian cucumbers, thinly sliced
½ bunch cilantro, leaves only
Coarse sea salt

MAKE THE AGUACHILE BROTH:

1. In a blender, combine the cilantro, garlic, black garlic, chiltepín peppers, orange zest and juice, lime juice, shallot, rice wine vinegar, and the serrano pepper. Blend the ingredients on high, then remove the center cap of the blender lid. Continue to blend while slowly drizzling the olive oil into the mixture through the lid. Once the mixture is smooth, pour it into a medium bowl and season with salt to taste. Place in the refrigerator for at least 2 hours before using so the flavors can develop.

GRILL THE STEAK:

2. Remove the rib eye from the refrigerator at least 30 minutes before grilling to take the chill off.

3. If using a charcoal grill: Fill a coal chimney to the top with charcoal, light it, and allow the coals to burn for about 20 minutes, until the coals turn gray with ash. Pour the coals into a pile at the bottom of your grill. Carefully push three-quarters of the coals to one side of the grill, and the remaining quarter to the other side, to create a "hot zone" and a "hold zone."

4. If using a gas grill: Turn the grill to medium-high heat, with a separate medium-low zone.

5. Clean and oil the grill grates.

6. Drizzle olive oil on the steak and season with salt and pepper on both sides. Massage the steaks to rub the seasonings in.

Recipe continues

7. Set the steaks on the grill over the hot zone. Grill, covered, until a probe thermometer inserted in the thickest part of the meat registers 85°F. Flip the steaks, monitoring the thermometer until it registers 100°F. Then, move the steak to the side "hold" zone of the grill until to your desired degree of doneness, 5 to 10 minutes. (Between 115°F and 120°F for rare, between 125°F and 130°F for medium-rare, and so on.)

8. Transfer the steaks to a cutting board. Tent them with aluminum foil and let them rest for 12 to 15 minutes to allow the juices to redistribute. Slice the steaks against the grain into ¼-inch-thick slices.

TO SERVE:

9. Spoon the aguachile broth onto a rimmed platter or individual plates. Lay the grilled steak in the center of the broth and garnish with red onion, cucumber, cilantro leaves, and coarse sea salt to taste.

SWEET CORN TAMALES

"*Somos de maíz*"—"we are of the corn"—is a sentiment felt throughout a massive swath of the entire Americas, since time immemorial. The smell of sweet corn tamales is like aromatherapy for me. They're a northern borderland staple, especially in my home. Unlike the tamales you'll find in most other areas of Mexico, these ones don't involve masa—they're made with fresh sweet corn kernels straight off the cob, and cornmeal, enriched with sweetened condensed milk and cinnamon.

Other sweet versions of corn tamales exist, such as *uchepos* in Michoacán, whose history goes back ten thousand years. Here in the north, though, I notice a marriage between North and Central American Indigenous cultures. These tamales are like our version of corn bread, eaten as dessert or to accompany other savory braised meat dishes.

The dry, arid climate of the Sonoran desert did not lend itself to growing corn like other regions ten thousand years ago, but it still has a long history in the region. As the ecology evolved, the lands became wetter, and as the Santa Cruz River began to flow, conditions became more favorable to the crop. The Indigenous Tohono O'odham and the Yoeme (Yaqui) peoples have been growing corn along what is now the Arizona–Sonora border, mainly in the summertime, for the last four thousand years. Then, between AD 400 and 700, new cultivars made it possible to grow corn for cornmeal production.

I have eaten these tamales my whole life, and am equally partial to eating them as a sweet snack, with cajeta, or savory-style, topped with Mexican crema, Tomato and Oregano Sauce (page 52), and crumbled queso fresco. Pro tip: This batter also makes a great spoonbread, in case the husks give you too much trouble. Butter a 10-inch square baking dish, pour in the batter, and bake at 350°F for 30 minutes, or until a toothpick comes out clean when poked in the center.

Makes 10 to 12 tamales

- 5 large ears sweet corn, in their husks (see Note)
- 1 (16-ounce) package dried corn husks, as needed
- 7 ounces sweetened condensed milk (half of a 14-ounce can)
- ½ cup finely ground yellow cornmeal, plus more as needed
- 1 teaspoon baking powder
- 1 teaspoon ground cinnamon
- ¼ teaspoon Diamond Crystal kosher salt (or a pinch of Morton salt)
- 4 tablespoons unsalted butter, softened
- Milk, as needed
- Optional add-ins: Raisins, dried cranberries, dried cherries, or chopped dried apricots

Special equipment

Steamer pot or basket

1. Cut the ears of corn half an inch from the bottom, effectively removing the base. Carefully remove the husks and set aside. Clean the corn thoroughly, removing all the silk strands.

2. Place the fresh and dried corn husks in a large bowl, cover them with hot water, and leave them to soak for 15 minutes to help them become pliable. Set aside until you are ready to build the tamales.

3. Set an ear of corn flat on its side on a cutting board. Holding firmly with one hand, carefully cut the kernels from one side of the cob. Rotate the cob cut-side down and cut the kernels from another side of the cob. Continue until you've removed all the kernels. Repeat with the remaining ears of corn.

4. Reserve ½ cup of the corn kernels in a small bowl and set aside. Add the rest of the kernels to a blender with the condensed milk. Blend on high until the mixture is smooth.

5. In a large bowl, stir together the cornmeal, baking powder, cinnamon, and salt. Add in the butter, along with the blended corn mixture, and stir to incorporate with a rubber spatula. Fold in the reserved ½ cup of corn kernels and any other add-ins (if using). The mixture should have a consistency similar to brownie batter. (If it's too thick, add milk a tablespoon at a time to loosen. If it's too

Recipe continues

thin, add cornmeal a tablespoon at a time to thicken—but be aware that the cornmeal will thicken a bit as the batter sits.)

6. Put the batter in the refrigerator to set, best if left overnight, but at least 4 hours—this will thicken it up a bit and make it more manageable to work with.

7. Fill the bottom of a steamer pot with about 1 inch of water, making sure the water does not reach the bottom of the steamer cage/basket. Add a couple of pennies or small stones to the bottom of the pot—I'm serious, they'll be important later! Line the steamer cage with one or two layers of the soaked dried corn husks, and insert the cage into the pot. Place the steamer over medium-high heat, and bring the water to a simmer.

8. Build the tamales. Grab one of the corn husks and flatten it out, with the wider end farthest from you. Spoon about 3 tablespoons of the sweet corn batter onto the wide part of the husk, and spread into a 2- to 3-inch square, about ¼ inch thick, with a ½-inch border of husk on the edges.

9. To wrap the tamales, fold one long side of the husk over the batter, then overlap it with the other long side. Fold the empty narrow part of the husk (the tapered end closest to you) up over the batter-covered part, from the bottom up.

10. Stack the tamales upright in the steamer cage, with the open ends facing up. Cover the pot and steam the tamales for 40 to 50 minutes, until fully cooked. As the tamales steam, the pennies will rattle in the water. If you notice the pennies have stopped rattling, it means the water is almost evaporated, so check your water level and add more as needed.

11. After 40 minutes, take a tamal out of the pot and test for doneness. (The husk should release easily from the tamal when you peel it back.) If not done, close the tamal back up, return it to the pot, and cook the tamales for another 10 minutes before checking again.

12. Once the tamales are ready, turn the heat off, remove the lid, and let the tamales sit in the pot to cool to room temp before removing them. Enjoy fresh (see headnote for serving suggestions).

Note: If you're not able to save the fresh corn husks from the corn, just use more of the store-bought dry ones—they'll do the job just fine.

CALDO DE QUESO

(CHEESE AND POTATO SOUP)

Something to know about the people of the Sonoran border: no matter how hot it is in the summer, caldo de queso (cheese broth) is fair game. Sonora really it is the land of caldos (soups). I have never seen another dish stretch as much as a family can stretch a caldo across meals. Feeding an entire large family or ranch hands and field workers with caldo made it possible to not eat all of your earnings, so to speak.

The ingredients and/or method in caldo de queso may differ from family to family, but they all tap into the same comforting core: the smoky, grassy flavor of charred Anaheim or poblano peppers, Mexican oregano, a little bit of tomato, sweet milk, and panela cheese, which gives the soup a wonderfully curd-like squeak as it warms in the broth.

Panela is a fresh farmer's cheese, sort of like queso fresco. Panela cheese, though, is made with skim milk, and it's great in the soup because it doesn't melt into the broth. (Let's get one thing out of the way: This soup is nothing like the broccoli-cheddar soup.) The broth should not be overly thick, and using waxy potatoes helps because they keep their shape well when cooked, prevent them from breaking in the hot soup.

The best beverage pairing for a bowl of caldo de queso is—you guessed it—a piping-hot cup of Café de Olla (page 202). Yep, you simply ignore the sweat drops sliding into your eyeballs, because it tastes good, and will keep you energized for the rest of the day's work.

Serves 4 to 6

- 3 poblano peppers
- 2 tablespoons grapeseed or other neutral oil
- ½ medium white onion, diced
- 2 garlic cloves, minced
- 3 Roma tomatoes, diced
- 3 waxy potatoes (such as Yukon Gold), peeled and diced
- ½ teaspoon Diamond Crystal kosher salt, plus more as needed
- ½ teaspoon freshly ground black pepper
- ¼ teaspoon dried Mexican oregano
- 1 bunch cilantro, tied into a bundle with twine
- 1 cup whole milk
- 12 ounces queso panela, cubed

1. Char the poblano peppers on all sides, over an open flame or under a broiler, until the peppers have puffed and the skin is evenly blistered. Place the peppers in a bowl; then cover the bowl with plastic wrap to steam for 5 minutes—this will help loosen the skin. Peel the charred skin off the peppers by rubbing the skin with a damp paper towel. Cut each pepper down the side from stem to tip, remove the seeds and stem and cut the peppers into strips.

2. Add the oil to a large pot over medium heat. When the oil is shimmering, add the onions and sauté them until translucent, about 4 minutes. Add the garlic and cook for 1 minute, until fragrant. Then add the tomatoes and cook them until soft, about 4 minutes.

3. Add the potatoes, salt, pepper, and oregano to the pot and stir to incorporate. Cook for 3 minutes, to give them a head start.

4. Add the bundle of cilantro to the pot, along with 6 cups of water. Bring to a boil, reduce to a simmer, and cover the pot with a lid. Cook until the potatoes are cooked through, about 20 minutes.

5. When the potatoes are cooked, stir in the charred poblano strips and cook the soup for 3 minutes.

6. Stir in the milk and the cheese cubes. Cook the soup just to heat up the milk and cheese, about 5 minutes. Remove the bundle of cilantro and discard. Season the soup to taste with salt and pepper and serve hot.

FRIJOLES MANEADOS

(BEANS "TIED UP" WITH CHEESE AND CHORIZO)

Another term we often use for what you probably know as refried beans is "frijoles maneados"—beans "tied up"—like roped or herded cattle. In this case, the beans are "roped" together with cheese and pork chorizo.

This dish has everything: A variety of textures; spicy notes from the chorizo; tender, earthy beans, and stretchy, melty cheese. You could write a love song about them. If you can't find Mayocoba beans, you can sub in any tender white bean. (This recipe uses home-cooked dry beans, but you can use canned in a pinch.) At the grocery store you'll often see two kinds of chorizo—you want the soft Mexican kind that you can crumble, not the firm, cured Portuguese chorizo.

Prepare these frijoles, warm up some freshly made flour tortillas, pour yourself a hot coffee, and allow yourself to be transported, experiencing how ranch hands and cowboys have eaten for centuries along the borderlands.

Serves 6

---

4 cups Stewed Beans (page 30), made with Mayocoba beans
1 cup Mortar and Pestle Tomato Salsa (page 43)
12 ounces fresh pork chorizo
1 cup manteca or lard
2 cups small-diced queso Chihuahua
Diamond Crystal kosher salt

Optional Garnishes
Flour Tortillas (page 27), not-really-optional
Crumbled queso fresco
Ground chiltepín peppers

1. Blend the cooked beans with the salsa until smooth. If you need more liquid to get the smooth texture, you can add water or some of the cooking liquid from the beans, ¼ cup at a time.

2. In a large skillet over medium heat, add the chorizo, using a wooden spoon to break it up into crumbles. Cook for about 5 minutes, until the fat is completely rendered out of the meat (the crumbles shouldn't be fully dried out or caramelized). Using a slotted spoon, transfer the chorizo to a bowl and set aside.

3. Add the manteca or lard to the rendered chorizo fat in the skillet. Once the lard is melted, carefully pour the blended beans and salsa into the pan. Stir frequently to incorporate the lard into the beans—you're basically "frying" the beans in the fat. Add the chorizo to the beans and continue stirring everything together.

4. Once the chorizo is three-quarters of the way mixed in, add the cubed cheese, and yes, keep stirring. Do not stop stirring until the last of the cubed cheese is completely melted and combined. At this point, remove from heat and add salt to taste.

5. Transfer the beans to a large serving bowl as a dip to share, or portion into smaller bowls to serve as a personal snack. Always serve with flour tortillas for dipping, full stop. Top with some queso fresco and some ground chiltepín peppers if you'd like.

TOHONO O'ODHAM NATION TEPARY BEAN ENFRIJOLADAS

Bean "enchiladas" enfrijoladas and I go way back, pretty much to day one. Or at least to the first day I could eat solid food, which for a Mexican kid is pretty much as soon as you cut your first tooth. Enfrijoladas are the bean-based version of enchiladas—instead of drenching semi-fried tortillas in a chile sauce (get it? En*chi*ladas?), you smother them in a savory, creamy bean purée before rolling or folding them over a filling.

This dish is made special by the use of tepary beans. The Indigenous Tohono O'odham people have been cultivating this beautiful small legume for at least a thousand years—on land stretching from north of what we know as Phoenix, east of Tucson, down well into Sonora and west all the way to the Gulf of California. Legend says that the tepary beans were scattered across the sky to form the Milky Way. This warrior of a legume is the most drought-tolerant and heat-resistant bean in the world, and it also happens to have a lovely creamy texture and a unique flavor. If you find and make Frijoles de la Olla (page 30) with brown tepary beans, expect a rich and earthy flavor for your sauce. If you use white tepary beans, you will have a milder and almost sweet, nutty flavor.

When frying the tortillas, remember you aren't making tostadas, and you don't want them crispy. The frying adds flavor and richness, but you want them pliable enough to roll.

Serves 4

- 4 cups Stewed Beans (page 30), made with tepary beans, liquid reserved
- ¼ small yellow onion
- 2 garlic cloves, smashed
- 2 chipotle peppers in adobo sauce
- 1 tablespoon red wine vinegar
- Neutral cooking oil, for frying
- 12 (5-inch) Corn Tortillas (page 23), or store-bought
- Diamond Crystal kosher salt
- 1 cup crumbled queso fresco

Optional Garnishes

- Mexican crema
- Crumbled Cotija cheese
- Cilantro leaves
- Quick-Pickled Red Onions (page 33)
- Salsa of choice

MAKE THE SAUCE:

1. In a medium pot over medium-high heat, combine the beans, 2 cups of bean liquid, the onion, garlic, and chipotle peppers. Bring to a simmer; then reduce the heat to low, cover, and simmer for 30 minutes, so the flavors can come together. Remove from heat, add the red wine vinegar, and taste and adjust seasonings as desired.

2. Carefully transfer the pot's contents to a blender. Cover with the blender lid, leaving a small gap for steam to escape. (I like to hold a clean dish towel over the blender lid to prevent splashing.) Blend on high until completely smooth, adding water a splash at a time as needed if it seems too thick. The sauce should be pourable, almost like a bean soup, not like a purée. Return the blended sauce to the pot and bring to a simmer over low heat.

MAKE THE ENFRIJOLADAS:

3. Line a tray or baking sheet with paper towels. Pour 1 inch of oil into a large sauté pan. Set over medium heat until the oil is shimmering. Test the temperature of the oil by dipping a tiny bit of a tortilla; you should see tiny bubbles form immediately. Once the oil is hot enough, add a whole tortilla to the hot oil and fry it lightly on the first side for 2 minutes. Flip the tortilla and fry for another minute. If the tortillas aren't super fresh and have dried out a bit, you will need less time. They shouldn't become too crispy or tough—you need them just sturdy enough that they can be dipped without falling apart. Remove the tortilla from the oil and place it on the prepared baking sheet to drain. Repeat until all of the tortillas are fried.

4. Using tongs, pick up a fried tortilla and quickly dip it into the bean sauce, making sure both sides are completely coated, and place it on a plate or a baking sheet to fill. Fill one side of the dipped tortilla with the queso fresco, then fold it over to close. Repeat with each fried tortilla until all are dipped and filled. Plate the enfrijoladas on a platter or individual plates. Ladle with more bean sauce on top, and garnish as desired.

JAMONCILLO

(CARAMELIZED MILK FUDGE)

Despite having a name that means "little ham," *jamoncillo* is actually a candy that you can find for sale at every corner store and mercado in Sonora. Hailing from colonial times, the milk-based candy became popular throughout the North as a result of ranches that had large herds of dairy cows. Nowadays, it makes a great holiday treat, especially since it can be made in large batches.

Jamoncillo is a beautiful, dark caramel fudge with a somewhat crystallized texture and warm floral notes from the vanilla and nut filling. If you are able to find goat milk, its tanginess also helps make for a more balanced dairy flavor. You can scoop out the fudge, roll it between your hands, and wrap it in wax paper, or for a more intricate look, you can pipe it out with a decorative star frosting tip and garnish it with chopped nuts. Take liberties with your garnishes—you can also try dried cranberries or shredded coconut.

Makes about 2 dozen pieces of fudge

½ cup pine nuts or pecans
2 cups goat milk or whole cow milk
2 cups sugar
1½ tablespoons vanilla extract
¼ teaspoon baking soda
Butter, for greasing

1. Toast the pine nuts or pecans in a dry pan over medium heat until golden brown and you begin to smell the nuts. Chop and set aside near the stovetop.

2. Line a tray or baking sheet with wax paper and set aside near the stovetop.

3. In a medium heavy pot, combine the milk, sugar, and vanilla. Stir just to incorporate the ingredients. Set over medium heat and bring to a boil.

4. Once the mixture starts to boil, add in the baking soda and whisk to incorporate. Reduce the heat to low and let the mixture come to a simmer, stirring periodically so that the bottom does not scorch. The mixture will begin to darken and become thicker. The timing can vary greatly depending on many external factors (including temperature and altitude), but color is most important here, so keep an eye on it. When the mixture is deep amber-colored and has thickened to the consistency of a caramel sauce, remove it from the heat.

5. Using a wooden spoon, stir the pine nuts or pecans into the caramel. It will start to crystalize and set into a fudge very quickly, no more than 5 minutes. Use a lightly greased (pan spray is great) spoon to scoop coin-sized mounds and drop them on the prepared wax paper to cool.

6. Once the fudge is cool enough to handle, rub a small amount of butter on your hands and roll the fudge into 1-inch balls. Wrap each piece of fudge in cellophane or wax paper.

Note: When making the fudge, after the mixture reaches a boil, make sure you stir intermittently to prevent scorching or burning.

TAQUITOS DE PAPA AHOGADOS

(CALDILLO-SMOTHERED ROLLED POTATO TACOS)

In taco shop lingo, taquitos are also known as rolled tacos. (They're not to be confused with flautas, which are made with flour instead of corn tortillas.) You'll see rolled tacos with all kinds of fillings, but in my opinion nothing beats the version filled with mashed potatoes, fried until crispy, and smothered in tomato caldillo. It's hard to stop eating these taquitos. Between the crunchy exterior, the hot filling, and the cold crema and cheese on top, they really hit the spot.

With a large population of migrants hailing from Jalisco during and after the Mexican Revolution, it's no wonder that the drenched-in-sauce style, or *ahogado* (meaning "drowned") arrived in Sonora as well. Jalisco has long been long known for *charro* culture, in which horse rearing is a generational rite of passage in families. During the revolution, many wealthy families in Jalisco lost their land, as soldiers began squatting on ranches and pushing the families out. Many of them moved to areas where their expertise could be of some use, ending up as far north as Sonora. When people migrate, they bring their dishes—and that's how you end up with Norteños drowning their taquitos in caldillo.

Makes 16 taquitos

---

2 small russet potatoes, peeled and diced
1 small celery root, peeled and diced
1 dried avocado leaf
1 bay leaf
Diamond Crystal kosher salt
1 teaspoon white pepper
1 quart half-and-half
¾ cup queso Chihuahua or mozzarella
16 (5-inch) corn tortillas, or use homemade (page 23)
Grapeseed or other neutral oil, for frying
2 recipes Tomato and Oregano Sauce (page 52)
1 recipe Chile de Árbol Salsa (page 37)

1. In a medium pot, add the potatoes, celery root, avocado leaf, bay leaf, a generous pinch of salt, and the white pepper. Pour in the half-and-half to cover the vegetables. Set the pot over medium heat and cook until the potatoes and celery root begin to fall apart when pressed with a fork, about 25 minutes.

2. Remove the bay and avocado leaves from the pot and discard. Using a slotted spoon, transfer the potato and celery root into a large bowl and mash them with a bean smasher—this will become the filling. The mixture should be dense, and not at all watery. Adjust the seasoning to taste; then fold in the cheese and set aside to cool. Once cool enough to handle, transfer the filling to a piping bag, or a large resealable plastic bag.

3. Preheat a dry comal or large pan over medium heat. To make the tortillas pliable, splash each one with a bit of water and warm them on the hot comal.

4. Set your taquito-filling station up with a cutting board, the softened tortillas, the filling in the piping bag, and a handful of toothpicks.

5. Line a baking sheet with paper towels and set a wire cooling rack on top. Set aside.

6. In a deep skillet or Dutch oven, add 2 to 3 inches of frying oil. Set over medium-high heat until the oil reaches 350°F on a frying thermometer.

7. Grab the piping bag (or plastic bag) and snip off a corner, about an inch from the tip. Pipe a "log" of the filling horizontally across the center of a tortilla. Carefully fold the bottom edge of the tortilla over the filling and roll the tortilla like you would to make a burrito: gently drag the filling toward you as you continue to roll the tortilla forward on itself. Fasten the tortilla shut with a toothpick.

8. Once the oil has come up to temperature (and all of the taquitos are rolled), add the taquitos to the oil, working in batches of four to prevent crowding. Carefully fry the taquitos until the tortillas crisp up and turn a rich golden brown, about 4 minutes each.

9. As each batch of the taquitos finishes cooking, remove them from the oil with a slotted spoon and set them on the wire rack to drain excess oil. Repeat with the rest of the taquitos, making sure that the oil returns to 350°F before you add a new batch of taquitos to the oil.

10. Remove the toothpicks after frying and draining the taquitos.

11. To serve the fried taquitos, arrange them on a platter and then smother them with a generous amount of sauce and salsa to your liking.

COYOTAS

(PILONCILLO-FILLED PASTRIES)

As Sonoran as wheat itself, coyotas are empanada-like pastries filled with piloncillo (unrefined cane sugar). *Coyota*, meaning "female coyote," was a Sonoran term for the mestizo daughters of Indigenous women and Spanish men. While the mothers baked, the girls would help their family by taking the baskets around town to sell pastries.

Some credit for the pastry goes to Doña Teodora de Moreno of Villa de Seris, a community of largely Indigenous Comcaac ancestry in Hermosillo, Mexico. Doña Teodora popularized coyotas after making them to support her family, but it wasn't until 1954 that the pastry was commercially produced by Doña Maria Ochoa. Doña Maria, originally from Chihuahua, arrived to Villa de Seris in 1925 and was given the recipe for coyotas by a neighbor, Agustina de Araiza. She began making her own coyotas and began producing them for commercial wholesale. Doña Maria's family still runs the business, sending coyotas across the border and even to Europe.

Coyotas made fresh in the wood-fired hearths in Hermosillo are incredibly delicious. Over the last few years, I have seen many more kinds of filling, including guava and quince paste, cajeta, and jams—so feel free to experiment yourself.

The key to the coyotas is that the pastry is rolled out thinly—when it's done, it should have a crunchy outer ring and be slightly softer toward the center. If you stick to the piloncillo filling, these are shelf-stable for up to one week.

Makes 12 cookies

- 3 (8-ounce) cones piloncillo
- 6 cups plus 4 tablespoons all-purpose flour
- 1 tablespoon plus 1 teaspoon Diamond Crystal kosher salt (or 2 teaspoons plus ½ teaspoon Morton salt)
- 1¼ tablespoons baking powder
- 1 cup manteca or shortening

1. Using a box grater or food processor, grate or grind the piloncillo cones to make a powder. Reserve a quarter of the grated piloncillo in a small bowl and set aside.

2. In a medium bowl, combine the remaining three-quarters of the grated piloncillo, 4 tablespoons of the flour, and 1 tablespoon of the salt. Set aside—this will be the filling for the cookies.

3. In a medium pot, combine the reserved grated piloncillo and 1 cup of water. Set over low heat until melted and dissolved; then turn off the heat so the liquid does not reduce. Set aside.

4. In a large bowl, add the remaining 6 cups of flour, the remaining 1 teaspoon of salt, and the baking powder and mix to combine. Begin cutting the manteca (or shortening) into the flour in the bowl, using a fork or your fingertips. Once you start to notice lentil-sized crumbs forming, your dough is ready for the wet ingredients.

5. Slowly drizzle the piloncillo and water mixture into the dough, mixing to incorporate. Continue mixing the dough with your hands until it forms a smooth ball.

6. On a clean work surface, roll the dough into a long, 2-inch-thick log. Mark the center of the log with a butter knife, then mark an indentation at the center of each half, and then the center of each quarter. Repeat until you have marked 24 equal-sized portions; then slice the dough.

Recipe continues

7. Grease your hands with a little bit of manteca or shortening and roll each portion of dough into a ball, lightly coating the dough balls with manteca in the process. Place each ball of dough on a baking sheet and cover them with a clean, damp kitchen towel to rest for 45 minutes to 1 hour.

8. Preheat the oven to 400°F. Line a baking sheet with parchment paper and set aside.

9. Once the dough balls have rested, use a rolling pin to flatten each ball into a thin round, about as thick as a flour tortilla. The manteca should allow you to stack the rounds as you roll them without them sticking to one another. Keep the rounds under the damp cloth to prevent drying out.

10. To assemble the coyotas, place one flattened round down and spoon 2 tablespoons of the piloncillo filling onto the center, then top with another flattened round. Gently press the edges of the coyote together, working your way around while squeezing out any air pockets. Crimp the pressed edges with a fork. Use the tip of a paring knife to poke 5 little holes on the top for steam to escape.

11. Place the cookies on the prepared baking sheet, 2 inches apart. Bake until golden brown on top and bottom, 30 to 40 minutes. Let cool slightly before serving.

12. You can store the coyotas in an airtight container on your counter for a few days, and reheat for a few minutes in a toaster oven to refresh the freshly baked texture.

13. Coyotas don't keep for long, so if you can't eat them yourself within a few days, I suggest sharing with friends. Or you can assemble the coyotas and freeze them raw between layers of wax paper—simply thaw before baking.

AGUA DE CEBADA

(TOASTED BARLEY AGUA FRESCA)

An agua fresca made with barley? Yes—in fact, it's one of my favorites! Think of this as another version of horchata, but using a different grain. And what area is better suited to grow grains than the borderlands of Sonora? Barley grows in the same environments as wheat, but has more fiber. When made into this drink, it's sweet and milky, with a nutty, toasty flavor. As a bonus, this also works as an energy drink.

Makes 8 cups

1½ cups barley
1 (3-inch) stick Mexican canela/Ceylon cinnamon, broken into small pieces
1½ cups evaporated milk
1½ cups sweetened condensed milk
1 tablespoon vanilla extract
Pinch of Diamond Crystal kosher salt
Sugar, as needed

1. In a large dry skillet over medium heat, toast the barley and cinnamon stick together, stirring constantly to avoid burning, until the barley becomes nutty and fragrant, about 5 minutes. Make sure while you're toasting the barley that you keep the grains moving to prevent burning, and cut the heat as soon as the barley develops a buttery, nutty smell.

2. Add the toasted barley and cinnamon to a blender with 3 cups of water. Blend on high until totally smooth, about 5 minutes.

3. Pour the blended mixture into a large pitcher or mixing bowl. Stir in the evaporated and condensed milks, along with 5 more cups of water, the vanilla extract, and a pinch of salt. Let the beverage rest for 15 minutes for the flavors to meld.

4. Stir the mixture once more; then strain through a fine-mesh sieve into a serving pitcher. Discard any pulp. Add 2 cups of ice to the pitcher, and allow the drink to settle for a few minutes. Taste and adjust sugar as needed, adding a tablespoon at a time and stirring to dissolve after each addition. Serve in glasses over more ice.

MESQUITE-CHOCOLATE TEA CAKES

Before you freak out, I'm not suggesting that you make a cake with mesquite charcoal. On the contrary, I'm talking about flour made from ground-up mesquite tree pods, which have long been a vital Indigenous food source in the Sonoran desert. Mesquite beans are an incredibly nutrient-dense legume with a sweet aroma. With the desert land bearing more mesquite pods than corn, the people adapted and used what they had. Some years, the harvest is in the millions of pounds.

These light, airy, gluten-free treats get their texture from whipped egg whites that are folded into the batter. I find the mesquite flour to be sweet and nutty, and making it a perfect duo with the natural bitterness of rich dark chocolate.

Serves 6 (Makes one 8-inch springform cake, or 24 mini muffins)

¼ cup almond flour
¼ cup plus 2 tablespoons mesquite flour*
⅛ teaspoon salt
6 ounces bittersweet chocolate
10 tablespoons unsalted butter, cubed, plus more for the pan
⅛ teaspoon almond extract
4 large eggs, separated
½ cup plus 2 tablespoons granulated sugar
⅛ teaspoon cream of tartar
Confectioners' sugar, for dusting
Whipped cream or vanilla ice cream, for serving

1. Preheat the oven to 375°F and place a rack on the middle shelf. Grease an 8-inch springform pan, or line two 12-cup mini muffin tins with paper muffin cups. Set aside.

2. In a large bowl, mix together the almond flour, mesquite flour, and salt. Set aside.

3. In a small pot, bring a few inches of water to a simmer over medium-low heat.

4. Add the bittersweet chocolate and butter to a medium heatproof bowl. Carefully set the bowl over the pot of simmering water to create a double boiler. Melt the chocolate and butter in the bowl, stirring as necessary with a heat-safe silicone spatula. Once the chocolate and butter have melted together, remove the bowl from the pan and stir the almond extract into the chocolate. Set aside. (You can leave the pot of water on the stove.)

5. In a separate medium heatproof bowl, vigorously whisk the egg yolks with ½ cup of sugar, until the sugar dissolves completely—you should no longer be able to feel sugar crystals between your fingers. Place this bowl over the same pot of simmering water and begin whisking constantly until the egg mixture is tempered and pale yellow. Once the eggs are warm, remove the bowl from the heat.

6. Using either a handheld electric mixer or a stand mixer, whisk the egg mixture on medium speed until it reaches the ribbon stage: When you lift the whisk from the yolks, the egg mixture should fall in thick ribbons. If you trace a figure-eight with the runoff, the shape should remain visible for several seconds.

7. Fold the egg yolk mixture into the chocolate mixture. Then gently fold the dry ingredients into the chocolate mixture. Do not overwork the batter!

8. In a clean, dry, medium heat-safe bowl, add the egg whites and the cream of tartar. With a clean whisk or electric hand mixer, whisk the egg whites until they are foamy. Then set the bowl over the pot of simmering hot water. Continue whisking; then gradually add the remaining 2 tablespoons of sugar, whisking at high speed (or as quickly as you can whisk by hand). Whisk until you achieve soft peaks, creating a meringue. Turn the heat off and carefully remove the bowl from the heat.

9. Gently fold the meringue into the chocolate mixture in thirds, taking care not to beat the air out of the whites. Once the batter is homogenous, pour it into the springform pan or the mini muffin cups.

10. Bake the cake on the middle rack in the oven for 25 to 30 minutes (or 20 to 25 minutes for a muffin tins), until a toothpick inserted comes out almost clean, similar to a brownie. The center of the cake will be slightly fudgy. Place the pan on a wire rack to cool completely before cutting.

11. Dust the cake (or muffins) with confectioners' sugar and serve with a dollop of whipped cream or vanilla ice cream.

Note: You can find mesquite flour online from many retailers.

CAFÉ DE OLLA

(SWEET CINNAMON COFFEE)

I can only speak for my own family, but from the moment us kids could walk, we were exposed to drinking "cafecito." Café de olla is for me what hot cocoa is to many others—a childhood drink comforting beyond measure, an ode to a slower paced life. It's flavored with orange peel, cinnamon, and piloncillo (sometimes called panela), an unrefined brown cane sugar with a delicious molasses flavor.

Like with many commonly used ingredients in our pantries, there are homeopathic benefits to the ingredients in café de olla. Cinnamon is believed to have many health benefits and antibacterial properties. Piloncillo has high mineral content. Drinking your café de olla could be your daily source of vitamin B_6, iron, magnesium, calcium, and much more.

My abue (grandmother) called it *café de calcetín* ("sock-brewed coffee") because of the cloth bag she used to filter the coffee, called a *talega*. It wasn't uncommon that she'd be unable to find her talega, but without missing a beat, she would go into her bedroom and cut the foot off of her pantyhose to make an impromptu filter.

In Sonora, the *talega* method of coffee brewing on the ranches goes back to before the time of automated or instant coffee. People living in rural areas needed a simple and practical method to brew their café. The talega was sometimes a bigger piece of cloth, filled with coffee grounds, tied around a stick and set over an olla. The coffee would be submerged in the hot water, and it could be easily removed to drain. You're welcome to try the talega method, but just in case, I'll save you the trouble of having to cut your pantyhose and give you the stovetop version.

Makes enough for 6 large mugs

1 (3-inch) stick Mexican canela/Ceylon cinnamon, plus more for garnish
1 cup Piloncillo Syrup (page 232)
½ cup medium-ground coffee
Peel of 1 orange, plus more for garnish
Pinch of Diamond Crystal kosher salt

1. In a large pot, add 2 quarts of water and bring to a boil over high heat. Add in the cinnamon, piloncillo syrup, ground coffee, orange peel, and a pinch of salt. Whisk the ingredients to hydrate the ground coffee, then shut the heat off.

2. Let the coffee steep for 5 minutes, then strain through a fine-mesh sieve. Discard the solids. Taste and adjust sweetness by adding more syrup or more water if you'd like.

3. To serve, garnish with a cinnamon stick or orange peel on each mug.

CHIHUAHUA

MUCH MORE THAN
DOGS AND CHEESE

In Chihuahua, we find a vast state—the largest in Mexico—where the deserts meet the mountains, where much of the land is parched, where we share an extensive border with West Texas, and where food has a history as colorful and layered as a perfect taco.

Chihuahua's culinary story starts with its Indigenous peoples, who originated the culinary history of this land. These early chefs were masters of survival, using native ingredients that could withstand the harsh climate and keep their spirits high. They were also savvy foragers, gathering everything from wild herbs to exotic cacti. Of the four nations that call Chihuahua home, the Tarahumara (Rarámuri) people, who live primarily in the Sierra Madre Occidental mountain range, are world-renowned for their impressive long-distance running. Their traditional lifestyle is closely tied to the rugged terrain, and the cuisine reflects their use of native staples like corn, beans, and chiles.

When Spanish colonizers arrived in the sixteenth century, they brought along their own culinary staples, including ingredients like beef, wheat, and dairy. The emergence of the *mestizaje*—mixed-race people and cultures—led to a delicious blending of flavors. Then came the Mexican Revolution and subsequent modernization, which dramatically influenced Chihuahuan cuisine. New ingredients and techniques were introduced, transforming traditional recipes and adding even more depth and variety. After the Mexican Revolution, food in Chihuahua shifted away from the Eurocentric styles pushed by the Porfiriato (the military dictatorship led by Porfirio Díaz) and embraced local, rural, and mestizo traditions. Dishes became more practical and rooted in everyday life, reflecting the values of the new post-revolutionary society. Ingredients like dried chiles, corn, and beans became central once again, along with beef farmed by vaqueros, and new borderland culinary fusions began to emerge.

My fellow cheese lovers will understand the greatness of *queso Chihuahua*, another hallmark of the region. This mild, melting cheese nods to dairy farming that was introduced by Spanish colonizers, and is now a staple in everything from quesadillas to hamburgers—here to make everything better in one melty bite!

The culinary history of Chihuahua is a story of adaptation, flavor, and tradition, where every dish tells a tale of its own. With the recipes in this chapter, you're savoring centuries of history, one delicious mouthful at a time.

BEEF BARBACOA

Barbacoa made on a ranch in the North is a kind of art form—it's cooked in a pit dug in the ground. Even though it seems like the simplest, most elemental cooking method, when you see it done by masters, there is attention to every detail: digging the pit, layering the meat and seasoning, managing the fire, coal, and ash that sits above the pit, and protecting the food from the heat just enough to achieve the perfect, slow roast, steam or simmer. And this all happens underground, so you're unable to see what you're cooking, let alone touch it. Every detail that's done right makes for delicious meat that's been gently cooked or roasted in its own juices.

With this recipe, I will help you replicate (or at least get close to) the same flavor explosion in a home oven. You'll simply have to close your eyes and imagine that you can hear trees moving in the wind, animals making noises nearby, and a ranch dog trying to catch every morsel that may potentially fall off the table or out of your mouth. In the center of the country, barbacoa is made with lamb, but in the ranch-heavy areas of Chihuahua and Texas, we have a lot of beef to go around.

Once the beef is cooked, it is served shredded on a platter and set in the center of the table with tortillas and the garnishes on the side. The cooking broth is served in cups for those who want it; you can add onions, chiles, and lime and either drink it straight up, or dunk your barbacoa tacos in it and then drink what's left. It has been said that the broth can raise the dead—and by "dead," I mean your uncle Pepe who has a hangover but has to watch the kids for your tía.

Serves 6

3 fresh banana leaves
6 dried guajillo chiles, stemmed and seeded
3 dried ancho chiles, stemmed and seeded
1 medium yellow onion, quartered
5 garlic cloves
2 teaspoons ground cumin
1 tablespoon dried Mexican oregano
2 tablespoons whole black peppercorns
Diamond Crystal kosher salt
4 pounds beef chuck, cut into 2-inch cubes
3 bay leaves

For Serving

At least 24 Corn Tortillas (page 23), warmed
Sliced avocado
Minced white onion
Chopped fresh cilantro
Lime wedges
Ground chile de árbol

1. Toast the banana leaves. Working with one banana leaf at a time, hold the leaf directly over a medium-low flame, or place it in a cast-iron skillet over medium heat, turning occasionally, until the leaf is glossy and pliable, 30 seconds to 1 minute. Repeat the process with the remaining banana leaves.

2. Line a large, deep roasting pan with aluminum foil, with 6 or more inches of overhang on all sides (you need enough to fold back over to cover the pan later). Layer the banana leaves over the foil, overlapping the pieces so that the entire interior of the pan is covered with the leaves, with 4 to 6 inches of overhang on all sides. Set aside.

MAKE THE ADOBO:

3. First, toast the chiles on a dry skillet or comal over medium heat until they start changing color; the reds will deepen and you will begin to smell the chiles.

4. Fill a medium saucepan halfway with water and bring it to a gentle simmer over medium heat. Add the toasted guajillo and ancho chiles, the onion, and garlic. Cook the chiles and onion, lowering the heat as needed to prevent the mixture from reaching a boil, until the onion is translucent and chiles are softened, 6 to 8 minutes. Remove the pot from heat.

Recipe continues

5. Using a slotted spoon, transfer the chiles, onion and garlic to a blender; reserve the cooking water. Add the cumin, oregano, and black peppercorns to the blender. Blend on high speed until smooth, about 1 minute. Add some of the reserved cooking water if needed to help achieve a smooth texture. Strain the adobo marinade through a fine-mesh strainer into a large bowl and season with salt to taste.

COOK THE MEAT:

6. Adjust the oven rack to the lower middle position and preheat to 350°F on the convection setting, or 400°F conventional.

7. Place the cubed beef into the banana leaf–lined roasting pan and mix in 4 tablespoons of Diamond Crystal kosher salt (or 2 tablespoons of Morton or table salt), massaging to thoroughly season the beef. Pour the adobo over the beef and toss to coat. Add the 3 bay leaves to the pan with the meat, and pour in 5 cups of water. Fold the overhanging banana leaves over to completely cover the barbacoa; then fold over the overhanging foil to cover the whole dish. Finally, cover with a lid.

8. Place in the oven and roast the barbacoa until the meat is completely tender and can be easily pulled apart with a pair of forks, about 4 hours.

9. Remove the pan from the oven and allow the beef to rest in the foil-covered roasting pan with the lid on for 20 minutes. After 20 minutes, remove the lid, unwrap the foil and banana leaves, and shred the beef with two forks. Transfer the beef to a large serving platter.

10. Pour the drippings and broth from the roasting pan into a small pot, skim the fat off the top, and replenish whatever amount of fat removed with an equal amount of water. Season the broth to taste with salt.

11. Enjoy the barbacoa family-style. Serve the shredded beef on a large serving platter, with cups of the barbacoa broth on the side. Eat with warm corn tortillas and your favorite garnishes.

CHARCOAL-GRILLED WHOLE CHICKEN

Rotisserie chicken, or *pollo rostizado*, is the unsung hero of the borderlands, commonly found at taco stands in many towns. In the States, you may hear it called *pollo loco*—crazy chicken—while on the other side of the border, you'll find the same dish served as "happy chicken"—*pollo felíz.* The birds' mental state aside, business is good.

The magic of a whole roasted chicken is that it can feed a family of four, and then the bones can become part of the soup the next day. You can absolutely make this chicken on a gas grill, but grill over charcoal if you can. Even those tiny round porch grills work—you know, the ones that your dad's favorite grill company makes? (That company didn't pay us to be named here, so you'll have to guess.) Maybe it's just the petrol smell in the air, but sitting on the curb of the chicken spot, ripping a chunk of chicken off with a tortilla in hand, and pouring a generous helping of salsa on top is heaven to me.

Makes 1 chicken

---

4 dried guajillo chiles, stemmed and seeded
1 small yellow onion, quartered
2 tablespoons dried Mexican oregano
Leaves from 1 sprig thyme
3 garlic cloves, peeled and smashed
1 cup freshly squeezed orange juice (from about 4 oranges)
2 bay leaves
1 cup distilled white vinegar
1 tablespoon freshly ground black pepper
Diamond Crystal kosher salt
1 (3- to 4-pound) whole chicken, giblets removed
Grapeseed oil

For Serving

Salsa para Pollo (recipe follows)
White Rice with Corn (page 33)
Stewed Beans (page 30)
Flour Tortillas (page 27)
Coleslaw (optional)

1. Make the marinade. In a blender, add the guajillos, onion, oregano, thyme, garlic, orange juice, vinegar, and black pepper. Blend until smooth and add salt to taste. Set aside.

2. Spatchcock/butterfly the chicken. Place the chicken breast-side down, with the cavity facing toward you. Use heavy kitchen shears to cut through the back ribs on both sides of the backbone; then remove the backbone and discard or save for stock. Open the rib cage and use a heavy knife to score down both sides the sternum.

3. Turn the chicken over so it's breast-side up and spread it open, like a book you're putting down to read later. Place the heel of your hand on the sternum (the spine of the book) and press down firmly using your full body weight. You should hear a crack, and the chicken will flatten.

4. Fold down the top of a large zip-top bag. Place your chicken into it, laid out as flat as possible. Place the first bag inside a second zip-top bag to prevent leakage. Pour the marinade into the bag and close both bags. Place the bags in a baking dish that allows the chicken to lie flat and marinate for 2 hours in the refrigerator, or overnight if possible.

5. Cook the chicken. Thirty minutes before cooking, take the marinated chicken out of the fridge to take the chill off.

6. If using a charcoal grill: Fill a coal chimney starter with charcoal and light it. Let the chimney coals burn for about 20 minutes, until fully covered in white ash. Make a large mound of cold coals at the bottom of your grill, about 12 to 14 inches high in the center, to maintain the heat during grilling. Pour the hot coals over the cold coals, and spread it out. Once the coals turn gray, your grill is ready to use.

Recipe continues

7. If you are using charcoal, carefully separate the coals into two sections, a "hot zone" with three-quarters of the coals, and a "hold zone" with the remaining coals. Place a clean grill grate on top; once hot, lightly oil the grate.

8. If using a gas grill: Turn your grill to medium-high heat.

9. Remove the chicken from the marinade (you can discard excess marinade). Pat the chicken down with paper towels to remove excess moisture.

10. Place the chicken, breast-side up, on the "hot zone" side of the grill. Cook with the lid off for 30 minutes. Brush the skin with oil and flip the chicken, cook for 15 minutes, breast-side down. Flip again and cook for another 15 minutes.

11. After this time, move chicken to the cooler side of the grill (or turn the gas grill to medium-low). Continue cooking until the thickest part of the breast reads 160°F on a probe thermometer. (It will reach 165°F during carryover cooking, after it's removed rom the grill.)

12. Remove the chicken from the grill and tent it with aluminum foil (don't wrap it). Let it rest for 8 to 10 minutes, so the juices can redistribute.

13. Split the pieces up or leave whole. Serve it with Salsa para Pollo, rice, beans, and flour tortillas . . . always flour.

SALSA PARA POLLO

Makes 1½ cups

2 ripe heirloom tomatoes, halved
1 jalapeño, stemmed
¼ cup lightly packed cilantro leaves
Sea salt

In the bowl of a food processor, combine the tomatoes, jalapeño, and cilantro. Pulse 4 to 5 times, until the ingredients are broken down but not puréed.

Pour the salsa into a small bowl and season with salt to taste.

CHILE PASADO

(BRAISED STEAK WITH CHILE AND POTATOES)

I grew up eating this exact dish, but my mom called it *bistec con papas* (steak with potatoes)—a guisado (braise) that fed us for several meals. In the borderland of Chihuahua and Texas, though, it's about more than those two ingredients. The star of the dish is actually the chile "*pasado*," meaning a chile that is past its prime. Usually, when we're talking about dried chiles, we're talking about chiles that have been dried from raw. Chile pasado, however, takes an unconventional route. The fresh *chilaca* chile is first charred, then peeled, and *then* dried, hung by the stem in a dry shaded area (or in a dehydrator). This results in a dried pepper with unique depth of flavor and a meatier texture. They're relatively easy to order online, but you can absolutely buy them fresh and char/dry them yourselves.

For me, these kinds of braises are key to remembering very specific moments or even people I have met. The hearty umami flavors leave indelible fingerprints on my food memory bank. The rich, savory beef flavor, with notes of sweetness from the Mexican holy trinity of tomato, onion, and peppers, will have you going back for seconds, guaranteed. I could easily eat this with flour or corn tortillas, so I'll allow you to choose your player. This is often served with Frijoles Rancheros (page 216) for a meat-on-meat-on-bean feast; on its own, you might want to double the recipe for a main dish.

Serves 2 to 4

- 3 dried pasado chiles (see headnote)
- 1 pound beef sirloin or tenderloin tips, cut into ¼-inch strips
- Diamond Crystal kosher salt
- Freshly ground black pepper
- 2 tablespoons neutral oil
- ½ medium yellow onion, diced small
- 2 garlic cloves, minced
- 1 tablespoon dried Mexican oregano
- 2 Roma tomatoes, diced small
- 1 large russet potato, peeled and diced
- ¾ cup grated queso Chihuahua

For Serving

- Stewed Beans (page 30)
- Corn Tortillas (page 23) or Flour Tortillas (page 27)

1. Stem and seed the chiles. Add them to 1 cup of boiling water and steep until softened, about 8 minutes. Remove the chiles and pat dry (save the soaking water). Cut the chiles into small pieces.

2. Season the beef with salt and black pepper. Set a large sauté pan over medium heat and add the oil. Once the oil is shimmering, add the meat to the pan in a single layer to sear (work in batches to prevent crowding). Allow the meat to cook undisturbed, for about 3 minutes, so it caramelizes on one side.

3. Once the meat is browned, add in the diced onions, garlic, and oregano. Sauté until the onions become translucent, about 10 minutes. Add the diced tomato and continue to sauté for 4 minutes, stirring and scraping up any caramelized bits at the bottom of the pan.

4. Add the diced potatoes, chile pasado, and the reserved chile soaking water. Adjust the salt to taste and reduce the heat to low. Cover the pan with a lid and simmer for 20 minutes.

5. After 20 minutes, stir the guisado to ensure nothing is stuck on the bottom. Test the potatoes for doneness—you want them soft but not falling apart. Once the potatoes are done, adjust seasoning once more to taste.

6. Sprinkle the queso Chihuahua over the entire pan. Allow it to melt directly in the pan, or transfer to the oven and broil for extra bubbly goodness. Serve with Stewed Beans and fresh tortillas.

FRIJOLES RANCHEROS

(COWBOY BEANS)

We can't talk about the borderlands without talking about our vaqueros, the men on horses who worked the cattle on the rancheros. *Vaca* means cow—that's where vaqueros get their name. (Yes, Mexico gave the world cowboys—you're welcome!)

The cowboys would make do with whatever meat they had available on the ranch, cooking giant pots of protein-filled beans outside over a live fire. These meals are probably best enjoyed when eaten sitting under a tree, sharing jokes and stories from the "good ol' days" . . . but they're pretty damn good eaten inside in your air-conditioned house, too.

There are many versions of these types of beans, but my favorite frijoles charros are made with lots of cured and smoked pork products, which accommodate the roaming ranchero lifestyle. The various textures, heat, creaminess, and the cool, fresh flavor of the cilantro on top makes this a complete meal, always better when tucked into a homemade Flour Tortilla. You can make beans fresh just for this, but I like to use this recipe to finish up leftover beans and amp them up with aromatics and pork.

Serves 4 to 6

---

6 strips bacon, diced
½ cup diced smoked ham
1½ cups diced andouille sausage
2 serrano peppers, stemmed, seeded, and minced
½ medium yellow onion, diced small
2 garlic cloves, minced
2 whole San Marzano tomatoes from a can
2 canned chipotle peppers in adobo sauce, minced
4 cups leftover Stewed Beans (page 30), liquid strained
Diamond Crystal kosher salt

Optional Garnishes
Flour Tortillas (page 27, not-really-optional)
Crumbled chicharrones
Fresh chopped cilantro
Crumbled queso fresco

1. In a large pot or Dutch oven set over medium heat, add the bacon, ham, and sausage. Cook to render out the fat, browning the sausage and ensuring the bacon is crisp, about 8 minutes. Pour most of the fat out into a ramekin and set aside; then return the pot to the heat.

2. Add the serranos, onion, and garlic to the pot with the meat. Sauté until the onion becomes translucent, 3 to 5 minutes. Then add the tomatoes and chipotle peppers, scraping the bottom of the pan to dislodge any caramelized bits.

3. Lastly, add the Stewed Beans and bring to a simmer; then reduce the heat to low. Smash everything roughly with a bean smasher or the back of a spoon until you have a chunky purée. Adjust salt to taste.

4. Serve hot with warm flour tortillas. I like to crumble chicharrones and chopped fresh cilantro on top, and if I'm feeling fancy, maybe some crumbled queso fresco.

S

CURED NOPAL AND WILD PURSLANE SALAD

Nopales, or cacti, have been an important food source for Indigenous communities in the desert borderlands for thousands of years. As a child, I mainly ate cactus (and purslane) in gloopy salsas or sautéed with eggs. (Try it, it's delicious!) Then, in 2015, I began working at a restaurant with another grown-up border kid, Chef Javier Plascencia. He had me cure the strips of cleaned cactus pads by covering them with a ton of salt. That technique draws out all of the liquid from the cactus—and simultaneously seasons it. You then rinse the cured cactus under running cold water until the water runs clear. You are left with bright green cactus with a delicious crunch, a perfectly seasoned, chlorophyll-filled nugget. If you live in a town with a Mexi-mart or bodega, run in and see if they have cleaned cactus. If you're the type to avoid leafy green salads at all costs (like me), this salad will give you all the texture, brightness, and salinity that your body wants and needs, and your grandma will be happy that you're eating your greens.

Serves 4

1 cactus pad, cleaned
Diamond Crystal kosher salt
Zest and juice of 2 limes (about ¼ cup)
Zest and juice of 2 lemons (about ½ cup)
1 teaspoon Dijon mustard
¼ cup olive oil
1 pound purslane (see Note)
2 Persian cucumbers, thinly sliced on the bias
4 green onions, thinly sliced on the bias
1 serrano pepper, stemmed, seeded, and minced
4 medium tomatillos, husked, rinsed, and thinly sliced into rounds
½ cup Japanese peanuts, crushed
Coarse sea salt

1. Cut the cactus pad into ¼-inch-wide strips and place in a medium bowl. Sprinkle with a generous amount of salt, massage the salt into the cactus, and set the bowl aside to allow the strips to cure for 30 minutes.

2. Place the cured cactus in a colander and rinse under cold running water, tossing the strips until the liquid is no longer thick or slimy, testing the viscosity in between your thumb and index finger. Taste a strip to check its salt level. If it's still extremely salty, continue to rinse for another 2 to 3 minutes. Set aside.

3. Make the vinaigrette: In a blender, combine the lime and lemon juice, mustard, and a pinch of salt. Begin blending on high. Remove the center lid cap and, with the blender still running on high, drizzle in the olive oil.

4. In a large bowl, toss together the purslane, cucumbers, green onions, serrano, tomatillo slices, and the lime and lemon zest. Add a few tablespoons of the vinaigrette and toss. Transfer everything to a serving platter or portion onto individual plates. Top with the cured cactus, crushed peanuts, and a pinch of coarse sea salt. Serve with remaining vinaigrette on the side.

Note: Purslane can be found in many Latin markets and farmers' markets across the States. It grows wild and in many different climates.

RED PIPIÁN WITH ROASTED SQUASH

Pipian is a rich, nutty, puréed pumpkin seed–based sauce. When you bring pipian up in conversation, some people will insist that it has to be green. While green pipian is perhaps more common, red pipian does exist—and it's the millionth example of people cooking what they have available to them (and making it taste great). Hot and arid regions tend to yield more recipes that use cured meat and dried peppers, including this one. The beauty of the borderlands is that it's the land of food convergence.

Dry ancho chiles (the dried form of the poblano pepper) provide heat and color, and differentiate this dish from green pipian, which uses fresh poblano peppers. The spices are the same ones that you will find in countless mole and curry recipes. This is a warm and soulful sauce, and when paired with the natural sweetness and earthy flavor of kabocha squash, it makes a great vegetarian meal (and filling for tacos).

Serves 4

---

1 large kabocha squash, cut into 8 wedges
Diamond Crystal kosher salt
3 tablespoons grapeseed oil, plus more as needed
2 medium ancho chiles, stemmed and seeded
½ cup raw pumpkin seeds
3 tablespoons sesame seeds
1 corn tortilla (store-bought is fine), torn into small pieces
1 small onion, chopped
3 garlic cloves, minced
½ teaspoon freshly ground black pepper
½ teaspoon ground allspice
½ teaspoon ground cinnamon
⅛ teaspoon ground cloves
¼ teaspoon dried Mexican oregano
½ teaspoon sugar
1 Roma tomato, diced small
2 cups vegetable stock

For Serving
White Rice with Corn (page 33)
Corn Tortillas (page 23)

1. Preheat the oven to 450°F. Line a baking sheet with parchment paper.

2. Lightly oil the kabocha wedges and season with salt. Spread them out on the prepared baking sheet. Roast the squash for 8 minutes, flip, and roast for an additional 10 minutes, until they are tender. Remove the squash from the oven and set aside.

3. Now, you're going to toast a series of ingredients and transfer them to a blender. At the end, you'll blend it all together to create the pipian.

4. In a large pan, dry-toast the ancho chiles over medium heat for 1 to 2 minutes on each side. Set the toasted chiles in a medium bowl and cover with 2 cups of hot water. Steep the chiles until softened, about 5 minutes. Drain the chiles and reserve the water. Transfer the softened chiles to a blender.

5. In the same pan, toast the pumpkin seeds over medium-low heat, stirring, until the seeds start browning. Transfer most of the seeds to the blender, reserving a tablespoon or two for garnish.

6. Now toast the sesame seeds over medium-low heat, stirring, until they start browning. Transfer them to the blender.

7. Toast the tortilla pieces over medium-low heat until they are dried and charred. Transfer to the blender.

8. Still in the same pan, this time over medium heat, add 1 tablespoon of grapeseed oil. Once the oil is hot, add the chopped onion and garlic. Sauté until the onions are translucent and begin to brown, about 8 to 10 minutes. Transfer to the blender.

9. Finally, add the black pepper, allspice, cinnamon, cloves, oregano, sugar, and tomatoes to the blender. Blend everything on high until smooth, scraping down the sides of the blender as needed. Add the reserved soaking water from the chiles a splash at a time until you have a thick sauce.

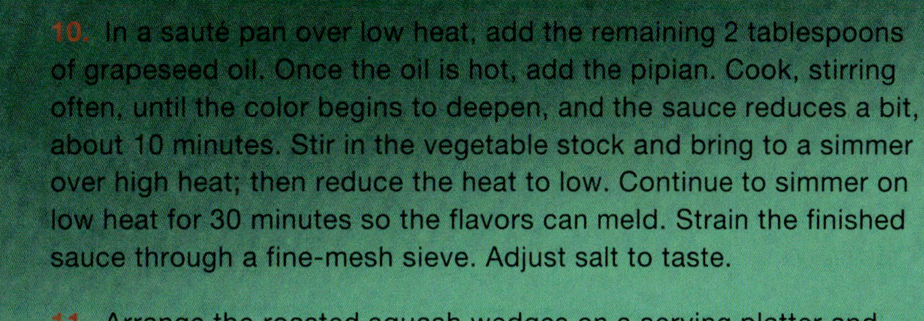

10. In a sauté pan over low heat, add the remaining 2 tablespoons of grapeseed oil. Once the oil is hot, add the pipian. Cook, stirring often, until the color begins to deepen, and the sauce reduces a bit, about 10 minutes. Stir in the vegetable stock and bring to a simmer over high heat; then reduce the heat to low. Continue to simmer on low heat for 30 minutes so the flavors can meld. Strain the finished sauce through a fine-mesh sieve. Adjust salt to taste.

11. Arrange the roasted squash wedges on a serving platter and spoon the pipian sauce over the squash. Garnish with toasted pumpkin seeds. Serve with White Rice with Corn and corn tortillas.

TESGÜINO OR TEJUINO

(FERMENTED CORN BEER)

The Tarahumara (Rarámuri) tribe, with a current population of around 120,000, have been able to maintain much of their way of life and customs while living in the Sierra Madre Occidental mountain range in Chihuahua.

Tesgüino (or *tejuino*) has origins in this community, who have been brewing the fermented corn beer for thousands of years. It is used as a ceremonial beverage, a gift to the gods, and even for bartering. The flavor has complex sweetness thanks to piloncillo, as well as earthiness from corn, and the characteristic tang from the process of fermentation.

I love to serve tesgüino with a scoop of lime sorbet—I find it helps brighten the flavor. It's not such a stretch—after all, lime is used across savory and sweet food throughout the Mexican diaspora. Making the drink does require a bit of patience—traditionally, the production lasts for almost one hundred days—but we'll boil it down to three days to make a batch for ourselves, using masa harina as a shortcut. Once you make it and drink tesgüino on a hot summer day with a giant scoop of lime sorbet, you will want more, with or without a ceremony.

Serves 4

2 (8-ounce) cones piloncillo
2 cups masa harina
Juice of 3 Key limes (about 2 tablespoons)
Sea salt
Ice

For Serving
Lime Sorbet (recipe follows) or lime wedges
Tajín to taste (optional)
Chamoy to taste (optional)

1. Place the piloncillo cones between two kitchen towels. Using a meat mallet or rolling pin, smash the cones until they're broken into roughly ½-inch pieces.

2. In a large pot, combine the piloncillo and 2 cups of water. Bring to a simmer over high heat; then reduce the heat to low and stir until the piloncillo is fully dissolved. Remove the pot from the heat and set aside.

3. In a large bowl, combine the masa harina and 6 cups of water. Whisk until fully incorporated. Add the masa to the pot with the piloncillo water, a few small handfuls at a time to prevent clumping, whisking to thoroughly incorporate.

4. Return the pot to the stove over medium heat and cook for 10 minutes, or until the mixture begins to thicken. Then remove the pot from the heat and allow it to cool completely. The mixture should have a consistency similar to that of horchata, with a viscosity somewhere between milk and cream. Add tablespoons of water as needed to reach the correct texture.

5. Once cool, pour the corn base into a sterilized 4-quart glass container and whisk in the lime juice. Cover the container with cheesecloth or a thin towel and secure it with twine. Place the container in a cool, shaded area of your kitchen for 72 hours to ferment.

Recipe continues

6. If the weather is warm, I like to check on it daily; anything over 80°F can accelerate fermentation or create a breeding ground for unwanted bacteria. Your nose is your best friend here. When the base has reached fermentation, you will see small bubbles all over the glass of the container, and the mixture should have a foamy top. You should not see any mold; if you see mold, discard the base and start over. If you notice bubbles on the first or second day, you may have tesgüino ready ahead of 72 hours—just taste it to ensure it's got that fermented beverage tang.

7. Once your tesgüino reaches fermentation, transfer it to the refrigerator. To serve, pour into ice-filled glasses with a lime wedge or a scoop of lime sorbet. If you'd like, squeeze lime around the rim of the glass and dip the rim in Tajín or chamoy; it's lovely.

NIEVE DE GARRAFA

(LIME SORBET)

Serves 4

2 cups sugar
1 envelope unflavored gelatin (2½ teaspoons)
2 cups freshly squeezed lime juice (from about 16 limes)
Pinch of salt

In a small pot, combine the sugar and 2 cups of water. Set the pot over medium heat and stir the sugar until completely dissolved—this is a simple syrup. Remove from heat and set aside.

In a medium bowl, add 2 cups of water and sprinkle the gelatin over it. Let the gelatin bloom until absorbed and the mixture is thickened.

Add the bloomed gelatin-water mixture to the pot of still-warm simple syrup, stirring to dissolve it. Allow this mixture to cool to room temperature. (If not churning immediately, you can refrigerate it until ready to churn.) Once cooled to room temperature, stir in the lime juice and a pinch of salt.

You can either churn the mixture in an ice cream machine or in stand mixer with the ice cream maker attachments, or you can churn the old-school way to make nieve de garrafa:

For nieve de garrafa, fill a large metal bowl with crushed ice. Sprinkle a generous amount of rock salt all over the surface of the ice. Then nestle a slightly smaller metal bowl on top of the ice in the larger bowl, creating an ice cradle for it.

Pour your sorbet base in the smaller bowl and begin spinning it inside the larger bowl, as my abue would say, "*con ganas!*" (with gumption!). Continue spinning the bowl until you see small ice crystals forming along the inside wall of the bowl. With a wooden spoon, begin scraping the crystals off the wall toward the middle of the bowl and keep spinning. Once you have a solid bowl of slushy ice, transfer to an airtight container with a lid and place in the freezer to finish setting.

CALDO DE OSO

(FISH STEW)

If you know any Spanish, you may know already that "oso" translates to bear, but rest assured this soup contains no bear! What it does contain is the story of how it came to be one of the most popular stews to make and eat in Chihuahua . . . not originally by the people's choice.

The story starts during the building of one of the state prisons in La Boquilla, Chihuahua, a process that took place over five years. The construction crews were given food, dropped into the commissary kitchen, which reportedly included a lot of catfish from the lake that formed from the building of the dam, which was often made into a soup.

By the third year of the project, the workers, sick of the soup, began calling it "caldo de oso," short for "*sopa odiosa*," or "*el caldo odioso*"—the hated soup. We Mexicans also deploy the word "oso" when someone is being obnoxious or a pest.

Since you don't have to eat this stew for five years straight; you can feel free to fall in love with it. The base has a slightly pomodoro-esque flavor, but uses butter instead of olive oil. (Remember, we're still in dairy country.) The sweet onion and garlic dancing with the butter and tomatoes is pure comfort food.

The caldo comes together rather quickly, and depending on how you like the consistency, you can add or subtract liquid. I use rockfish in my stew, but feel free to use shrimp instead. To this day, this soup is a hangover cure for many, or as we say, "*vuelve a la vida*"—return to life.

Serves 4 to 6

3 tablespoons salted butter
½ small white onion, diced small
2 garlic cloves, smashed
2 bay leaves
4 Roma tomatoes, diced
Diamond Crystal kosher salt
Freshly ground black pepper
1½ pounds whole rockfish, catfish, or fish of your choice (see Note), or shrimp
2 medium carrots, peeled and cut into chunks
2 medium yellow waxy potatoes (such as Yukon Gold), peeled and cubed
½ tablespoon dried thyme
½ tablespoon dried Mexican oregano
2 canned chipotle peppers in adobo sauce
½ cup chopped cilantro

For Serving
Limes, cut into cheeks
Tostadas raspadas (store-bought is fine)

1. Set a large pot over medium heat and melt the butter. Add the onion, garlic and bay leaves and sauté until translucent, about 4 minutes.

2. Add the diced tomatoes to the pot, season with salt and black pepper to taste, and reduce the heat to low to sweat out the juices and cook down the ingredients, about 5 minutes.

3. Once you have a mixture with tomato paste-like consistency, add in 8 cups of water, the fish head(s) and bones, carrots, potatoes, thyme, oregano, chipotles in adobo, and cilantro. Cook the ingredients together for 15 minutes, stirring occasionally and gently, to keep the broth clear. Adjust the seasoning to taste.

4. Cut the fish fillets into large bite-sized pieces. Carefully lower the fish pieces into the soup and simmer for 10 minutes, stirring occasionally, but taking care not to break the fish up too much. Adjust seasoning to taste and serve the soup with limes and tostadas.

Note: Have your fishmonger fillet the fish for you, and save the head and bones for the stock.

ISKIATE

(CHIA SEED AGUA FRESCA/ENERGY DRINK)

Put down that mystery-chemical-laden energy drink and instead make iskiate (or chia fresca), a natural energy drink powered by chia seeds and flavored with lime and honey (or piloncillo). Chia seed drinks have found their way into the spotlight of the health industry a few times, but like most trends, they tend to fade from the limelight quickly.

So, let's take a moment to understand where iskiate got started, or at least where its history is thousands of years old.

Chia seeds, native to Mesoamerica, have been cultivated and used as food since 3500 BC in Uto-Aztecan Indigenous groups. These tiny magic seeds boast incredible amounts of omega-3 fatty acids, iron, calcium, and antioxidants. The fiber in chia seeds helps slow the release of energy into the body. When the seeds come into contact with liquid in the stomach, they form a gel-like coating that slows the digestion of carbohydrates (and the conversion of those carbs into sugar). The Tarahumara, an Indigenous people of Chihuahua, drink iskiate as an endurance fuel to support their long-distance running. They refer to themselves as the Rarámuri—meaning "runners on foot" or "those who run fast."

Makes 4 cups

¼ cup chia seeds
Juice of 5 Persian limes (about ½ cup), plus more to taste
Honey or Piloncillo Syrup (page 232) to taste
Ice, for serving
Orange, lemon, or lime zest strips, for garnish

In a medium pitcher, stir together 4 cups of water, the chia seeds, lime juice, and your sweetener of choice. Allow the chia seeds to hydrate for 10 minutes, forming a gelatinous texture, and then stir again. Taste and adjust the amount of lime juice or sweetener as needed. Serve over ice.

SOTOL Y TUNA

(PRICKLY PEAR COCKTAIL)

Say hello to your new welcome drink for all your family and friend gatherings: This well-rounded, earthy, tart, floral cocktail, like many others, comes with an interesting story.

Along the US–Mexico border, mixologists and consumers are still being introduced to spirits that the Indigenous Anasazi (Ancestral Puebloans) and Tarahumara peoples have been producing for the last eight hundred-plus years. The sotol plant is agave's lesser-known cousin, a much smaller plant whose nectar is definitely worth the squeeze. The production of sotol is also much more environmentally sustainable than that of agave spirits. Harvesting the piña (the heart of the plant), does not end the sotol plant's life—it will regrow, unlike agave, which cannot grow back after harvesting.

This cocktail celebrates sotol, combining it with prickly pear and floral elderflower, which sometimes reminds me of desert flowers. When you try it, you will immediately notice its earthy flavor and floral aromas. Of course, if you don't have sotol, you can make this drink with the agave spirit of your choice instead.

Makes 4 cocktails

- 6 prickly cactus pears/tunas, peeled and quartered
- 1 tablespoon plus 1 teaspoon confectioners' sugar
- 6 ounces sotol spirit (or agave spirit of choice)
- 4 ounces St-Germain Elderflower Liqueur
- Juice of 2 limes (¼ cup)
- 1 cup ice
- Crushed ice, for serving
- Lime wedges, for garnish

1. In a blender, combine the prickly pears and sugar. Blend on high until completely puréed; then strain the liquid through a fine-mesh sieve into a small bowl. Discard the leftover pulp.

2. Measure out ½ cup of prickly pear juice and add it to a cocktail shaker. Add in the sotol, elderflower liqueur, lime juice, and a few ice cubes. Cover and shake for 3 to 4 minutes, or until the ice cubes make almost no noise. Strain the drink into 4 rocks glasses filled with crushed ice. Garnish with lime wedges.

AGUA DE PINOLE

(TOASTED CORN AND CINNAMON AGUA FRESCA)

Pinole—a ground toasted corn flour mixed with piloncillo (and sometimes cinnamon)—is used in a lot of food items in the North, including in Coricos (page 237), atoles (see sidebar), and more. I'm aware that making a drink with corn flour mix might seem odd—it's even odd for me, and I know the final product. But you're just going to have to trust me.

I'd be remiss not to mention that for thousands of years, pinole has been a food source for Chihuahua's Indigenous Tarahumara people, who use this agua fresca as a fuel source for their long-distance running (much like Iskiate, page 226).

But even if you're not getting ready for a hundred-mile run, give this drink a shot. I find the nutty, toasted pinole a bit addictive. It's best served up over giant ice cubes and enjoyed while staring out at nature . . . or out your front door at your neighbor's abandoned car-repair projects. We consume agua de pinole year round, but in the colder months, I like to change it up by adding other warming spices.

Makes 5 cups

1 cup Pinole (recipe follows)
4 cups coconut milk or whole cow's milk
½ cup grated or ground piloncillo
Ice, for serving

1. In a blender, combine 1 cup of water, the pinole, coconut milk, and piloncillo. Blend the ingredients on high for 2 to 3 minutes, until smooth.

2. Strain the mixture through a fine-mesh sieve into a pitcher. Stir in 2 more cups of water. Adjust sweetness to taste as needed. Serve over ice.

PINOLE

(SWEETENED TOASTED CORN FLOUR)

Makes 2 cups

2 cups masa harina
¼ cup plus 3 tablespoons grated or ground piloncillo
1½ teaspoons ground cinnamon

Set a large sauté pan over medium heat. Add the masa harina to the dry pan and toast, stirring the flour continuously to prevent burning. After about 10 minutes, you will start to smell its nutty aroma, and it will turn a deep tan, a couple of shades darker than light brown sugar. Remove the pan from the heat and transfer the toasted masa harina to a large bowl to cool completely.

Once the flour is completely cooled, add the piloncillo and cinnamon to the bowl and stir to thoroughly incorporate. Store the pinole it in an airtight container in the pantry for up to 1 month, or for up to 4 months in the refrigerator.

WHAT TO DO WITH PINOLE

- In Mexico, we have thousands of *dichos* (sayings), and there are more than a dozen about pinole and life. My favorite is "*No se puede chiflar y comer pinole al mismo tiempo*"—"You can't eat pinole and whistle at the same time"—meaning that you can only do one thing well at a time.

- But unlike people, pinole can do lots of things well! You can add a spoonful or two into your morning smoothie to give it body, a sweet, toasty flavor, and a dose of fiber and nutrients. For a refreshing, nutty cold drink, you can make an agua fresca. You can use it as a flour for baking, such as in Coricos (page 237). Or, go for an atole de pinole, a thick, sweet beverage that's enjoyed hot, perfect to sip on a cold day.

- To make an atole de pinole, in a small bowl, combine ¼ cup pinole, 1 tablespoon cornstarch, and 1½ cups cold milk. Whisk until fully combined. Add 3 cups of milk to a medium pot set over low heat. While whisking the milk continuously, stream in the pinole mixture. Add ground piloncillo to taste (or Piloncillo Syrup, page 232), and continue stirring constantly until the mixture starts to thicken. Once it thickens, remove from heat. If you want a thinner consistency, add more milk, ¼ cup at a time.

BUÑUELOS

When making piped churros from scratch seems like too daunting a task, take a bite of these cinnamon sugar–dusted frisbees—I promise you'll barely know the difference. Okay, okay, buñuelos are really more of a cousin to the piped churro; the two are not interchangeable. But these are still full ASMR-cronch-mode. And in the northern borderlands, they definitely command respect.

The tomatillo husks help alter the pH of the water, giving the perfect crunch to the buñuelos. What makes tortillas soft, help with the snap of these.

Instead of cinnamon sugar, you can also make Piloncillo Syrup (page 232) and dunk them into that; the result reminds me of the deep-fried Indian sweet *jalebi.*

Makes 10 buñuelos

---

1 cup Tomatillo Husk Water (page 25), or tap water
4 cups all-purpose flour, sifted, plus more for rolling
2 tablespoons granulated sugar
1 teaspoon Diamond Crystal kosher salt (or ½ teaspoon Morton salt)
2 large eggs, lightly beaten
2 tablespoons salted butter or lard, melted
Vegetable oil, for greasing and frying

Topping and Glaze
¾ cup sugar
2 tablespoons ground cinnamon
Pinch Diamond Crystal kosher salt
Piloncillo Syrup (recipe follows)

MAKE AND SHAPE THE DOUGH:

1. In a small pot over low heat, heat the Tomatillo Husk Water until it reaches body temperature. Set aside.

2. In the bowl of a stand mixer fitted with the hook attachment, add the flour, 2 tablespoons of sugar, and 1 teaspoon salt. Mix on low for 1 minute to incorporate.

3. With the mixer still running on low, add in the eggs and the melted butter and mix until incorporated. Then slowly stream in the warmed tomatillo husk water. Increase the mixer speed to medium and knead the dough for 10 minutes. The dough should be supple and smooth and be pulling away from the walls of the bowl.

4. Transfer the dough to an oil-coated bowl and cover it with a clean, damp kitchen towel. Allow the dough to proof at room temperature for one hour, then do the "poke test"—press your thumb into the dough. If the dough springs back quickly, it needs to proof longer. If it springs back slowly, your dough is ready!

5. Flip the dough onto a lightly floured surface and divide it into 10 even portions. Roll each portion into a ball. Place the balls under the damp towel while you continue to roll the other portions to prevent the dough from drying out.

6. Dust your surface with more flour. With a rolling pin, begin rolling out the circles of dough as you would with a flour tortilla, in diameter and thickness, dusting the dough and the surface with flour as needed. Keep the rolled dough under the damp cloth until you are ready to fry.

7. Prepare the cinnamon sugar. In a large, shallow baking dish or bowl, toss together the granulated sugar and cinnamon, plus a generous pinch of salt. Set aside near the stovetop. (If glazing with piloncillo syrup, skip this step and see recipe to follow.)

Recipe continues

FRY THE BUÑUELOS:

8. Fill a large frying pan with 2 inches of oil and set over medium heat until the oil reads 350°F on a thermometer. Line a baking sheet with paper towels and set a wire rack on top.

9. Carefully slide one round of dough into the hot oil. Fry until golden brown, 3 to 5 minutes, then use tongs to carefully flip the dough. Fry on the other side until equally golden brown, about another 3 minutes.

10. Use tongs to lift the buñuelo out the oil and transfer it to the wire rack to drain excess oil. Repeat with the remaining dough rounds, making sure your frying oil has returned to 350°F before you fry each subsequent round of dough.

11. After all the buñuelos have drained and are cool to the touch, transfer them to the baking dish with the cinnamon sugar. Turn to coat evenly on both sides. Alternatively, glaze the buñuelos with Piloncillo Syrup.

PILONCILLO SYRUP

Makes 3 cups

- 2 (3-inch) sticks Mexican canela/ Ceylon cinnamon
- 4 (8-ounce) cones piloncillo
- 1 whole clove
- 2 whole allspice berries
- 1 star anise
- Peels of 2 oranges
- Diamond Crystal kosher salt

In a small pot set over medium heat, add 2 cups of water and bring to a boil. Add the cinnamon, piloncillo, clove, allspice, star anise, orange peels, and a pinch of salt. Allow the mixture to boil for 20 minutes, stirring occasionally to ensure the piloncillo is completely melted and dissolved.

Turn off the heat, cover the pot with a lid, and allow the syrup to cool completely. Strain the syrup through a fine-mesh sieve, discarding the spices and orange peels. Store the syrup in in the refrigerator in a glass jar with a tight-fitting lid, or in a clean bottle with a bar spout for ease of use. Syrup will keep, refrigerated, it will keep for months but hopefully you use it regularly!

SWEET PINEAPPLE EMPANADAS

Almost every cuisine boasts some kind of pastry pocket with a sweet or savory filling, the pinched edge of the dough locking in the hot, molten interior. Towns on both sides of the border have *panaderías* making bread in the old-school and new-world ways; some have been open continuously for the past hundred years. This sweet empanada with a cinnamon-scented pineapple filling is a nod to my childhood trips to the bakery. I would go with my dad, and I could smell the empanadas a mile away.

Since I usually make too much dough (I freeze it in flat layers), I sometimes use leftover dough from this recipe to make savory empanadas stuffed with Picadillo (page 67). If you want to try other fillings, I also love cajeta with crushed pecans, apple pie filling, sweet potato pie filling, or even chocolate with marshmallow!

Makes 12 small empanadas or 6 large ones

Pineapple Filling

2 cups canned crushed pineapple, drained
1 (8-ounce) cone piloncillo, cut into small pieces
1 tablespoon ground cinnamon
Pinch of salt
1 teaspoon five-spice powder (optional)
1 tablespoon cornstarch
½ cup chopped pecans (optional)

Empanadas

3 cups bread flour, sifted, plus more for rolling
1 cup (2 sticks) salted butter, chilled cubed
3 tablespoons granulated sugar
½ teaspoon Diamond Crystal kosher salt
1¼ cups heavy cream
1 large egg, beaten
1 tablespoon vanilla extract
Raw sugar, for topping

MAKE THE FILLING:

1. In a small pot, combine the drained crushed pineapple, the piloncillo, cinnamon, and a pinch of salt. Bring to a simmer over medium-low heat, stirring often to prevent burning, until the piloncillo is completely dissolved, 8 to 10 minutes. Stir in the five-spice powder (if using).

2. While the pineapple mixture is cooking, in a small bowl, combine the cornstarch and ¾ cup cold water. Whisk together to create a slurry; then pour the slurry into the pot with the pineapple.

3. Return the pineapple mixture to a simmer until it thickens and becomes glossy, 3 to 4 minutes. Remove the pan from the heat, set aside, and fold in the pecans (if using). Allow to cool completely before using.

MAKE THE DOUGH:

4. Add the sifted flour to the bowl of a stand mixer fitted with the paddle attachment. While running the mixer on low speed, slowly add in the butter, followed by the sugar and salt. Mix until you have small, pea-sized crumbles, scraping down the sides of the bowl as necessary.

5. With the mixer still on low, stream in 1 cup of the heavy cream, the beaten egg, and the vanilla. Increase the mixer speed to medium and mix for 6 to 8 minutes. The dough should be soft to the touch and should not stick to the bowl. it. If the dough is too dry, add a splash of milk. If it's too sticky, add in a little more flour.

6. When the dough is ready, remove it from the mixer and portion it into two disks. Wrap each disk individually in plastic wrap and chill for 30 minutes.

Recipe continues

MAKE THE EMPANADAS:

7. Preheat the oven to 375°F. Line 2 baking sheets with parchment paper and set aside.

8. Portion the chilled dough from one of the disks into 12 golf ball–sized pieces. Roll into balls and cover them with a towel to prevent drying out. Using a rolling pin or your tortilla press, flatten each ball of dough to into a circle, ¼ inch thick and 4 inches in diameter.

9. Fill a dough round with 2 tablespoons of the pineapple filling. Fold one side over the filling to create a semicircle shape and press gently around the filling to squeeze out any air pockets. Then press down the edges with your fingertips or the palm of your hand to seal the edges. Transfer the filled empanada to the prepared baking sheet. Repeat to make 12 small empanadas (or 6 large ones), spaced an inch apart on the baking sheet.

10. Use the tines of a fork to crimp the dough around the sealed edge of each empanada. Brush the tops with the remaining ¼ cup heavy cream, and then sprinkle on the raw sugar.

11. Bake the empanadas until golden brown, 20 to 22 minutes. For a darker golden-brown crust, turn the broiler on high and broil for less than one minute. Transfer the empanadas onto cooling racks. Let cool for a few minutes; then, once cool enough to handle, enjoy warm or at room temperature.

CORICOS

(TOASTED CORN FLOUR COOKIES)

When I was offered coricos as a child, I honestly thought I was being punished—I would whine, "¡¿*Una galleta*?!" ("*That's* a cookie?!") I couldn't see how this plain, no-frills, golden-brown ring fit in the same category as my favorite treat. To me, a cookie meant vanilla shortbread sandwiches with marshmallow, shredded coconut, and a jam filling (you may know them as the popular Sponch cookies).

A corico is on the humbler end of the cookie spectrum, a regional Northern biscuit made with toasted corn flour (called pinole) and unrefined piloncillo sugar. I've had people in Mexico City look at me like I am crazy when I ask for them at panaderías. They have no idea what I'm talking about.

I may have scoffed at them as a kid, but nowadays, I crave coricos' mild, sweet, toasted corn flavor, especially when I'm missing my abuela Paula. She taught me how to properly enjoy coricos: They're best when dunked in a piping-hot cup of Café de Olla (page 202).

Makes 12 cookies

¾ cup vegetable shortening
¼ cup ground or grated piloncillo (or dark brown sugar)
½ large egg, beaten
1½ teaspoons vanilla extract
1 teaspoon baking powder
¼ teaspoon Diamond Crystal kosher salt (or a pinch of Morton salt)
1¼ cups masa harina or pinole (page 229)
2 tablespoons flour, sifted, plus more for dusting

1. Preheat the oven to 350°F.

2. Into the bowl of a stand mixer with the paddle attachment add the shortening and mix it on medium speed until light and fluffy; it will have a bit more volume but not much.

3. Into a medium saucepan, heat 1 cup of water and the piloncillo on low until the piloncillo dissolves. With the mixer running on low speed, stream the piloncillo syrup into the shortening until well incorporated.

4. Continue running the mixer while you add the egg, scraping down the sides of the bowl between each addition.

5. Add the vanilla to the batter and scrape the bowl once more.

6. In another medium bowl, combine the baking powder, salt, pinole, and flour and whisk the ingredients to combine.

7. Drop the mixer to low speed. Add the dry ingredients and mix until a dough forms, scraping the bowl sides as needed. The dough will have a shortbread texture and come off the sides but still be slightly tacky to the touch.

8. Divide the dough on a lightly floured counter into 12 equal portions, rolling each portion one by one into a ½-inch-thick by 6-inch rope.

9. Once you have rolled your strands, loop each rope into a circle, pressing lightly down to join the ends. Place each circle of dough spaced 2 inches apart on a baking sheet lined with parchment paper.

10. Bake the cookies until they are set on the outside and firm to the touch, about 12 minutes.

COAHUILA, NUEVO LEÓN, AND TAMAULIPAS

THE BIRTHPLACE OF TEX-MEX

This region of the borderlands forms a dynamic culinary crossroads where Mexican and American traditions mix, giving rise to distinctive regional flavors and hybrid cuisines that reflect centuries of cultural exchange, migration, ranching, and adaptation to arid landscapes. These borderlands are the birthplace of Tex-Mex cuisine as we know it today, blending Indigenous, Spanish colonial, and Anglo-American foodways. The culinary identity of the Coahuila–Nuevo León–Tamaulipas–Texas borderland is bold, smoky, beef-driven, and fusion-rich. It blends northern Mexican tradition, ranching life, and Texan influence, producing one of the most distinct and influential food cultures in North America.

I could not give you recipes from this area without also mentioning two hugely influential men from the region. The first is Ignacio "Nacho" Anaya, a maître d' whose hospitality and ingenuity led to the invention of Nachos (page 249). The second, of course, is El Centauro del Norte—the Centaur of the North—Francisco "Pancho" Villa, the father of the Mexican Revolution. Learning about Pancho Villa's sweet tooth through the process of writing this book made the history geek in me so happy.

In this chapter, we'll see dishes that originated in Mexico, crossed the border, and eventually transformed into iconic, larger-than-a-sombrero creations. The northeastern regions covered in this section continue to show the borderlands as a melting pot for culinary innovation, where traditional recipes are constantly adapted and reimagined.

As you delve into the vibrant food culture of the northeastern borderlands, you'll discover how the culinary landscape fosters a sense of community and identity that bridges the two nations through the universal language of food.

Elote En
Vaso $2
Refrescos: COCA & ESQUIR
Coca-Cola
Squirt

Ranch in Ures Sonora

PAN DE PULQUE

The hearts of *maguey* (agave) plants are filled with a sap called *aguamiel* ("honey water"). Aguamiel is carefully harvested from the plant by *tlachiqueros* ("maguey scrapers") and then fermented into a viscous drink called *pulque*, which was enjoyed by the Aztecs. Men and women have dedicated their lives to preserving this tradition dating back to 200 BC.

When you extract aguamiel from maguey, it tastes a bit like green tea sweetened with honey, but the flavor and texture of the aguamiel changes regionally from the highlands to the lowlands. Once it's fermented into pulque, it develops an unusual sour, fizzy flavor profile that many say is an acquired taste . . . and a definite fuzzy blanket for the senses.

So where does the "pan" come in? Well, the fermented pulque provides an incredibly active breeding ground for yeast, especially helpful before commercial yeast was available. Breads made with pulque are commonly found during *Día de Muertos* celebrations. The smell of the freshly baked bread is naturally sweet, evoking brown sugar and warm spices, with a soft texture similar to an enriched dough. The sweet-yet-savory bread is a great vehicle for slathering on a layer of Frijoles Rancheros (page 216) topped with shredded cheese and then broiled. It's also great toasted and spread with salted butter and a sprinkling of cinnamon sugar.

Makes 2 loaves or 12 rolls

- 5 large eggs, whites and yolks separated, plus 1 egg, beaten
- 1 cup natural pulque (see Note)
- 1 cup granulated sugar
- 4½ cups all-purpose flour, sifted, plus more for dusting
- 1 tablespoon dry instant yeast
- 1 cup (2 sticks) salted butter, softened, plus more for greasing
- 2 tablespoons sesame seeds

1. In the bowl of a stand mixer fitted with the whisk attachment, add the egg whites of 5 eggs and pulque. Whisk for 6 minutes at medium speed, until frothy.

2. Switch to the dough hook attachment. With the mixer running on medium speed, add in the egg yolks, sugar, flour, instant yeast, and softened butter. Knead for 10 minutes, until you have an elastic dough.

3. Transfer the dough to a greased bowl and cover it with a clean, damp kitchen towel. Place the bowl in a warm spot in your kitchen and let rest until the dough doubles in size, 1 to 3 hours, depending on the temperature in your kitchen.

4. Turn the dough out onto a floured work surface. Portion the dough into 2 large, round loaves or 12 small rolls. Place the loaves or rolls on a baking sheet, spaced out evenly. Cover the dough with the damp towel and allow it to rest for 20 minutes.

5. While the dough rests, preheat the oven to 430°F.

6. Brush the loaves or rolls with the beaten egg and sprinkle with sesame seeds. Bake the loaves for 30 minutes (or 20 minutes for rolls). The bread should be golden brown on the top and bottom, and should sound hollow when you tap on it. If the bread is not yet ready, rotate the baking sheet and add time in 10-minute increments, checking color and bottom crust after each interval. Allow the bread to cool completely before enjoying.

Note: If you can't find pulque, you can substitute natural kombucha, or a cup of lager and the juice of a lime.

ESQUITES/ELOTE EN VASO

(STREET CORN IN A CUP)

It's not a mystery to me why this simple dish of corn kernels in a cup, dressed with mayo, crema, cheese, chile, and lime, has become ubiquitous all over the US. Having tried many versions, I would say that it's often imitated, but seldom duplicated.

The secret to many elote stands on the Mexican side of the border is that the corn isn't necessarily grilled—and the corn used is usually starchier white corn, almost never sweet yellow sweet corn (see Note). The corn cobs are stewed whole in their husks in a broth seasoned with herbs. Then they're shucked and placed back in the same broth. The result is a cleaner, more savory corn flavor. This recipe uses a similar technique, simplified for the home kitchen.

The cooked corn kernels are served in a cup with a little bit of the corn broth and topped with the sauces and seasonings. In Coahuila, tortilla chips are often topped with esquites, along with their classic garnishes and a spicy salsa. The combo is affectionately known as "*chorreado de Coahuila*" (the mess of Coahuila). Feel free to experiment with flavors—you can even add some masala curry powder to the broth.

Serves 4

4 ears white corn
3 tablespoons unsalted butter
½ white onion, diced small
3 garlic cloves, minced
2 epazote leaves
Diamond Crystal kosher salt

Optional Garnishes

½ cup Mexican crema or sour cream
½ cup mayonnaise
½ cup crumbled Cotija cheese
4 limes, halved
Salsa Huichol hot sauce or chile powder

1. Remove the corn kernels from the cobs and place them into a medium bowl. Reserve the cobs and set them aside.

2. In a large saucepan set over medium heat, add the butter, onion and garlic and sauté until the onions become translucent, about 3 minutes. Add the corn kernels and cobs to the pan and cook them, stirring occasionally, for 5 minutes.

3. Add 5 cups of water to the pot, along with the epazote and salt to taste. Bring to a simmer and let cook for 20 minutes; then remove and discard the cobs.

4. Using a slotted spoon, transfer the simmered corn to bowls or cups. Spoon a bit of the corn broth on top. Top with the crema, mayonnaise, crumbled Cotija, a squeeze of lime juice, and a sprinkle of chile powder or hot sauce . . . and maybe one more squeeze of lime juice. Must be served hot!

Note: In the US, sweet corn is easier to find in the markets; feel free to use that if you can't find starchier Mexican corn.

MONTERREY-STYLE GUACAMOLE

When you ask anyone about mole, ten out of ten people will start talking about black mole or mole poblano. Few people realize they're forgetting an even more popular mole: avocado mole. Yep, guaca*mole* is technically a mole made from avocados—the Aztecs ate it with ground chiles and tomatoes and considered it a gift from the gods.

Nuevo León, whose capital is Monterrey, is the home of one of the three wild varietals of avocado; you can still find *aguacates criollos* (Creole avocados) in the valleys and mountains. They have a different texture, and the pit takes up three-quarters of the inside of the fruit, which has a thinner, longer shape. For this recipe, you can use the more common Hass avocado.

The addition of blended zucchini and crema in this recipe adds tang, richness, and sweet "green" flavor, making this guacamole taste more like the kind meant to be spooned onto tacos at taquerias. It also helps to slow down the avocado's oxidation.

Serves 4 to 6 (or one of me when I'm hangry)

---

1 small zucchini
1 garlic clove
Juice of 3 limes (about 6 tablespoons), plus more to taste
6 whole dried chiles piquines (pequin peppers)
½ teaspoon sea salt, plus more to taste
6 large ripe Hass avocados
1 small white onion, minced
½ cup minced cilantro
2 teaspoons Mexican crema (optional)

Optional Garnishes
Mexican crema
½ cup diced tomato
Cilantro leaves
2 green onions, green parts only, thinly sliced

1. Roughly chop the zucchini and purée in a blender or food processor. Set aside.

2. In a large molcajete, combine the garlic clove, lime juice, chiles, and salt. Use the pestle to grind them into a paste. Transfer to a medium mixing bowl. (If you don't have a molcajete, grate the garlic and grind the pepper, and combine with the lime juice in a mixing bowl.)

3. Peel and pit the avocadoes (reserve the pits). Dice them, or, for a shortcut, push the avocado halves through the wire grid of a cooling rack into the mixing bowl. Add in the minced onion, cilantro, and blended zucchini and season with more salt to taste. Mash and mix all the ingredients thoroughly to combine. Stir in 2 teaspoons of crema, to prevent oxidation, or place the pits back in the guacamole.

4. When ready to serve, transfer the guacamole to a serving bowl, top with the garnishes (if using), and enjoy with *totopos* (crispy tortilla chips).

1940 NACHOS

If you were to say out loud to me that nachos were Mexican food, my instinct would be to roll my eyes. You might be rolling your eyes too—but I have to admit the story is more complicated than that, and I must give credit where credit is due: Enter Ignacio "Nacho" Anaya Garcia ("Nacho" is the common nickname for "Ignacio"). In 1940, Nacho was working as the maître d' at the Club Victoria restaurant in the border town of Piedra Negras, Coahuila, when a group of American military wives walked through his doors. People debate the time of day, but no one disputes the fact that there was no one in the kitchen to prepare food.

Not wanting to tell the women that there was nothing for them to eat, Nacho headed into the kitchen, grabbed some totopos (fried tortilla chips), topped them with cheese and slices of pickled jalapeño, and threw the whole thing in the oven. And thus, Nachos were born. (When I learned this story, I couldn't believe that college students around the world—and my own kids—had been making the OG Nachos this whole time.) The snack was a hit, and ended up being added to the menu as "Nachos Especiales." Eventually, the dish took off on both sides of the border. Ignacio eventually opened his own restaurant, appropriately called Nacho's. There are tons of variations today, but this recipe stays true to Nacho's original creation.

Serves 1 or 2

1 tablespoon vegetable oil
3 corn tortillas
1 cup shredded Cheddar cheese
24 pickled jalapeño slices

1. Preheat the oven to 350°F. Line a baking sheet with parchment paper.

2. Brush the oil on both sides of each tortilla and cut each into 8 wedges. Spread the pieces evenly on the prepared baking sheet. Bake for 10 minutes; then flip the tortilla wedges and bake for another 10 minutes, or until the tortillas are golden brown.

3. Take the baking sheet out of the oven and top the tortillas with the shredded cheese, distributing it equally. Place a slice of jalapeño on each chip.

4. Return the chips to the oven and bake for about 5 more minutes, until the cheese is melted and bubbly. Alternatively, you can place them under the broiler for 1 minute or so, but don't walk away—they'll be quick to burn! Serve hot.

NACHA'S NACHOS

If you read the headnote for the 1940 Nachos, you'll know that "Nacho" is a nickname for "Ignacio." Well, my mom's name is Ignacia, hence the nickname "Nacha." So here's my version of nachos, in honor of her, made border-kid style, mixing the original nachos with what we see more commonly in the US these days—crispy tortillas covered in a savory queso sauce.

The sauce uses mild, creamy, and perfect-for-melting Chihuahua cheese and is seasoned with what I like to call magic powders—garlic, onion, cumin, and coriander. It's optional, but I recommend topping the chips with meaty Cowboy Beans and pickled vegetables for a pop of acidity.

Serves 4

Corn tortilla chips (totopos), measured with your heart

Queso Sauce

3 cups freshly shredded queso Chihuahua (or Muenster or Jack in a pinch)
1 tablespoon cornstarch
¼ tablespoon unsalted butter
¼ yellow onion, diced small
2 garlic cloves, minced
1 small Roma tomato, diced small
1 (13-ounce) can evaporated milk
¼ cup diced charred poblano pepper
¼ teaspoon onion powder
¼ teaspoon garlic powder
¼ teaspoon ground cumin
¼ ground coriander
Diamond Crystal kosher salt
Whole milk, as needed

Optional Garnishes

½ cup Cowboy Beans (page 216)
Pickled Vegetables (page 32)
Chopped fresh cilantro

1. Preheat the oven to 350°F. Line a rimmed baking sheet with parchment paper and set aside.

MAKE THE QUESO SAUCE:

2. Place 2½ cups of the shredded Chihuahua cheese in a medium bowl. Add the cornstarch and toss to coat the cheese evenly.

3. In a medium saucepan set over medium heat, melt the butter. Add in the onion and garlic and cook until the onions are translucent, about 3 minutes. Add the diced tomato and cook for 3 minutes, or until softened.

4. Pour in the evaporated milk and add the shredded cheese. Whisk until the cheese is melted. Add in the charred poblano pepper, onion powder, garlic powder, cumin, and coriander, and season with salt to taste.

5. Continue to whisk until the sauce becomes smooth and thickens a bit. If the sauce is thicker than you like, add a couple tablespoons of milk to thin it out. Remove from heat.

MAKE THE NACHOS:

6. Spread the tortilla chips in a single layer on the prepared baking sheet. Sprinkle the remaining ½ cup of shredded cheese over the chips. Bake in the oven for 10 minutes, or until the cheese is melted and bubbly.

7. Remove the chips from the oven and, if desired, spoon Cowboy Beans evenly over them. Then ladle the cheese sauce over the nachos. Garnish the nachos with Pickled Vegetables and cilantro.

Note: Do *not* use pre-shredded cheese here—freshly shredded cheese makes all the difference.

SALSA DE SUERO CON QUESO DE RANCHO

(WHEY AND FARMER'S CHEESE SALSA)

I learned how to make my own fresh farmer's cheese almost twenty years ago, and I still remember how proud I felt. As the name implies, this cheese is made on most—if not all—dairy ranches. It is easy and quick to whip up, which makes it great to bring to market to earn money faster. Even my twenty-year-old son, who (perhaps thankfully) has no desire for a career in cooking, knows how to make it.

This salsa is a product of innovation, using cheese *and* the by-product of cheesemaking—whey. Who wouldn't want to see how good that would turn out? Well, the verdict is in, and it turns out this is a very delicious creation indeed. When you taste this salsa, hopefully with a warm tortilla, the dance between the salinity of the whey and cheese and the acidity of the tomatillos is magic. It's the collab you never knew your life was missing.

Serves 4

4 cups whole milk
Juice of 3 limes (about 6 tablespoons)
Sea salt
4 serrano peppers, stemmed and seeded
2 poblano peppers, stemmed and seeded
2 tablespoons salted butter
2 garlic cloves, minced
½ cup minced white onion
2 tomatillos, husked, rinsed, and diced small
Sea salt
Flour Tortillas (page 27), warmed, for serving

Optional Garnishes
Chopped fresh cilantro
Chicharrones
Limes, cut into cheeks

MAKE THE FARMER'S CHEESE:

1. In a medium heavy pot set over medium heat, add 3 cups of the milk. Heat the milk until it reaches 180°F on a kitchen thermometer. Add the lime juice and a generous pinch of salt and stir slowly. The milk will begin to separate into curds and whey. Turn the heat off and let the milk sit for 30 to 40 minutes for the curds to set. Once the raft forms and is solid, use a butter knife to cut the curds into rows, then into squares about 1 inch apart.

2. Once the curds are set and firm, allow the curds and whey to cool to room temperature.

3. Using a fine-mesh strainer lined with a piece of cheesecloth, strain the curds out of the whey, reserving both. Squeeze the curds through the cheesecloth to remove as much of the whey as possible. Place the cheesecloth with the solids in a small colander set over a bowl to continue straining. Place something heavy on top, such as a large tomato can or a small dumbbell weight. Place the bowl in the refrigerator for a few hours or overnight so the cheese can set.

MAKE THE SALSA:

4. Char the serrano and poblano peppers over an open gas stove flame or under the oven's broiler, turning occasionally. Once blackened all over, transfer the peppers into a bowl and cover it with plastic wrap to steam the skins loose. Once cool, carefully peel the skin off the peppers (do not run under water) and remove the seeds. Discard the skin and seeds. Mince the serrano peppers and dice the poblanos small.

5. In a sauté pan over medium heat, melt the butter. Add the garlic, onion, and charred serrano and poblano peppers and sauté until the onion is translucent, about 5 minutes.

6. Add the diced tomatillos and cook until the majority of their liquid has evaporated, about 8 minutes, stirring often to ensure nothing sticks or burns.

7. While the tomatillos are cooking, remove the cheese from the cheesecloth and cut it into small pieces. Set aside.

8. Add the whey and the remaining 1 cup of milk to the pan and stir to combine. Adjust the salt to taste. Simmer the salsa for another 10 minutes, stirring occasionally.

9. Add the pieces of farmer's cheese to the pan and stir to incorporate. Cook the cheese and salsa together for 6 more minutes—the cheese will be soft, but the pieces will remain intact.

10. Pour the salsa into a bowl, add garnishes (if using), and serve with limes, if desired, and warm flour tortillas.

CHILES RELLENOS

(STUFFED POBLANO PEPPERS)

Chiles rellenos come in many forms, but the only ones I really love are these cheese-stuffed and battered poblanos, served nestled in warm, oregano-laced tomato caldillo, with a side of warm corn tortillas. (To make it even better, enjoy with Red Rice, page 29). These are eaten often during Lent, since they're an easy but satisfying meat-free option.

The recipe is deceivingly simple, but it uses a few key techniques to achieve the perfect flavor and texture: You char the peppers just enough for the skin to peel off, but not so much that the flesh gets too soft. You make a light, fluffy egg batter to perfectly coat the peppers. (The egg whites are done when you can turn the bowl upside down over your head, and the whipped eggs stay put. My mom used to do it to scare us when we were little—in my eyes, she was a wizard.)

Makes 4 servings

---

4 whole poblano peppers with stems
1 pound asadero cheese or queso Chihuahua cheese, cut into rectangular blocks (2 inches long, ½ inch wide)
¼ cup all-purpose flour or rice flour
Diamond Crystal kosher salt
Freshly ground black pepper
1 recipe Tomato and Oregano Sauce (page 52)
6 large eggs, separated
Vegetable oil, for frying
Corn Tortillas (page 23), for serving

1. First, char the peppers. Place the poblanos directly over the burner of a gas stove set to high heat. Char the skin completely, using tongs to rotate as needed, until the skin is blistered and blackened on all sides. Alternatively, place the chiles on a baking sheet in an oven set to broil. For best results, place them as close as possible to the broiler. Watch closely, and rotate the peppers as needed to ensure that they char on all sides.

2. Place the charred peppers in a bowl and cover with a clean, damp kitchen towel or plastic wrap for 5 to 10 minutes. When the peppers are cool enough to handle, peel them. Hold on to the stem of the pepper with one hand, and use your other hand to sweep the skin off the pepper. The skin should come off easily. (Don't rinse them with water!)

3. Cut a slit from the stem down the full length of one side of a pepper, stopping just before the tip. Gently open the pepper and clean out its seeds. Then fill the cavity of the pepper with a block of cheese. Close the pepper back up, with the edges slightly overlapping, and secure it with a toothpick. Repeat with the rest of the peppers and cheese.

4. Add the flour to a shallow dish and season with a couple pinches of salt and black pepper. Coat the cheese-stuffed peppers in the flour, shake off the excess, and place them on a plate.

5. Make the batter. In a medium bowl, whip the egg whites to stiff peaks with a whisk or a handheld electric mixer. In a separate bowl, lightly beat the egg yolks, and then gently fold them into the whites until smooth and fluffy. Set aside.

6. Line a tray or baking sheet with paper towels and set a wire rack on top.

Recipe continues

7. Fill a large skillet with about an inch of oil and set over medium heat. To test if the oil is hot enough, drop some of the egg batter into the skillet. If the oil is hot enough, the batter will sizzle and fry immediately upon contact.

8. Once the oil is ready, hold a flour-coated pepper by the stem and dip it all the way into the egg mixture, turning to ensure that it is coated evenly. Place it immediately in the oil, seam side facing up. Repeat with a second pepper.

9. Fry the peppers on the first side for about 3 minutes. Using a large heatproof spoon, bathe the top side of the peppers with the hot oil to ensure the opening is sealed. Carefully flip the peppers and fry them for another few minutes, until they are golden brown on both sides. Use tongs or a slotted spoon to carefully lift the peppers out of the oil, pausing to let excess oil drip off, and place them on the wire rack.

10. Repeat the battering and frying steps with the remaining peppers. When the toothpicks have cooled down enough that you can touch them with your bare hands, remove and discard them.

11. Warm up the Tomato and Oregano Sauce, and spoon it onto the surface of a rimmed serving platter to cover. Arrange the chiles rellenos in the center. Serve hot, with warm tortillas and the extra caldillo in a bowl on the side for dipping.

MENUDO NORTEÑO

We've all heard that food is medicine, and menudo is one of the longest-held food medicine secrets in the North, especially if you happen to come down with a case of the "brown bottle flu." Hangovers are rough, but the best stories are told amongst the plastic tables serving menudo for breakfast on Sunday mornings.

In the North, this tripe stew is rich and deep red, made with a dry chile adobo base. Apart from being delicious, it also helps keep you full and energized. The herbs used in this soup—particularly yerba buena and oregano—have medicinal properties that can help settle the stomach and fight bacteria.

I have a vivid memories of my grandma using a metal laundry washboard to scrub the tripe clean. She stressed the importance of the tripe needing to be as clean as possible before soaking it in milk overnight. (Today, most tripe sold is pre-cleaned.) Cooking the tripe low and slow in a chile adobo with hominy makes for an incredibly satisfying and complex bowl. And you'll notice the undeniable power of the oregano and mint in the broth, lightening up the otherwise deep, rich flavor.

Serves 6

Menudo

2 pounds beef tripe, cleaned, cut into 2-inch pieces
2 pounds beef broth bones, wrapped in cheesecloth
1 medium white onion, halved crosswise, with the root still attached
2 to 4 sprigs fresh Mexican oregano
2 to 4 sprigs fresh yerba buena or spearmint
1 bay leaf
8 cups hominy, freshly nixtamalized or canned

Adobo

3 dried guajillo chiles, stemmed and seeded
½ medium white onion, chopped
8 garlic cloves
2 tablespoons distilled white vinegar
1 teaspoon whole black peppercorns
1 teaspoon dried Mexican oregano
Diamond Crystal kosher salt

Garnishes/For Serving

Corn Tortillas (page 23)
Chile de Árbol Salsa (page 37)
Minced white onion
Minced fresh mint
Dried Mexican oregano
Limes, cut into cheeks

MAKE THE BROTH (MENUDO):

1. In a large stockpot, combine the tripe, stock bones (in the cheesecloth), onion, oregano, yerba buena or mint, bay leaf, and 5 quarts of water. Bring to a boil over high heat, then reduce the heat to reach a low simmer, and cover the pot. Cook the broth for 2 hours, undisturbed.

MAKE THE ADOBO:

2. On a dry comal or in a sauté pan, toast the guajillo chiles until the color brightens and they start to release whispers of smoke, but are not yet blackened.

3. In a medium pot, combine the toasted chiles, onion, garlic cloves, and 4 cups of water. Bring to a boil over high heat; then turn off the heat, cover, and let steep for 5 to 10 minutes, until the chiles have softened.

4. Strain out the steeped chiles, onion, and garlic into a blender, reserving the soaking water. Add the vinegar, peppercorns, and oregano to the blender. Blend the ingredients into a smooth purée, adding in some soaking water if needed. Season the adobo with salt to taste.

MAKE THE MENUDO:

5. After 2 hours, use a slotted spoon and/or tongs to remove the onion, herb bundle, and stock bones from the pot of broth, allowing as much liquid back to drain back into the pot as possible. Discard the solids.

6. Strain the adobo through a fine-mesh sieve directly into the stockpot, and stir to incorporate the adobo into the broth.

7. Add the hominy to the pot, and reduce the heat to low. Continue cooking the broth, uncovered, for 2 more hours. After 2 hours, taste and adjust salt as needed before serving.

8. Serve the menudo in bowls, with warm corn tortillas, Chile de Árbol Salsa, and garnishes on the side.

GORDITAS DE QUELITES

(GORDITAS WITH BRAISED WILD GREENS)

I know what you're thinking: "Finally! Some vegetables!" The reality is that along the borderlands, there is both extreme poverty and extreme wealth. The wealthy are those who own the land and ranches, and the poor are those who work on the cattle ranches or harvest the vegetables, fruit, and nuts that the rest of the world consumes.

The workers usually eat what they are harvesting, often eating directly over the same dirt they care for. I have learned so much about humanity, and my own heritage and culture, in seeing how these people cook, making rich and highly nutritious meals with foods that others might look past or even throw away.

That brings us to *quelites*. Quelites are the native edible plants and weeds that are usually sauteed into "guisados" (braises) and used as a filling for *garnachas*, a corn masa–based street food that's either fried in a copper pot or griddled on a comal over wood fire.

These gorditas are a beautiful representation of culture and history, all wrapped up in a portable masa hand pie. This recipe calls for a mix of commonly available greens, but think like a local and use what you like and have available.

Makes 6 gorditas

3 tablespoons olive oil, plus more as needed
2 small shallots, minced
1 garlic clove, minced
1 chile de árbol
1 bay leaf
1 teaspoon ground cumin
1 teaspoon ground coriander
½ pound beet greens, cleaned and cut into 1-inch chiffonade
½ pound chard leaves, cleaned, stemmed, and cut into 1-inch chiffonade
½ pound spinach, cleaned
Diamond Crystal kosher salt
1 cup Stewed Beans (page 30)
1 recipe masa dough for Corn Tortillas (page 23)

Optional Garnishes
Salsa Verde Morita (page 41)
Mexican crema
Crumbled Cotija cheese
Chopped fresh cilantro
Sliced avocado

COOK THE GREENS:

1. In a large skillet set over medium-high heat, warm the olive oil. Add the shallots, garlic, whole chile de árbol, bay leaf, cumin, and coriander and sauté until the shallots are translucent, about 3 minutes.

2. Add the beet greens, chard, and spinach to the pan, stir to incorporate, and sprinkle with a pinch of salt. Cover the pan with a lid, so that the greens cook in their own steam. Lower the heat to medium, and cook the greens for 7 minutes, until tender.

3. Remove the lid from the pan and stir the greens thoroughly. Continue to cook the greens, uncovered, until all of the liquid has evaporated. Remove the bay leaf and chile de árbol from the greens and discard. Fold in the Stewed Beans, taste, and adjust the salt as needed.

MAKE THE GORDITAS:

4. Divide the prepared masa into 4-ounce portions and roll them into well-formed balls. Keep the balls of dough under a clean, damp kitchen towel until ready to use.

5. Set a comal or cast-iron griddle on the stovetop over medium heat. Set a wire cooling rack nearby the stovetop.

6. Place a masa ball in the middle of a tortilla press lined with a square of thin plastic. Lay a second plastic sheet over the masa, pressing down gently with the palm of your hand to help adhere it to the base plastic. Bring the tortilla press lid down, lightly pressing the masa ball into a round, roughly ½ inch thick and 4 inches in diameter. (If you flatten the masa any more than this, it may be too difficult to fill.)

7. Lift the press lid, carefully remove the top plastic square, and lift the gordita from the press, placing the uncovered side face-down in the palm of your nondominant hand. Then carefully peel off the second plastic square.

8. Gently pass the gordita back to your dominant hand and lay it on the comal. Cook on the first side until a few char marks form on the surface, about 2 minutes, then flip and cook the other side for another 2 minutes. Flip the gordita back to the first side to cook for another 30 seconds, then transfer it to the wire cooling rack. Repeat these steps to shape and cook the remaining gorditas.

9. Once the gorditas are cool to the touch, use the back of a spoon or a butter knife to cut a slit along the edge halfway around the gordita, sort of like a pita pocket.

10. Fill each gordita with ½ cup of filling (or as much as you can fit inside). Add any optional garnishes and serve hot.

ENCHILADAS ROJAS

Yes, these enchiladas are first dipped in a wet salsa . . . and *then* fried in hot oil. Why? I suppose because in the state of Monterrey, they like to live on the wild side. Adding a water-based sauce to frying oil is sort of like finding a wild black stallion in the mountains of the Sierra Madre Occidental and trying to jump on.

This specific high-stakes method is not necessarily unique to this area, but these enchiladas are a favorite of Norteños. And the risk is not without reward. With this admittedly perilous technique, the adobo fries *into* the tortilla, helping concentrate the flavor and create a texture somewhat like that of a sauce-covered chicken wing. And it's doable if you're careful and prepared. Wear long sleeves. And a last piece of advice: If hot oil splatters on your hand, *do not* launch your piping-hot tongs into the air. You can do this—I believe in you!

Makes 4 to 6 enchiladas

2 cups crumbled queso fresco
¼ medium white onion, minced
3 epazote leaves, minced
½ cup minced cilantro
2 cups Red Wine–Braised Short Ribs (recipe follows)
Freshly ground black pepper
Diamond Crystal kosher salt
3 dried cascabel chiles, stemmed and seeded
2 dried ancho chiles, stemmed and seeded
1 teaspoon ground cumin
¼ cup whole milk
Vegetable oil, for frying
12 (5-inch) corn tortillas, store-bought or homemade (page 23)

Garnishes

Mexican crema
2 cups thinly-shaved Iceberg lettuce
Queso Cotija, finely grated (optional)

PREPARE THE FILLING:

1. In a small bowl, combine the queso fresco, onion, epazote, cilantro, and prepared shredded beef. Stir to incorporate and season with salt and pepper to taste. Set aside.

MAKE THE ENCHILADA SAUCE:

2. First, toast the chiles on a dry skillet or comal over medium heat, until they start changing color; the reds will deepen and you will begin to smell the chiles.

3. Fill a saucepan halfway with water and set it over medium-high heat. Once the water reaches a simmer, turn the heat off and add in the toasted chiles. Cover the pan and allow the chiles to steep in the hot water for 10 minutes.

4. In a blender, combine the softened chiles, cumin, black pepper, and 1 cup of the soaking water (discard the rest of the water). Blend until smooth; then taste and season with salt as needed. Strain the sauce through a fine-mesh sieve back into the saucepan that you used to soak the chiles. Whisk the milk into the chile sauce; then place the pan over low heat to keep the sauce warm.

MAKE THE ENCHILADAS:

5. Set up an enchilada assembly station nearby where you're frying, with a serving platter, the filling mixture, and the pot of warm enchilada sauce. Keep the filling nearby as well.

6. In a skillet, add about ½ inch of frying oil and set over medium heat until the oil shimmers, or reaches 350°F on a cooking thermometer. Make sure you are wearing long sleeves, have a splatter screen, or are using a pot lid to shield yourself!

Recipe continues

7. Using tongs, dip a tortilla into the enchilada sauce, coating it completely. Shake the tortilla to allow any excess sauce to drip back into the saucepan. Then carefully ease the coated tortilla into the skillet with the hot oil. The oil will splatter right away, so protect yourself!

8. Fry the tortilla in the oil for about a minute on each side, then remove from the oil and set it on the serving platter. Fill the fried tortilla with ¼ cup of the queso fresco filling, and fold the tortilla over the filling to close the enchilada. Repeat with the remaining tortillas, arranging them in a row on a platter.

9. Cover the filled enchiladas with the remaining sauce and garnish them with crema, lettuce, and more finely grated Cotija (if using).

Note: If you don't have an oil screen (a.k.a. a splatter screen) to set over your pan, use a pan lid. Hold the lid in your nondominant hand like a knight's shield to make sure the oil doesn't splatter on you. Fill the tortillas with the cheese and beef, or just the cheese, for all I care. You are ready, so go for it!

RED WINE–BRAISED SHORT RIBS

Makes about 2 quarts shredded meat

1 bay leaf
2 dried avocado leaves (optional)
1 hoja santa leaf (optional)
1 fresh thyme sprig
1 bunch cilantro
2 pounds boneless beef short ribs, cut into 2-inch pieces
Diamond Crystal kosher salt
1 teaspoon freshly ground black pepper
2 teaspoons garlic powder
2 teaspoons onion powder
Grapeseed oil
2 tablespoons tomato paste
1 medium white onion, diced
2 carrots, diced
2 ribs celery, diced
1½ cups red wine
2 tablespoons white distilled vinegar

Tie the bay leaf, avocado leaves, hoja santa leaf (if using), thyme, and cilantro together into a bouquet with twine. Set aside.

Spread the short rib pieces in a single layer on a paper towel-lined baking sheet to bring to room temperature, about 30 minutes. Pat the beef dry with another paper towel.

Season the beef all over with salt, black pepper, and the garlic and onion powders.

Set a large Dutch oven over medium heat and add a generous glug of oil. When the oil is shimmering, add the beef in a single layer (work in batches if needed to avoid crowding the pan). Sear the beef on one side for 5 minutes; when nicely browned, flip and sear on the other side. Repeat until the beef is well-browned all over—this can take 15 to 20 minutes total. Remove the browned beef from the pot and set aside in a medium bowl.

Add the tomato paste to the skillet and cook for 2 minutes, until fragrant and darker in color, using a wooden spoon to keep scraping the bottom of the Dutch oven to keep the tomato paste from burning. Add in the onion, carrots, celery, and a pinch of salt. Cook for 4 minutes, until softened, continuously scraping the bottom of the pot to remove stuck bits.

Add the herb bouquet, red wine, vinegar, and 1 cup of water. Continue to scrape up the caramelized layer on the bottom of the pan.

Turn the heat to low, and add the seared beef back to the Dutch oven. Stir to incorporate and cover the pot with a lid. Cook for 2 hours on low heat.

After 2 hours, check the meat for doneness using a fork—it should fall apart easily. If too much of the liquid evaporates before the beef is finished cooking, add an additional cup of water; you want it to have created its own sauce, but not watery. When the beef is cooked, remove and discard the herb bouquet. Adjust the seasoning to taste.

If shredding, transfer the meat to a bowl to cool until you can handle it with your bare hands. Use your hands or two forks to shred the meat. (You can also shred it in a stand mixer fitted with the paddle attachment, on low speed for about 2 minutes.) Store the shredded beef with its sauce in a resealable plastic bag (or bags, depending on the portion sizes you want). The beef can be stored in the fridge for 3 days, or frozen for up to a month.

TAMALITOS REGIOMONTAÑOS

(MONTERREY-STYLE TAMALES)

I have to get a simple grammar lesson out of the way before we make the steamed masa pockets we call tamales. A single one is a "tamal." More than one, and they are "tamales." That is to say, there's no such thing as "*a* tamale."

Now, this part might confuse you further: If the word has an "-ito" at the end, it means a small, cute version of that thing—a tamalito, for instance. Or, you can have many small and cute tamalitos.

In many parts of Mexico, making tamales at home is reserved for the holidays. There's an exception in the North, along the border, where we always need food that's easily portable because of the prevalence of ranching.

In Monterrey, the capital of and largest city in Nuevo León, beef and lamb are featured in most classic dishes. Tamales in Monterrey are often filled with shredded beef and red chile salsa and enjoyed as an everyday treat.

Makes 16 tamalitos

Tamales

16 dried corn husks (7 to 9 inches long), plus more to line the steamer
2 pounds masa for Corn Tortillas (page 23)
1⅓ cups lard or shortening
1 teaspoon baking powder
2 teaspoons Diamond Crystal Kosher salt (or 1 teaspoon Morton)
1 cup chicken or beef stock
½ cup sauce (recipe follows)

Sauce and Filling

20 dried guajillo chiles, stemmed and seeded
8 tomatillos, husked and cleaned
3 garlic cloves
Diamond Crystal kosher salt
¼ teaspoon ground cumin
¼ teaspoon freshly ground black pepper
1 recipe Red Wine–Braised Short Ribs (page 265) shredded, Cowboy Beans (page 216), or smashed Stewed Beans (page 30)

Optional garnishes

Adobo sauce (page 73)
Queso fresco
Mexican crema

1. Soak the dried corn husks in hot water for at least 30 minutes. Make sure your corn husks are at least 7 inches wide at the center, to ensure they can accommodate the filling.

MAKE THE SAUCE AND FILLING:

2. On a dry comal or sauté pan, toast the guajillo chiles until the color brightens and starts to release whispers of smoke, but the peppers are not fully blackened.

3. Fill a medium pot three-quarters of the way with water and a couple of pinches of salt and bring to a boil over medium-high heat. Add the toasted guajillo, tomatillos, and garlic cloves. Turn off the heat, cover, and steep for 15 minutes.

4. Transfer the guajillos, tomatillos, garlic, and 3 cups of the soaking liquid to a blender (you can discard the rest of the liquid). Add the cumin and black pepper and blend until smooth. Strain the sauce through a fine-mesh sieve back into the pot and adjust salt as needed.

5. Portion out ½ cup of the sauce and set it aside for the masa. Add the prepared shredded beef (or other filling) to the remaining sauce in the pot. Simmer together for 30 minutes on medium low heat, stirring occasionally.

MAKE THE TAMAL MASA:

6. In the bowl of a stand mixer fitted with the paddle attachment, add the tortilla masa, lard, baking powder, salt, and stock. Mix the ingredients on low speed for 2 minutes, until the masa is light and fluffy, sort of like a cookie dough, but a bit shinier.

Recipe continues

7. Pour the reserved ½ cup of sauce into the masa. Raise the mixer speed to medium and mix the masa for 6 minutes, until the sauce is fully incorporated, and the lard is evenly distributed. At this point, the masa should have the texture of buttercream.

8. Proceed to make tamales. If you aren't assembling the tamales right away, you can cover the masa with plastic wrap and store in the refrigerator for a day, no more. When ready to use, mix it once more with the paddle attachment for 3 to 5 minutes to fluff it back up.

MAKE THE TAMALES:

9. Remove the corn husks from the water. Lay one out on a flat surface, with the wider end closest to you. Place a baseball-sized scoop of masa at the wider end of the husk. Use a spatula to spread the masa across three-quarters of the husk starting at the wider end, leaving a small border. Spoon 2 tablespoons of the shredded beef and sauce over the center of the masa.

10. Tightly fold one side of the husk in vertically over the filling, then fold the opposite side in over that. Pick up the tamal in your nondominant hand and squeeze it gently to push out any air pockets. With your dominant hand, take the tapered end of the husk (the end not covered with masa) and fold it up to meet the open, wider edge of the tamal.

11. At this point, you have a few options: You can leave the tamal as is, or use twine or a thin strip of corn husk to tie the opening closed. Alternatively, you can skip folding up the narrow end of the husk, and instead tie both ends shut, so the tamal is tied like a wrapped piece of caramel. You should end up with a long, thin tamalito, approximately 5 inches long and 1 to 1½ inches wide.

COOK THE TAMALES:

12. Fill a large pot with 3 inches of water. Throw a couple of coins or pebbles into the pot—really, they'll be important later! Set a wire steamer rack inside the pot, so that it sits just above the water. Line the surface of the grate with a few corn husks, cover the pot with a lid, and bring to a simmer over medium heat.

13. Once the pot starts steaming, open the lid and gently place the tamales on the steamer grate one by one, standing with open sides up. Start from the inner edge of the pot and work your way toward the center. Once you've placed all the tamales on the steamer grate, cover them with a few more corn husks and replace the lid.

14. Steam the tamales for 1½ hours. This is where the coins or pebbles come in—as long as there is water, they will rattle continuously. If you no longer hear the rattling, it means the water has evaporated and you should add more right away.

15. After 1½ hours, use tongs to carefully remove one tamal from the pot. Let cool for 5 minutes; then test for doneness: Open one of the husk sides. The husk should release easily from the masa when you peel it back, and the masa should be matte in appearance. If the masa is still shiny, close the tamal back up, return it to the pot, and cook the tamales for another 20 minutes before checking again. Once the tamales are ready, turn the heat off, remove the lid, and let the tamales sit in the pot to cool to room temp before removing them.

16. We eat tamales fresh, straight from the pot. But if you have guests to impress, you can garnish the bottom of a plate with the sauce, place the tamal in the center, and drizzle with as much crema and crumble with as much queso fresco as your heart desires. A popular side for tamales are beans of any kind. I suggest Beans with Cheese and Chorizo (page 187), but you can't go wrong with simple smashed beans either.

Note: For leftover tamalitos, the power move is to pan fry them until golden brown and serve them next to refried beans and rice with a hot salsa. Or you can freeze them before cooking and steam them in small batches as you want them, a good option if you don't have fifteen people to share them with.

Squirt
Squirt
Coca-Cola

PALANQUETAS DE CACAHUATE

(PEANUT PRALINE BARS)

Long before the Spanish landed in Mexico, Indigenous people were making sweets with native peanuts, amaranth, and chia seeds, bound together with honey. This treat isn't *that* ancient (since it uses butter, which isn't native to Mexico), but its name does comes from the Nahuatl word *papaquili*, meaning happiness or joy. As a matter of fact, I find these treats delightfully addictive—the piloncillo's earthy molasses flavor combines beautifully with the salted butter and crunchy peanuts.

This was also the snack of choice of Francisco "Pancho" Villa, a.k.a. the "Centaur of the North," a leader in the Mexican Revolution that overthrew the dictatorship of Porfirio Díaz. The fierce leader was also known to ride between Coahuila and El Paso or San Antonio on horseback to indulge in his favorite soda fountain treat, a strawberry milkshake. On his day-to-day rides, it is also said that he ate an impressive pound of palanquetas a day!

Since candy-making is really a (sweet) science, I should note the corn syrup used in the recipe. Corn syrup is what's called an "inverted" sugar, and is helpful in making candy because it can prevent the sugar from crystallizing. Think of it as an insurance policy against bad texture. If you live in a humid area, I would recommend buying some silica packets to store the candy with—they will absorb moisture, helping to keep the bars fresh.

Makes 8 bars

Nonstick cooking spray or vegetable oil, for greasing
1 cup granulated sugar
¼ cup grated or ground piloncillo
¼ cup honey
1 tablespoon light corn syrup
4 tablespoons salted butter
4 cups roasted skinless peanuts
Flaky finishing salt

Special equipment
Candy thermometer

1. Lightly grease the inside of an 8 × 8-inch baking dish with cooking spray or vegetable oil. Line the pan with enough parchment paper to overhang on each side by 3 inches, creating a sling.

2. In a small, heavy saucepan, combine the sugar, piloncillo, honey, corn syrup, and ½ cup of water. Gently stir to incorporate, brushing the inner sides of the pot with more water to ensure no sugar granules are stuck on the sides of the pot. Secure a candy thermometer to the side of the pot and set over medium heat.

3. Cook the mixture for about 20 minutes (resist the urge to stir—don't touch it!), until the syrup is at the dark caramel stage, with a temperature of 345°F to 350°F. If you notice a small dark circle forming in the mixture, gently swirl the pot, but don't use a utensil!

4. When the caramel comes to temperature, turn off the heat. Immediately add the butter and peanuts, mixing them in vigorously with a metal spoon to ensure that all of the peanuts are evenly coated with the caramel.

5. Pour the mixture into the prepared baking dish, and use a rubber spatula to press the candy into the pan in an even layer. Allow the candy to cool in the pan for about 15 minutes, until cool to the touch.

6. Using the parchment paper sling, lift the candy out of the pan and place on a cutting board. With a serrated knife, cut the square in half, then cut it into 2-inch bars. Store in an airtight container with silica packets to absorb moisture. You can process leftover candy into a rough crumble, and store in an airtight container to use as a topping for ice cream.

GLORIAS

(GOAT MILK CARAMEL CHEWS)

American grandmothers carry butterscotch . . . and abuelitas in the North carry Glorias. This caramelized milk candy has a slight tang to it thanks to the goat's milk used in the recipe. It's not overwhelmingly sweet, and the pecan pieces give it a great texture. Like with many iconic foods, there is debate over the name—people argue over whether the name refers to a person, or the religious exclamation—"*Gloria!*"—that you'll say when you taste them! The recipe we enjoy today is a product of culinary innovation and fusion, likely influenced by Jewish and Middle Eastern peoples as well as Franciscan Missionaries—all immigrants in the city of Linares, Nuevo León, where Glorias were first invented.

Makes 25 to 30 caramels

1 quart goat milk
2½ cups granulated sugar
2 tablespoons vanilla extract
3½ tablespoons light corn syrup
½ teaspoon baking soda
1½ cups roasted pecans, finely chopped
¼ teaspoon Diamond Crystal kosher salt, or a pinch of Morton salt
Softened butter, for greasing and rolling

1. In a large (4- to 5-quart) pot, combine the goat milk, sugar, vanilla, and corn syrup and set over medium heat. Cook the ingredients, stirring to dissolve the sugar. Once the mixture comes to a boil, adjust the heat to low and stir in the baking soda.

2. Adjust the temperature as needed to maintain a continuous simmer. Continue stirring the mixture until it reaches a caramel color and thickens to a condensed milk–like consistency, about 45 minutes.

3. Once the mixture has thickened, turn off the heat and stir in the pecans and salt. Allow the mixture to rest and cool for 30 minutes.

4. Line a baking sheet with parchment or wax paper, and lightly coat 2 large spoons with butter.

5. Scoop a generous tablespoon of caramel out of the pot with the first spoon, and use the second spoon to scrape the excess back into the pot. Drop the caramel onto the prepared baking sheet. Repeat to spoon out 25 to 30 equal-sized pieces of caramel.

6. Coat your hands with a small amount of butter, and then roll each piece of caramel into a small sphere.

7. Wrap each piece of caramel in a square of parchment paper, twisting the ends to secure (or store the pieces together in a sealed container). They will keep at room temperature for up to 2 weeks.

CAPIROTADA

(PILONCILLO "BREAD PUDDING")

I debated whether or not to add this recipe—one of my favorite seasonal desserts—to the book . . . but here it is. Before we begin, I am fully aware that you might find this dish odd. Capirotada, a dessert often eaten during Lent, includes ingredients that are more commonly used in savory applications: cheese, as well as a syrup infused with tomatoes, tomatillos, and onions. I'm translating it as "bread pudding," but that's a bit of a stretch of the imagination, since it does not use eggs or custard (though it does include syrup-soaked bread).

I encourage you to try making capirotada—the end result is beautifully dense, speckled with the incredible texture of nuts and fruit and studded with Cotija cheese, which brings a touch of salinity to balance out the sweetness. And in the ingredients' defense, tomatoes are fruits, tomatillos are gooseberries, and everyone knows how sweet onions are once cooked. The syrup's smell will probably send your senses for a loop, but stick with me here.

Capirotada is made in the same quantities as tamales, if that helps describe how much we love it. And during Lent, even if we were not religious, we'll all of a sudden remember the whole, "our father," thing . . . if it means getting a serving.

This specific recipe originates in Jalisco, but it's one of hundreds of variations. Migrants from Jalisco just so happen to make up the highest population in the North—my own family included. So, here's our version! I recommend eating it slightly warm and topped with ice cream.

Makes one 13 × 9 × 4-inch baking dish

- 4 (8-ounce) piloncillo cones
- 2 (3-inch) sticks Mexican canela/Ceylon cinnamon
- 4 medium tomatillos, husked and rinsed
- 2 Roma tomatoes, quartered
- ½ medium white onion, halved
- 3 whole cloves
- 6 whole black peppercorns
- 1 star anise
- 1 cup vegetable oil
- 3 baguettes, 4 days stale and cut into ½-inch slices
- 6 store-bought corn tortillas
- 1 teaspoon Diamond Crystal kosher salt (or ½ teaspoon Morton salt)
- 1 cup roasted peanuts, chopped
- 2 cups crumbled Cotija cheese
- 1 cup minced dried fruit, such as apricots, prunes, and cherries
- ½ cup shredded coconut (optional)

MAKE THE SYRUP:

1. In a medium pot, combine the piloncillo, cinnamon sticks, tomatillos, tomatoes, onion, cloves, peppercorns, star anise, and 6 cups of water. Set over low heat, bring to a simmer, and allow the ingredients to steep for 45 minutes, stirring occasionally, until the piloncillo has dissolved completely. Strain the syrup through a fine-mesh sieve into a bowl (discard the solids) and set aside.

MAKE THE CAPIROTADA:

2. Preheat the oven to 350°F.

3. First, fry the bread: Line a baking sheet with paper towels and set a wire rack on top. Set aside near the stovetop.

4. Add the oil to a large skillet and set over medium heat. When the oil is hot and shimmering on the surface (350°F if you have a frying thermometer), test it by putting in a piece of bread. If small bubbles immediately form and begin to fry the bread, you are good. Place a batch of the baguette slices in a single layer in the pan and fry them until golden brown. Turn and fry until golden brown on the other side. Continue to fry the rest of the baguette slices. Set the fried bread slices to drain on the wire rack.

5. Now, assemble the capirotada: Lay two tortillas flat at the bottom of a 13 × 9 × 4-inch baking dish.

Recipe continues

6. Using tongs, carefully dip slices of fried baguette in the syrup, and place them over the tortillas in a single layer. Sprinkle the layer of bread with a handful of peanuts, Cotija crumbles, and dried fruit.

7. Repeat this process, starting with another two tortillas, then the dipped fried bread, then the peanuts, Cotija, and dried fruit. Repeat with additional layers until all the tortillas and bread are used up, with the bread as the final layer.

8. Carefully pour any remaining syrup evenly over the bread. Use a wooden spoon or spatula to gently press down on the capirotada to compact it. Sprinkle coconut over the surface (if using).

9. Cover the dish with aluminum foil and bake the capirotada for 45 minutes. Remove the foil and bake for an additional 15 minutes, until the top is nice and golden.

10. Serve the capirotada warm or chilled, with an ice-cold glass of milk or a cup of black coffee. It's also great with ice cream on the side. Leftover capirotada will keep in the refrigerator for 3 to 4 days.

John

DAMIANA
Coca-Cola
Coca-Cola

ACKNOWLEDGMENTS

To my kids, James and Hailey, my soulmates and greatest teachers, my constant north. Your love steadies my spirit and fuels every dream I dare to chase. This book carries the world I hope to hand to you someday, one rooted in pride, courage, and knowing exactly who you are.

To mi Amá, mi tía Lore y mi Abue, the quiet, relentless warriors who shaped me. You showed me that true strength is woven softly, through sacrifice, tenderness, and an unshakable faith in the generations to come. Your stories are the bones of this work; your love is its heartbeat.

To my chosen family, my Phoenix tribe, my Six, and the fierce women of my village, thank you for lifting me when the world felt heavy and my back began to curve. You met me with honesty and warmth, with grit and grace, and you reminded me of the power I carry even on the days I forget.

To the people of the borderlands, forever stretching, bending, and reshaping yourselves to feel like enough on both sides of the line: You are seen, you are worthy, and you are whole. We are so much more than the world ever taught us to believe. We are our ancestors' wildest, most radiant dreams. Stand tall and proud, mis norteños queridos. Your existence is resistance, and your spirit is unbreakable. ¡¡Somos de aquí y de allá!!

And to las cocineras, the keepers of fire, memory, and ancestral truth. Thank you for showing me that food is not just nourishment, but legacy, rebellion, and prayer. Your hands taught my hands, and every recipe here carries the echo of your wisdom.

To my Apá, mi Lic, the original dreamer in my life. El Señor Hugo. Who saw life and food in technicolor. ¡Lo logré Apá, tu niña está llevando el apellido de Zepeda por todo el mundo! Te quiero mucho. Gracias por enseñarme cómo gozar de la comida rica.

To my brothers, my original Guinea pigs. Love you dudes. Your Tete forever.

XO
Mum aka Clau aka La Niña de Hugo aka Cheffy/La Jefa

INDEX

Clarkson Potter/Publishers
An imprint of the Crown Publishing Group
A division of Penguin Random House LLC
1745 Broadway
New York, NY 10019
clarksonpotter.com
penguinrandomhouse.com

Library of Congress Cataloging-in-Publication Data is on file with the publisher

ISBN 978-0-593-79613-9
Ebook ISBN 978-0-593-79614-6

Editor: Francis Lam
Editorial assistant: Darian Keels
Designer: Ian Dingman
Production editor: Serena Wang
Production manager: Kim Tyner
Prepress color manager: Kim Tyner
Compositors: Merri Ann Morrell and Hannah Hunt
Food stylist: Ryan Norton
Sous Chef: Isamar Checo
Prop stylist: Jaclyn Kershek
Production Design: Britt Keller
Photo assistant: Jason Sutherland Hsu
Floral headpiece: Jessica Resendiz
Tamal Cart: Revolution Carts
Copyeditor: Allie Kiekhofer
Proofreaders: Patricia Dailey, Heather Rodino, and Surina Jane
Indexer: Jay Kreider
Publicist: Natalie Yera-Campbell
Marketer: Brianne Sperber

Manufactured in China

10 9 8 7 6 5 4 3 2 1

First Edition

The authorized representative in the EU for product safety and compliance is Penguin Random House Ireland, Morrison Chambers, 32 Nassau Street, Dublin D02 YH68, Ireland, https://eu-contact.penguin.ie.

RECINTO PORTUARIO
ENSENADA